# CHRISTOPHER MARLOWE
## Merlin's prophet

# JUDITH WEIL

# CHRISTOPHER MARLOWE
## Merlin's prophet

CAMBRIDGE UNIVERSITY PRESS
CAMBRIDGE
LONDON . NEW YORK . MELBOURNE

Published by the Syndics of the Cambridge University Press
The Pitt Building, Trumpington Street, Cambridge CB2 1RP
Bentley House, 200 Euston Road, London NW1 2DB
32 East 57th Street, New York, NY 10022, USA
296 Beaconsfield Parade, Middle Park, Melbourne 3206, Australia

First published 1977

Printed in Great Britain by
W & J Mackay Limited, Chatham

*Library of Congress Cataloguing in Publication Data*
Weil, Judith, 1938–
Christopher Marlowe: Merlin's prophet
Bibliography: p.
Includes index
1. Marlowe, Christopher, 1564–1593 – Criticism and interpretation
PR2674.W4   822'.3   76–62586
ISBN 0 521 21554 4

# Contents

FOR
HERBERT WEIL

# Acknowledgements

I wish to thank Professors Paul Kocher and Lawrence Ryan of Stanford University, who patiently guided the early development of this study. Their preference for literary parallels and resemblances, their scepticism about direct causes and effects, has strongly influenced its final form. Professor Kenneth Muir kindly read parts of the manuscript and asked stimulating questions about Marlowe and his contemporaries. I am especially grateful to Barbara Rosen for exposing hidden assumptions and challenging doubtful ones with so much tact and learning. Anne Barton and Michael Black offered many thoughtful suggestions about ways to assist the reader without simplifying the playwright. My dependence on the discoveries and arguments of other scholars will appear throughout text and notes. The greatest reckoning has to be made in a very small space: I hope to express some measure of thanks for continuing encouragement and criticism through the dedication to my husband.

# I

# Introduction

The descriptive phrase in the title of this study, 'Merlin's prophet', refers primarily to a style, rather than to a man. It derives from the passage with which Rabelais concludes his *Gargantua*. There, Gargantua and Friar John both comment on the meaning of a 'prophetic riddle' engraved on a plate and discovered in digging the foundations of the abbey of Thélème. Gargantua interprets the riddle – a muddled account of an Antichrist, an apocalypse, and a triumphant elect – to mean 'the Continuance and Upholding of Divine Truth'. Friar John, however, disagrees:

That is not my Explanation; The Style is that of Merlin the Prophet. Put upon it all the Allegories and Grave Expositions that you will, and dote about it, you and the Rest of the World, as much as you like.

For my Part, I believe there is no other Meaning enveloped in it than a Description of a Game at Tennis hidden under obscure Words.[1]

Friar John's brief argument with Gargantua can serve to introduce two basic sources of disagreement among the spectators and readers of Marlowe's work. First, Marlowe seems to have been a rhetorical provocateur, as well as, quite possibly, a political one. He could tantalize and manipulate the imaginations of an audience in a masterful fashion. Rarely does he disappoint our expectations without first over-inflating them. He thereby encourages us to 'dote' about his heroes and his ideas. Second, his plays mingle sense with nonsense, allegory with the violent energies of farce and tragedy. In language so 'obscure' that it may have baffled even his contemporaries, Marlowe 'enveloped' plots disturbingly similar to games, wagers, and jokes.

Marlowe's style has inevitably drawn attention to his personal character and beliefs. Most students of the plays soon become familiar with those speculations about the writer which began during his own life-time and survive into ours.[2] The few facts which remain suggest that Marlowe may have attempted to act conflicting roles. Although he had studied theology in Reformation Cambridge and had worked briefly for the Privy Council (perhaps actually spying upon the Jesuit community at Rheims), he later baited his peers with scurrilous, anti-Christian harangues. These peers seem to have included great and gifted gentlemen as well as underworld rogues. Simultaneously, he wrote plays which mask their strong dependence upon the Bible and the commonplaces of Christian thought. Such a man might have courted misunderstanding and aggression. Provoked by his dramatic history, we may neglect J. B. Steane's cautious warning: 'The impression is so very vivid that we tend to forget that what we have is only a small part of the truth.'[3]

If this impression of a personality owes much of its sharpness to the playwright's skill, we may need to revise some of the questions we have posed about him. Instead, for example, of asking why he was a rebellious free-thinker, we might ask why he wanted some of his contemporaries to *believe* he was a rebellious free-thinker. My study does not entirely beg these biographical questions, for all that it concentrates on Marlowe's ironic style. The essential argument in the following chapters is that Marlowe mocks his heroes in a remarkably subtle fashion. Their knavish speeches sleep so well in our ears because he has carefully obscured the folly of the speakers. Nevertheless, these speakers, with their mighty lines, are often the objects as well as the agents of his irony. Like Erasmus, another independent and subtle ironist, he exposes disorders of the spirit – self-love, literalism, and violence. My first concerns are to analyse the verbal and visual deceptions which have encouraged us to believe that Marlowe shares the attitudes of his heroes, and to show how these deceptions function within entertaining, popular plays. Should my argument about the style seem convincing, it may bring some common assumptions about Marlowe's personal knavery into doubt.

Whether or how well other writers of Marlowe's age actually understood his stylistic obscurity are problems we may best approach by studying their own plays and poems.[4] Pertinent comments are few. When read in light of the awareness that Marlowe alludes frequently to Biblical and classical literature, and that his style is sometimes proverbial, Drayton's nostalgic praise (1621) acquires more substance:

> Neat Marlow bathed in the Thespian springs
> Had in him those brave translunary things,
> That the first Poets had, his raptures were,
> All ayre, and fire, which made his verses cleere,
> For that fine madnes still he did retaine,
> Which rightly should possesse a Poets braine.[5]

Because simple proverbs were believed to conceal ancient insights, their roughness might have augmented the oracular quality produced by more 'cleere' and rapturous verses.

Another comment which may imply recognition of Marlowe's deceptive style is Robert Greene's contemporary attack on the language of Tamburlaine in *Perimedes the Blackesmith* (1588). Greene is settling a score with 'two Gentlemen Poets' who '...had it in derision, for that I could not make my verses iet upon the stage in tragicall buskins, euerie worde filling the mouth like the faburden of Bo-Bell, daring God out of heauen with that Atheist *Tamburlan*, or blaspheming with the mad preest of the sonne'. Justifying himself, Greene continues, 'but let me rather openly pocket vp the Asse at *Diogenes* hand: then wantonlye set out such impious instances of intollerable poetrie, such mad and scoffing poets, that haue propheticall spirits, as bred of *Merlins* race'.[6]

After this cryptic outburst, Greene apologizes to the Gentlemen Readers of his prefatory epistle for speaking 'darkeley' – for engaging, that is, in the Rabelaisian sport of enigmatically describing enigmatic obscurity. Like the popular prophecies of Merlin to which he refers, his own comment is partly open to subjective interpretation. Does Greene's defensiveness hint that Marlowe's jetting verses may have been an advertisement – or a defence – for Marlowe? The cynic Diogenes, according to Diogenes Laertius, called himself a 'Socrates gone mad' and dismissed *his* critics as follows: 'When some one said, "Most people laugh at you", his reply was, "And so very likely do the asses at them; but as they don't care for the asses, so neither do I care for them."'[7] It is surely a moot point whether the brunt of Greene's attack falls upon Marlowe or upon the poet-hero Tamburlaine as created by and distinct from Marlowe. We cannot be certain whether he is a Gargantua accusing Tamburlaine of religious impiety, or a Friar John accusing him of nonsense. In either case,

Greene's dark irony seems to pattern itself on Marlowe's, as if he had known that too direct an assault would be less effective. When we seek out the impious man behind the 'intollerable poetry', we are apt to discover an accomplished literary trickster.

By linking Marlowe's style with that disreputable genre, the prophecy, I may have implied that his relationship with his audience is an opportunistic and one-sided affair, that the dramatist manipulates naive readers and spectators according to rules which he can slyly break at will. Such an extreme view resembles its opposite, the view that because Marlowe speaks through his characters, the irony of his plays must be incidental – a privy scoff here, a fleering frump there. It would be impractical to discard all sense of these extremes when encountering so fiery an ironist as Marlowe. Although this book will emphasize mutually constructive relationships between playwright and audience, it will not pretend that these relationships should always please and reassure us. Every reader and spectator of Marlowe's plays can expect to find passages where artistic control threatens to shatter and communication to fail.

In speaking of Marlowe's beliefs or concerns, I mean by 'Marlowe' a set of intentions derived from study of his plays. All criticism which relies heavily on the concepts of intention and reaction runs three risks: 1) of creating an apology for the writer, making up for his real deficiencies with an integrating response, 2) of treating the writer as a moralizing pedagogue and the audience as a group of docile pupils, and 3) of using the term 'audience' as a means of giving one's personal responses more authority.[8] Even if it were desirable completely to skirt these risks, it might not prove possible. To turn a critical procedure into a myth: The most rewarding route toward discovery of integrating elements *within* Marlowe's plays may lie through their ironic traps. If my approach is considered too apologetic, moral, and personal, I hope it will at least deserve this excuse – that it adds to our understanding of Marlowe's ironic art, and of the range of responses his art produces.

Surprisingly, Marlowe's relationship to his audience may seem more one-sided and manipulative when his attitude is militantly serious. His plays sometimes presuppose a relationship between playwright and audience similar to that suggested between the prophet and his congregation in Second Corinthians 11:17-19.[9]

That I speak, I speak it not after the Lord: but as it *were* foolishly, in this *my* great boasting.
 Seing that manie reioyce after the flesh, I will reioyce also.
 For ye suffer fooles gladly, because that ye are wise.[10]

Particularly in those plays whose irony is more satiric – *The Jew of Malta*, *Doctor Faustus*, and *The Massacre at Paris* – Marlowe may seem to scorn the worldliness of his audience. Although he compels us to suffer the boasting of his heroes gladly, he ultimately exposes both their folly and ours.

Marlowe is a writer who continually invites us to compare the distinct and distinguish the comparable. He rarely lends himself to static formulations. Having suggested that his relationship to his audience sometimes resembles St Paul's, I must quickly add that the true prophet speaks to the few, the playwright to the many.[11] He cannot persist in the linguistic inversions of paradox if he wishes to represent mutability. His characters who rejoice after the flesh are not altogether foolish. Those who end their careers as allegorical abstractions begin them as realistic human beings. Moreover, had Marlowe consistently taken the Pauline view of his art and his audience, he could not have written those plays whose irony has a more tragic quality. *Dido Queen of Carthage*, the two *Tamburlaine* plays, and *Edward II* all invite a more independent and imaginative response by the audience. They encourage diversity in interpretation because they relate personal transformations to general historical ones.

By emphasizing two tendencies in Marlowe's ironic relationship with his audience, one satiric and the other tragic, I have tried to avoid the misleading rigidity of another distinction – that which has often been drawn between Marlowe the man and Marlowe the artist.[12] Marlowe's style will always confuse both biographical and formal critics, unless they are willing to exchange insights. We are not merely indulging a Romantic penchant for biography when we regard Marlowe's plays as unstable compounds of air and fire, ready to dissolve with each new translunary rapture. They *are* unstable, full of rapture. On the other hand, those who have discovered and analysed new evidence for Marlowe's intellectual control of his art sometimes seem to have neglected his air and fire.[13] We cannot isolate our reactions to the discipline of art from our reactions to the power of character and the energy of verse.

To surmise that Marlowe's 'prophetic spirit' accommodates all these reactions may be to risk comparison with Faustus and his desire for heady, magical solutions. The non-chronological approach to Marlowe's plays in the following chapters has the design of concentrating on actual changes in the relationship between ironist and audience. Chapter 2 describes essential features of Marlowe's boisterous style and suggests well-known Renaissance analogues for his ironic methods. Detailed analysis of his work begins in chapter 3 with *The Jew of Malta*, a play which inhibits our impulse to 'dote about it', as Friar John says. Because of its negative temper and constricted form, one can put a few 'Allegories and Grave Expositions' upon the play with greater likelihood that they are meanings Marlowe intended. Analysis ends with the tragedy of *Edward II*. For all its resemblance to *The Jew of Malta* in rapid pace and tight construction, *Edward II* is more humane in temper, more expansive and dynamic in form.

One benefit of studying relationships between style and audience has been the way in which this moving focus can clarify the anomalous nature of *Doctor Faustus*. No simple generic label seems to describe this particularly unstable compound of air and fire or to explain why it frustrates expectations based on familiarity with other dramatic forms. Central to the following interpretation is the argument that *Doctor Faustus* begins as a dark satire and ends as a satiric tragedy of knowledge, which only a knowing audience can fully experience. The superior insight acquired by the audience enables it to measure the hero's progress from foolishly clever impiety towards a desperate recognition of God. Even the painful terror of this recognition is not enough to dispel the detachment which Marlowe's firm satiric purpose generates. Faustus owes his seemingly tragic stature to an elaborate series of rhetorical deceptions. Unless we grant that he is a *potentially* tragic hero, he will always disappoint us. It may be that only two of Marlowe's characters acquire the large dimensions of tragic heroism, Tamburlaine and Edward II. And even so their gains are tenuous, depending less upon the power or awareness of the dramatic character than upon the reactions of the audience. Finally Marlowe's prophetic spirit moves out of his plays into the consciousness of those who read or watch.

# 2

# Marlowe's prophetic style

Marlowe designed his plays as striking reversals which heap disaster upon the protagonists they have seemed to celebrate. His heroes endure exacting retributions which are carefully matched with their particular failings. The catastrophes adjust plot to character, trapping protagonists within a rigorously moral form. Their appropriateness may invite critics to read the plays backwards, discovering anticipations of these last judgments. John Russell Brown, for example, has argued that a play by Marlowe 'is always more significant than any of its characters can realize: the hero is viewed ironically or relatively'.[1] This argument depends, I think, on the privilege of hindsight. It fails to explain why an audience might experience a final disaster with great surprise and shock.

Guided by the morality of Marlowe's catastrophes, the audience does ultimately discover that a protagonist's fate has always been implicit in the strong desires which move him. Douglas Cole has shown that Marlowe's plots seem to provide rationalizations of an Augustinian moral psychology: 'The soul is weighed in the balance by what delights her, as St Augustine put it, which is another way of saying that what a man loves tells most about what that man *is*.'[2] By creating disasters which fulfil mistaken desires and identify the characters with their loves, Marlowe casts brilliant light on basic spiritual perversions. Surely a process so intelligible in retrospect cannot be all that puzzling when experienced scene by scene. But, in fact, it can be very puzzling indeed. Few playwrights have been as willing as Marlowe was to obscure disaster in the offing, to postpone the resolution of ambiguities. Few have disguised self-deception so well or exposed it so belatedly. We might expect that Marlowe would have been anxious to guide the judgment of the audience. We probably do *not* expect that he would have sought to suspend our judgments and to let them go straying through the dark.

Even when Marlowe's irony brightens in a more satiric play like *The Jew of Malta*, it is subdued to the power of a protagonist who is a plausible spokesman for his own position. Marlowe's protagonists move energetically through contexts and relationships which reinforce their vigour and potency. This potency may prevent the audience from seeing the protagonists 'ironically or relatively' until the end of the play approaches. It is doubtful that 'Marlowe's staged suffering clearly underlines the irony of the kind of human "fulfillment" to which his major characters aspire', or that 'the dream of the poetic word is consistently confronted with the reality of the dramatic action'.[3] Marlowe encourages his audience to dream with his characters. While he intimates the 'reality' held in reserve, he also tempts the audience to ignore it. Marlowe's dramatic strategy inhibits detachment. In its overall function and effect upon an audience it bears a strong resemblance to the rhetorical questions asked so frequently by his characters. Repeatedly they adopt this method of affirming their values:

> Who hateth me but for my happiness?
> Or who is honored now but for his wealth?
>> Barabas, I.i.110–11

> Is to dispute well logic's chiefest end?
> Affords this art no greater miracle?
>> Faustus, I.i.8–9

> What greater bliss can hap to Gaveston
> Than live and be the favorite of a king?[4]
>> I.i.4–5

We might pause to answer such questions, were the questioners themselves less persuasive or the pace of the action less swift. Our attention moves onward, and we are disturbed, if at all, only by a suspicion that Marlowe's questioners cannot really be answered in the terms they employ.

The dramatic conventions which Marlowe adapts to his obliquely ironic purposes are traditional ones which he shares with other playwrights of his time.[5] As they work together, these conventional methods reveal Marlowe's preoccupation with particular types of character and theme. Risking repetition and a logical circle, I will consider these preoccupations before the ironic use of conventions. Both have been widely misunderstood. A brief discussion of his basic concerns may help to make the subsequent survey of Marlowe's methods more pertinent.

In *An Apology for Poetry*, Sir Philip Sidney states a distinction which can be brought to bear on Marlowe's kind of irony. When he turns to those objections to poetry which might be put in a 'counter-ballance' against his own defence, Sidney mentions first a group of 'Poet-haters' and anti-poets. He describes them as:

All that kinde of people who seek a prayse by dispraysing others, that they doe prodigally spend a great many wandering wordes in quips and scoffes, carping and taunting at each thing, which, by styrring the Spleene, may stay the braine from a through [sic] beholding the worthines of the subiect.[6]

Many of Marlowe's characters belong to this group. The cowards in both *Tamburlaine* plays, the scheming Machiavels in *The Jew of Malta*, *The Massacre at Paris*, and *Edward II*, and the Bad Angel and Mephistophilis in *Doctor Faustus* all know how to 'seek a prayse'.

Sidney then distinguishes these jesters, who deserve only our ridicule, from a second, more serious group:

So of the contrary side, if we will turne *Ouid*'s verse, *Ut lateat virtus proximitate mali*, that good lye hid in the neerenesse of the euill, *Agrippa* will be as merry in shewing the vanitie of Science as *Erasmus* was in commending of follie. Neyther shall any man or matter escape some touch of these smyling raylers. But for *Erasmus* and *Agrippa*, they had another foundation then the superficiall part would promise.[7]

Marlowe's raillery seems to have been more sardonic than the 'smyling' version which Sidney commended in Agrippa and Erasmus. But like their raillery, Marlowe's does seem to have had 'another foundation then the superficiall part would promise'. We need not identify him with the clever scoffers in his plays. Sidney went on to observe that 'scoffing commeth not of wisedome'.[8] When scoffers like Barabas and Faustus celebrate their wisdom they are actually praising their folly. Such paradoxical encomia may be highly persuasive, for, like Erasmus himself, Marlowe knew well how to 'stay the braine from a through beholding the worthines of the subiect'. His glorious fools are especially plausible when their exciting ideas and activities coincide with the ways of their worlds. That the pleasing spokes-woman of *The Praise of Folly* often has enough sense to understand such ways hardly recommends their value. Erasmus permits her to identify and satirize other fools, but he reminds us of her folly by suggesting now and again that her use of authorities and her reasoning are dubious. We will see that Marlowe uses a similar procedure in presenting his characters.[9]

Through the allusions which occur in all of his plays, Marlowe reveals an abiding preoccupation with wisdom. We can discern, behind his mistaken praisers of wisdom, the shadow of that lady who praised herself in the books of Proverbs and Wisdom as the bride of God and mother of all creation. The Church Fathers chose to replace this mediating Wisdom figure with the second person of the Trinity, Christ. Nevertheless, she preserved a feminine identity congenial to Erasmus and to such Christian poets as Dante, Spenser, and Donne.[10]

There appears to be a natural congruity between the darkness of Marlowe's ironic style and 'Wisdom's' shadowy life in literary convention. As a symbol for mediation and intuition, it is simply not in her character to support any literary 'foundation' too obviously. We will see that only Faustus and Tamburlaine, the boldest of overreachers, insist on giving wisdom a literal human shape. Many of Marlowe's allusions to wisdom appear to derive from the Hebraic sources of the wisdom tradition – the books of Job and Proverbs, and the 'ecclesiastical' books of Wisdom and Ecclesiasticus.[11] In *The Jew of Malta* and *Doctor Faustus* he suggests a foolish distortion of wisdom through allusions to Christ – in St Paul's words, 'the power of God, and the wisdome of God' (First Corinthians 1:24). Perhaps these plays also make some reference to the distinction stated in the Epistle of St James between genuine and devilish wisdom (3:13-18). Other allusions to wisdom ultimately derive from classical sources but seem to have taken on a proverbial, topical character in the Renaissance. Marlowe could easily hint at the folly of a character by comparing him with Actaeon or Icarus.

Within their dramatic contexts, these allusions imply that Marlowe's characters pervert 'sapientia' – a knowledge of things human as well as things divine.[12] Until more definitive studies of Marlowe's own Biblical learning have been made, it might be best to regard the wisdom which his characters abuse as eclectic and traditional in nature. Renaissance thinkers adapted the ancient wisdom tradition to their own attitudes and purposes. These ranged from the mysti-

cism of the Florentine neo-Platonists to the prudent virtue commended by Erasmus and Vives. Where Marlowe is concerned, there
may be little point in attempting to define the tradition too rigidly.
We will see that the resemblance between the ironic styles of Erasmus
and Marlowe extends to their specific subject matter as well,
particularly in *Doctor Faustus*. Therefore it might be suggested that,
like Erasmus, Marlowe valued a wisdom more ethical than esoteric.
The first principle of the moralized and humanistic wisdom to which
Erasmus so frequently refers seems to have been, 'Know Yourself.'[13]
Even though Marlowe mentions the Delphic oracle only once, in
*Doctor Faustus*, his idea of wisdom seems to depend largely upon the
same principle.

Marlowe's use of allusions can be described as one of his essential
ironic methods.[14] But in studying this method as a dramatic technique, it is important to remember that spectators unfamiliar with
his plays might fail to notice the allusions or to understand their
significance. Again, if we abuse our privilege of hindsight, we will
distort the quality of Marlowe's irony, which is dark or oblique. To
judge his intentions we must consider not only the sources of the
allusions and the diverse abilities of a popular audience, but also the
exact manner in which the allusions are presented. Otherwise we are
apt to identify responses to allusions by an Elizabethan audience
with our own most recent discoveries about their sources. In that case
we would not see that Marlowe has often made it difficult to recognize allusions to more familiar materials. The most learned spectator,
theoretically responsive to his classical as well as to his Biblical references, might not grasp some of them unless he came to 'hear' a play
several times.[15]

Perhaps I can clarify this point by citing briefly two different
approaches to a common problem – that readers who should have
known the Bible well understood it poorly. In his Prologue to *The
Ship of Fools*, Sebastian Brant gives as his general reason for writing,
the ignorance of men who had had greater access to 'Holy Writ'
through printed books but had not benefited from it.[16] In his
address 'To the Reader' in *Of the Vanitie and Uncertaintie of Artes
and Sciences*, Cornelius Agrippa observes:

I see many ware proude in Humane learning and knowledge, that therefore they
do despise and lothe the Sacred and Canonicall Scriptures of the Holie Ghoste, as

rude and rusticall, bycause they have no ornamentes of wordes, force of sillogismes, and affectate persuasions, nor the straunge doctrine of the Philosophers: but are simply grounded upon the operation of Vertue, and upon bare Faith.[17]

Brant's solution is to provide a catalogue of follies simply illustrated with woodcuts for the less literate readers:

> The viewer learns with certainty:
> My mirror leaves no mystery.[18]

Agrippa's solution implicitly repudiates Brant's. Certainty and authority were among the intellectual attitudes this sceptic questioned. He therefore approaches his readers by encouraging them to discover their own ignorance. Although Agrippa does occasionally pause to indicate that he is criticizing the abuses, rather than the uses of learning, he fills his critique with distortions and confusions. The main concern of this 'rayler', as Sidney called him, is the reader who gradually recognizes that almost every statement must be tested and then compared with other statements.

Marlowe's method resembles Agrippa's rather than Brant's. Of course, he emphasizes the experience of his heroes more than the learning of his audiences. But he does implicate his audiences by veiling allusions which might have exposed the heroes, had he presented them more directly. My references to 'dark' allusions will remain subject to several qualifications: All allusions might have been grasped by very acute spectators, by spectators who had been forewarned, or by spectators who had already guessed from past experience that Marlowe's ironic catastrophes emphasize meanings latent in his plays through allusions. Some of his devices for obscuring allusions were probably familiar both to more and to less well learned spectators. For example, when Faustus quotes selectively from Romans 6:23 and I John 1:18, Marlowe may have expected most of his audience to supply the missing verses. Not only were the texts themselves likely to have been well known.[19] Many in the audience were probably also accustomed to the trick of quoting or alluding to part of a saying. In order to characterize the sycophancy of courtiers, the Folly of Erasmus recites a few words of Homer, then interrupts herself and challenges her learned reader: 'You know the rest of the verse, which Echo can give you better than I.'[20] 'Echo' was often relied upon to provide parts of less esoteric material, like proverbs.[21] Shakespeare assumed an acquaintance with proverbs when he had Lady Macbeth ask her husband:

> Wouldst thou have that
> Which thou esteem'st the ornament of life,
> And live a coward in thine own esteem,
> Letting 'I dare not' wait upon 'I would,'
> Like the poor cat i' the adage?[22]

I.vii.41-5

Shakespeare probably thought that his popular audiences would know all about the poor cat.[23]

Clear allusions easily recognized create an effect of strong irony. They provide an instance of what Cole terms Marlowe's 'characteristic tendency to employ his formal knowledge with particular precision'.[24] So relevant are their original contexts as commentary on Marlowe's action that we cannot view them as either casual or decorative. A play which contains any number of obvious allusions can stand, in reference to the norms they provide, as a gigantic inversion, a world upside down. *Doctor Faustus* and *The Jew of Malta* both embody such worlds. But Marlowe does not always emphasize his allusions. Few are as conspicuous as the two half-texts read aloud by Faustus. Commonly, Marlowe alters the wording of his Biblical allusions; he works them unobtrusively into his swelling periods and exciting conflicts. We might consider, for a moment, the effect of that rhetorical question thrust at us by Faustus before he signs away his soul: 'When Mephistophilis shall stand by me,/What power can hurt me?' (II.i.24-5). Surely it will boggle the minds of those who fail to compare it with St Paul's affirmation of divine mercy, 'If God be on our side, who că be agaïst vs?' (Romans 8:31). In this particular case the memorable rhythms of the two questions might prompt a recognition strong enough to break through our absorption in events. But in other cases Marlowe may provide no more than a word or two which imports to the discourse a vaguely allusive quality. This quality might cause an audience to feel uneasy about Marlowe's characters; it would hardly encourage stronger judgments of the sort induced by the more obvious allusions.

The other ironic methods on which Marlowe relies are tendentiously direct forms of address to the audience, dramatic structures contrived through puzzling analogies, and spectacles or shows. All three will require careful distinctions in describing their nature and use. Knowledge of a convention like the soliloquy prepares us to recognize that Marlowe's direct addresses give speakers special claims on the attention of an audience, and that they articulate key attitudes and ideas. It does not warn us that the will of the speaker seems to come between Marlowe's meanings and our ready apprehension of them.[25] It is as if the speaker seizes upon the advantages of soliloquy to commend himself and his desires. Once our ears are attuned to the persuasive, moving speech of a Tamburlaine or a Faustus we are less inclined to heed allusions which suggest illogic or self-deception.

One reason why Marlowe's soliloquies discourage an immediate critical response is their energetic pace. Another is their timing; we are less likely to question the implied self-praise of a Barabas or Faustus when it comes very early in the action of a play. A third cause of their persuasiveness is the fact that Marlowe's speakers resemble Sidney's 'Poet-haters'; their soliloquies include many figures of speech particularly suited to stirring the spleen and staying the brain. In judging the effect which these figures can have upon a spectator, it will be helpful to remember that figures, as Puttenham pointed out, are not just 'instruments of ornament'; they are:

Also in a sorte abuses or rather trespasses in speach, because they passe the ordinary limits of common vtterance, and be occupied of purpose to deceiue the eare and also the minde, drawing it from plainnesse and simplicitie to a certain doublenesse, whereby our talke is the more guilefull & abusing.[26]

Significantly, in Marlowe's soliloquies which praise folly we often encounter those figures which, Puttenham concluded, may 'inueigle and appassionate the mind': metaphor ('an inuersion of sence by transport'), allegory ('duplicitie of meaning'), aenigma (riddles), paremia (adages), irony ('merry skoffe'), sarcasm ('bitter tawnt'), periphrase or circumlocution, and hyperbole ('incredible comparison').[27]

Marlowe's dramatic structures sometimes invite the audience to make its own 'incredible comparisons'. Like his predecessor, John Lyly, Marlowe often appears to think dramatically in terms of analogies.[28] The analogy may emerge between types of assertion and attitude in a play. For example, we eventually notice how very similar are all the speeches given by rulers in the *Tamburlaine* plays. Some analogies broaden to include the arrangement of incidents through which the characters move. We can find such parallel plot lines running through all of the plays except *Edward II*. This analogical method, although potentially repetitious, implies a disciplined concentration on a set of problems or issues. Such concentration is what shapes the catastrophes so firmly. But Marlowe creates a compensatory relationship between his own discipline and the freedom of his audience; his handling of structure reveals a decided willingness to let the reader or spectator interpret connections for himself.

When its analogies are fairly strong, the play is probably one which generates a more satiric kind of irony. Such connections are all the more gratifying if the reader or spectator must bring them out from behind a facade of differences. He plays the poet, in Bacon's sense, when he finds that the Turks, Jews and Christians of Malta or the popes and vintners of Rome are similar. Such a process of discovery seems to confirm Bacon's belief that poetry 'raises the mind and carries it aloft, accommodating the shows of things to the desires of the mind'.[29] In contrast, the *Tamburlaine* plays and *Edward II* frustrate these desires by giving 'things' greater substance and duration. They offer revealing identities which develop into profound differences.

By considering some of the analogies in Marlowe's earliest play, *Dido Queen of Carthage*, we may begin to see why this ironic technique can have a provocative effect.[30] *Dido* begins with an induction which shows Jupiter, the most powerful of the gods, playing amorously with Ganymede, his cup-bearer and lover of the moment. Venus interrupts this hyperbolic frivolity when she bursts in to report that her son, Aeneas, is endangered because of a storm which Juno has stirred up at sea. Jupiter reassures her that Aeneas's 'wandering fate is firm' (1.i.83) and prophesies the future greatness of both Aeneas and Rome. Jupiter's own dalliance with Ganymede may anticipate the mutual dalliance of Aeneas and Dido, although it is curious that Jove does not bother to mention Dido or Carthage. Jupiter's power, the power to 'control proud fate', eventually forces Aeneas to desert Dido, just as he has already deserted three Trojan women. One begins to surmise that for Virgil's grand conflict between heroic duty and love, *Pietas* and *Amor*, Marlowe has substituted a mere juggling contest between selfish power and equally selfish lust. The surmise could be reinforced when, at the end of the play, two blind and foolish lovers imitate Dido by committing suicide.

Marlowe appears to have turned Virgil's historical motives into psychological, subjective ones.[31] His strategy debunks both gods and men by intimating that passion can make puppets of us all.

We might confidently reach such reductive decisions about the meaning of *Dido*, if it weren't for the inconvenient fact that Marlowe's structural analogies are almost too firm for his play. They communicate attitudes towards the main characters inconsistent with the dramatic behaviour of these characters. Critics have been unable to agree on the exact connection between Dido and Aeneas, and either the narrative induction or the subordinate lovers whose passions Marlowe emphasizes.[32] Should we simply explain away this situation by agreeing that Marlowe was inexperienced or that he was collaborating with Nashe? These explanations cannot account for the similar lack of consensus about how we should respond to the relationships between Tamburlaine and other rulers, Edward II and his barons, Faustus and the clowns. The following chapters will test an hypothesis about Marlowe's reliance on elliptical, teasing analogies. The hypothesis is that Marlowe must have wished his audience to sense a disproportion between the strong forms and forces which control his characters and the natures of those characters. He has prevented us from taking the justice of his plots for granted.

By looking briefly at Marlowe's presentation of Dido and Aeneas, we may see why an audience might not be guided by Jupiter's initial promise that 'Aeneas' wandering fate is firm'. Jupiter's own proud, wilful power finds more of an echo in the cruelty of the Greek soldiers, whom Aeneas describes as twirling Hecuba by her heels, than it does in Aeneas himself. This plain-spun soldier would have been much more at ease in the worlds of *The Wars of Cyrus* or *Alexander and Campaspe* than he is at Dido's exotic court. How reluctantly he puts on Dido's robes and participates in her ceremonies! Virgil's Aeneas had suddenly disclosed himself to Dido, shedding his miraculous invisibility and dazzling her with his shining, goddess-born splendour. Beggared by misfortune, Marlowe's Aeneas doubts that Dido will see him at all. 'Well may I view her, but she sees not me' (II.i.73). This Aeneas is confused by shipwreck, haunted by the nightmare of Troy's defeat, thoroughly dependent upon his mother Venus and his loyal, protective retainers.[33] How can a figure so sentimentally complicated and humble have become involved with the imperial destinies of Rome? Never does he tell Dido, as Virgil's Aeneas does, that he has been promised a home and kingdom of his own in Italy. Perhaps Marlowe would have agreed with Sidney's view of Aeneas, because he presents him as, 'Obeying the Gods commandement to leaue *Dido*, though not onely all passionate kindenes, but euen the humane consideration of vertuous gratefulnes, would haue craued other of him.'[34] Against Dido's ceremonious and fanciful enchantments Marlowe sets the ungarnished fact that Aeneas must necessarily obey the inscrutably wilful behest of Jove. Courtly bliss yields to an obligation for which Marlowe has provided decidedly inadequate motives.

Dido, too, is a more complex, attractive figure than the gods who manipulate her or the lovers who mirror her. Therefore her destiny does not shadow her, as it does in the *Aeneid*, where she is 'infelix' Dido, doomed from the moment she is poisoned by love. Towards the end of the play, Aeneas learns from Hermes that Venus has substituted Cupid for his son Ascanius, and he observes:

> This was my mother that beguiled the queen
> And made me take my brother for my son.
> No marvel, Dido, though thou be in love,
> That daily dandlest Cupid in thine arms.
>
> v.i.42–5

No marvel, not much of Virgil's Bacchic frenzy, and little blame for Dido herself. To a great extent, Marlowe's development of subordinate lovers – Iarbas who loves Dido, and Anna who loves Iarbas – accentuates Dido's almost amoral freedom.[35] By suggesting that until scratched by Cupid's dart, Dido had favoured Iarbas over many rivals, Marlowe makes her resemble not her Virgilian prototype but the Dido of the seventh Epistle in Ovid's *Heroides*. As she baits Iarbas and enchants Aeneas, Dido seems to exist in an intensely emotional space – a world of great power, but little purpose or consequence.[36] Instead of worrying about her honour or her enemies, she attempts to rival the Sirens (III.i.129, III.iv.38), alludes to Circe (IV.iv.11), longs for a 'charm to keep the winds/Within the closure of a golden ball' (IV.iv.99), and finally sends her sister after Aeneas to 'look upon him with a mermaid's eye' (V.i.201).

Dido refuses to believe that the gods are responsible for calling Aeneas away from her:

Wherein have I offended Jupiter
That he should take Aeneas from mine arms?
O, no! The gods weigh not what lovers do.
It is Aeneas calls Aeneas hence.

v.i.129–32

And, until the catastrophe, analogies between her character and those of the two other lovers seem tenuous. All three characters are fanciful. But Dido, who struggles against her passion and celebrates it in cosmic terms, will not seem as fatuous as Iarbas or as weak as Anna. The soliloquy she speaks as she commits her love tokens and finally herself to the fire is eloquent and compelling. Marlowe forces one of his more incredible comparisons upon us when he abruptly follows Dido's attempt to 'cure my mind that melts for unkind love' (v.i.287) with two anti-climactic suicides, and when he gives Anna, the least and most hopeless lover, the last words in his play. To create a tragedy, rather than an Ovidian epyllion, a playwright must possess what Ovid lacked – a strongly ethical apprehension of natural or providential law. *Dido Queen of Carthage* leaves us with an unpleasant contradiction between the magnitude of Aeneas and Dido and the triviality of their universe. Later plays present contradictions which at first may seem similar to this one, but prove to be thoroughly different. The trivial worlds of Marlowe's other heroes are worlds which they themselves have helped to construct.

The last convention which Marlowe uses ironically is spectacle. By spectacle I do not mean all representation. In that sense most plays of the period are highly spectacular, for as Theodore Spencer once pointed out, 'the medieval tradition of play-writing made the Elizabethan spectators expect to see everything acted out before them'.[37] I am concerned primarily with representation as emphasis – the use of what is visible to focus attention on behaviour or situations seemingly significant in the play as a whole. I see little point in continuing to regard Marlowe's spectacular technique as a pioneering attempt to harmonize speech and action by substituting words for deeds.[38] Marlowe's achievement may have been gravely underestimated when judged in an evolutionary and pre-Shakespearean context. A clearer understanding of how his 'spectacles' function can bring us closer to an understanding of his basic subjects and style.

Again, because of its contradictory quality, *Dido Queen of Carthage*

may help us to define the extremes towards which Marlowe's spectacular ironies tend. On the one hand, Marlowe organizes his characters into shows of which they are unaware so as to sharpen the
audience's awareness of external forces or fates. The conspicuous
dandlings of Ganymede by Jupiter and of Cupid by Dido constitute
such shows.[39] By the time we see Dido's old nurse dandle Cupid too,
the universal power of passion will be clear. Like the use of obvious
allusions, such a technique produces strong and relatively simple
ironic effects. On the other hand Marlowe uses spectacle to develop
character. Surely it is no accident that 'sight' and 'see' are among
Marlowe's favourite terms. His heroes and heroines share a pre-
dilection for spectacular display, whether it be expressed through the
pageants and ceremonies of the monarchs, the extravagant revenges
of the Machiavels, or the magic demonstrations of Faustus. The love-
struck characters of *Dido Queen of Carthage* refer repeatedly to ceremonies, processions, costumes and costume changes, portraits, and
other visible properties. Throughout the play he associates spectacularly ceremonious types of behaviour with fanciful, conceited attitudes.[40] Later plays will work out a pattern seemingly
truncated in *Dido*; they will thoroughly involve these attitudes with
the choices and destinies of the protagonists.

It is Marlowe's characters, then, but not Marlowe, who fail to
criticize their visions when they attempt to turn them into actions.
As students of Marlowe's spectacles we can approach the show
through the character. We need not depend too far on unreliable
stage directions for information about appearances and gestures,
because these are matters of central importance which Marlowe
commonly emphasizes in dramatic statement and conversation. His
method encourages the spectators to compare what they see with
what the characters see. The more satiric the spirit of the play is, the
more confidently the audience may make the kind of discrimination
Achates makes when his master Aeneas confuses a stone Priam with
the real one:

> Thy mind, Aeneas, that would have it so,
> Deludes thy eyesight. Priamus is dead.
>
> II.i.31–2

Such discriminations grow more difficult when the characters themselves disagree about their visions. In the *Tamburlaine* plays and in

*Edward II*, sight becomes a problem for the audience as well as for the characters.

The spectacular element in Marlowe's plays has always helped them to succeed on stage. My argument that spectacle is part of Marlowe's obliquely ironic style may seem suspiciously pedantic. Why should a playwright have needed that astounding collection of thrones, chariots, cauldrons and costumes if, like Aeneas, he doubted the value of display? The question is related to a more general question about this dark ironist. Why would he have lavished so much art on characters whom he considered merely foolish and self-deceived? Any answers to these questions must grow from detailed studies of the plays themselves. I believe they will grow more naturally if we begin with a play which seems to have been written in a pedantic, negative temper. The spectacles and shows of *The Jew of Malta* were created by a playwright who might have assented to this observation from *The Praise of Folly*: 'The mind of man is so constructed that it is taken far more with disguises than with realities.'[41] By letting his characters embody their pretensions in spectacle, he makes these pretensions far more accessible to the judgment of his spectators. An emblem, to use Bacon's terms, 'reduceth conceits intellectuall to Images sensible'.[42] Marlowe's spectacles often associate the minds of his characters with their 'sensible' eyesight. As a measure of wisdom, spectacles may be more reliable than plausible speeches and riddling plots.

Renaissance writers or artists who designed pageants sought to interest a variety of spectators. Some would be more pleased than instructed by the fine show. Others would judge the pageant much as they would judge an emblem, considering the designer's use of visual symbols which had established meanings.[43] Marlowe's way with icons resembles his way with allusions; he often makes even a commonplace image difficult to identify. In this respect his shows differ both from the ready intelligibility of the street pageant and the deliberate obscurity of the printed emblem. His most emphatic spectacles provide focal summaries of a character's past behaviour, and therefore derive much of their force from their dramatic contexts. In his more tragic plays Marlowe's stage imagery may actually reveal a basic schism between his attitude and that of some emblem-makers. In *A Choice of Emblemes and Other Devices* (1586), Geffrey

Whitney describes emblems as 'Hauinge some wittie deuise expressed with cunning woorkemanship, somethinge obscure to be perceiued at the first, whereby, when with further consideration it is vnderstood, it maie the greater delighte the behoulder.'[44] Marlowe is not obscure because he is entertaining clever initiates. He is obscure because he wants his audience to discover that a delight in 'some wittie deuise' can be a self-destroying virtue.[45] For Marlowe, human imagination lies at the centre of tragic experience.

Marlowe allows his dark art to imitate the disappointments endured by his heroes. Even the imaginations of Faustus and Tamburlaine can fail to carry more sceptical readers and spectators over plateaux of trivia or mountains of dead. To a surprising extent, Marlowe's muse follows, as do his heroes, the path of Icarus, with this essential difference. His 'intollerable poetry', which confounds Heaven in earth, can eventually create vision in his audiences. Like a prophetic mirror, Marlowe's ironic art gives us more awareness of our own minds and values, but only if we continue to examine the mirror as well as the artist who holds it up.[46] His willingness to be misunderstood can then be viewed as an aspect of his skill in provoking an active, persistent kind of attention to his plays.

One might compare this attention to the way we respond when we study a puzzling Renaissance picture. Because it uses similar commonplace motifs, Brueghel's 'Landscape, with the Fall of Icarus' provides a helpful analogy. Is this painting an allegory? Is it a riddle? The incongruity between the drowning hero and the bright, busy landscape stimulates us to draw upon our knowledge – about Icarus, about the symbolism of sailing ships, even about the proverbial occupations of peasants. One of these peasants, ignoring Icarus, seems to be driving his plough towards some over-painted bones of the dead. Brueghel also invites us to exercise our ingenuity on the problem of our own perspective; he presents another peasant who apparently stares up at an invisible Daedalus flying into the darkness where we, the innocent onlookers, watch. Like Marlowe's, Brueghel's is a highly speculative art; it may lead us to reason very curiously. But that, I believe, is part of its excuse for being. One day, looking at Brueghel's 'Landscape', we begin to wonder how Icarus can have lost his wings when the warm sun, the simple focus of the entire design, lies barely above the horizon.

# 3

# Wicked fools of fortune

The life of man upon earth is a warfare, and his days are like the days of a hireling.
Job 7:1

Job's metaphors of strife and slavery aptly suggest the nature of life in Marlowe's Malta.[1] Job's terse, gnomic way of speaking resembles the proverbial style of Marlowe's own art in this play. By treating *The Jew of Malta* as an expanded proverb, I hope to shed more light on Marlowe's learned fooling. This fooling carries the stamp of the proverb-speaker in at least three respects. It is dark or 'hard', it is generalized in power, and it is dense with traditional meanings. Allusions to the Bible and to Machiavelli, as well as to more current literary genres and political events, form a kind of palimpsest covering the basic 'foundation' of the play – its topsy-turvical inversion of Job's wisdom and patience. Given the lively vigour of the fooling and the deadliness of Malta, Walter Benjamin's description of proverbs as 'ideograms' for stories seems to fit Marlowe's play remarkably well: 'A proverb, one might say, is a ruin which stands on the site of an old story and in which a moral twines about a happening like ivy around a wall.'[2]

Proverbs bring discipline, even censorship, to insight. They concentrate their wisdom in a form so simple that it seems innocuous. Wise men use them strategically for self-defence. Where prophecy would expose the speaker, a formulaic proverb disguises him. Or, to employ Benjamin's metaphors, the ivy hides the ruin and the ruin hides the site. Take these ingredients apart, and the proverb disappears. Analyse *The Jew of Malta* in the discrete formal terms of character, plot, or meaning, and the proverbial style vanishes.[3]

My discussion of this play stresses the general features of the proverbial style as they might affect an audience experiencing the play

for the first time. This audience would probably pass quickly over
Abigail's resolve to enter a nunnery for the *second* time. To Father
Barnardine the Jew's daughter explains her earlier rejection of 'that
holy life':

> Then were my thoughts so frail and unconfirmed,
> And I was chained to follies of the world,
> But now experience, purchasèd with grief,
> Has made me see the difference of things.
> My sinful soul, alas, hath paced too long
> The fatal labyrinth of misbelief,
> Far from the Son that gives eternal life.
>
> III.iii.59–65

The audience must be let down with a catastrophic bump before it
realizes that Malta itself is a 'fatal labyrinth of misbelief'. The self-
righteous characters, the tight-knit plot, and the subdued follies
discourage it from seeing 'the difference of things'. If a ruin is
exciting to explore, one forgets the danger of pits and traps.

## Dark sayings

Much of the action in *The Jew of Malta* is taken up by the 'professions' of the characters.[4] Marlowe reduces differences among these
characters by stressing the ways in which they justify themselves. He
encourages the audience to observe these self-justifying professions
through the eyes of his focal character, Barabas the Jew. For example, after the Knights of Malta have fleeced the Maltese Jews in
order to pay tribute to their Turkish overlords, they go off to collect
the wealth, saying

> For if we break our day, we break the league,
> And that will prove but simple policy.
>
> I.ii.159–60

Barabas indulges in a bit of word-play when he immediately remarks:

> Ay, policy; that's their profession,
> And not simplicity, as they suggest.
>
> 160–1

To the Knights, 'simple' meant 'imprudent' or 'improvident', meanings Barabas will later employ when he falls to scorning the witless-
ness of other Jews who haven't anticipated this financial disaster
(I.ii.215). Here, however, by opposing simplicity to policy he equates

policy with duplicity, and simplicity with sincerity or good faith.
The problem with the many 'professions' in this play is to decide
which kind of 'simplicity' they express.

At first this may seem easy enough to do. Barabas discovers that
his having 'cast with cunning for the time to come' has not improved
his fortunes. For although he has hidden a treasure under the floor of
his house, the Knights have quickly seized the house, turned out his
daughter Abigail, and established a nunnery. Put to his 'shifts',
Barabas immediately schemes to have Abigail turn nun and recover
the treasure. In order to persuade away her reluctance at dissembling,
he argues:

> As good dissemble that thou never mean'st
> As first mean truth and then dissemble it.
> A counterfeit profession is better
> Than unseen hypocrisy.
>
> I.ii.290–3

'Why not?' would be the probable response of the audience at this
point. They could assume that the Jew's distinction has ethical as
well as logical validity, and they would prefer a deliberate counterfeit profession which is at least self-knowledgeable to an 'unseen
hypocrisy' which is self-deceived.[5]

Marlowe has here contrived a war-like situation in which his hero
discovers that bad faith is necessary for survival. This bad faith thereby acquires the power to corrupt the hero's reason in a remarkably
plausible and subtle way.[6] The actual process of corruption becomes
more observable if we compare the 'profession' Barabas uses in persuading Abigail with the one he will use when he prepares to revenge
himself upon the Governor's son, Lodowick:

> Now will I show myself to have more of the
> serpent than the dove; that is, more knave than fool.
>
> II.iii.36–7

Through Barabas, Marlowe is here alluding to Christ's advice to his
disciples: 'Beholde, I send you as shepe in the middes of wolues:
be ye therefore wise as serpents, and innocent as doues' (Matthew
10:16).[7]

No wolf in sheep's clothing can be expected to credit a sheep with
wisdom! Barabas cannot see that a man may be *both* wise and simple.
Blinded by his own bad faith, he insists on clever distinctions, on a

choice between wisdom and simplicity, serpent and dove. Ironically, he thereby confirms his own folly. This brief profession offers us a glimpse of the negative, distorting-mirror effects achieved so swiftly through parodistic irony. The elastic analogy between serpent and dove in Christ's paradox 'returns', as Kenneth Burke puts it, in the shape of a more confining, trap-like relationship.[8] For, once distinguished, serpent and dove, wisdom and simplicity begin to contaminate one another. The knave now equals the fool. Or, to return to my first example from Act I, scene ii, the clever counterfeit 'professor' is actually an 'unseen hypocrite'. By persuading Abigail that they differ, Barabas is merely using reason for show. Severed from good faith and dove-like innocence, reason becomes folly.

Yet few of the numerous professions in *The Jew of Malta* are either transparently knavish or foolish. The puzzling 'unseen hypocrisy' appears everywhere, darkening the sayings of all self-righteous characters. The attitude of a character who simultaneously intends to deceive and deceives himself would seem less complicated if we could call it 'wilful ignorance'. That is how 'God's Judgment' describes wise knavery in the epilogue of William Wager's morality play, *The Longer Thou Livest The More Fool Thou Art*:

> But those are the greatest fools properly
> Which disdain to learn sapience
> To speak, to do, to work all things orderly
> And as God hath given intelligence;
> But contrary to nature and God's will
> They stop their eyes through wilful ignorance.[9]

Wager's plays openly associate knavery with folly, the abuse of knowledge and wisdom with the growth of evil. He makes it clear that characters who can 'first mean truth and then dissemble it' are wilfully ignorant. After 'God's Judgment' speaks, 'Piety' goes on to define herself as 'the highest sapience' (l. 1925), and 'Discipline' adds that we need both cunning ('scire') and wisdom. 'Exercitation' then argues (probably following Proverbs 26:18) that,

> A wicked man having learning and cunning
> And doth many sciences understand
> Is like one whose wits are running
> I mean a madman having a sword in his hand.
>                    1943–6

Marlowe's conception, although similar, is far more obscure.

Barabas retains his plausibility as he assures Abigail that Lodowick may be duped because he is 'not of the seed of Abraham' (II.iii.227) or when he triumphantly argues:

> It is no sin to deceive a Christian,
> For they themselves hold it a principle,
> Faith is not to be held with heretics;
> But all are heretics that are not Jews.
> This follows well, and therefore, Daughter, fear not.[10]
>
> II.iii.306–10

The Jew's ridiculous slave Ithamore temporarily puts the whole matter of self-justification in a comic perspective when he introduces himself with, 'My name's Ithamore, my profession what you please' (II.iii.162–3). But not until Marlowe's apocalyptic catastrophe explodes all the misleading distinctions of morality or dramatic advantage among characters can we recognize that counterfeit professions *are* weapons in Wager's humanistic sense. Wisdom without good faith grows murderous; it generates the warlike and slavish qualities of life on Malta. St James was thinking of wisdom in this way when he advised the twelve tribes:

> But if ye haue bitter enuying and strife in your hearts, reioyce not, nether be liers against the trueth.
> This wisdome descendeth not fró aboue, but *is* earthlie, sensual, and deuilish.
> For where enuying and strife *is*, there *is* sedition, and all maner of euil workes.
>
> 3: 14–16

Marlowe risks a parody of devilish wisdom and its effects when the fool, Ithamore, woos the whore, Bellamira, with a love song:

> Thou in those groves, by Dis above,
> Shalt live with me, and be my love.
>
> IV.iv.93–4

Marlowe knew well how powerful the charm of an utterance motivated by bad faith and self-deception could be. He allows this charm to work with, and sometimes in spite of, the distorted quotations and dubious maxims dear to so many citizens of Malta. Were it not for such charm, these citizens would all be as obviously foolish as Ithamore. They would manifestly be bearing out one of the principles set down in *The Praise of Folly* – 'That where a man wants matter, he may best frame some.'[11] But as T. S. Eliot seemed to see, the play, far from being merely ridiculous, is a 'terribly serious, even savage' farce.[12] Its temper resembles that of the religious comedy studied by

V. A. Kolve in *The Play Called Corpus Christi*.[13] The wicked fools of *The Jew of Malta* can induce an audience to suspend judgment. Darkness obscures our understanding of the play's central issues and influences our responses to the hero, Barabas the Jew.

The early debate between Barabas and Ferneze, Governor of Malta, can be approached as a remarkable piece of moral and thematic obfuscation. Each speaker self-righteously defends himself and challenges his opponent. Each can at least recognize his own folly when it appears in an antagonist; the two debaters are wise enough to expose each other:[14]

> *Ferneze :* Content thee, Barabas; thou has nought but right.
> *Barabas :* Your extreme right does me exceeding wrong.
> I.ii.153–4

There can be little doubt that Ferneze is victimizing Barabas. He begins his session with the Jews by explaining that wars have robbed the treasury, but when Barabas asks if Jews are to contribute equally with Christians, he bursts out:

> No, Jew, like infidels;
> For through our sufferance of your hateful lives,
> Who stand accursèd in the sight of heaven,
> These taxes and afflictions are befall'n.
> II.ii.62–5

Ferneze takes rapid advantage of the Jew's reluctance to choose either of the alternatives offered to him and to his fellows – payment of half their wealth or conversion to Christianity. He quickly and unjustly seizes all of Barabas's wealth. When Barabas asks whether theft is the ground of Ferneze's religion – the other Jews have still had to pay only half – Ferneze replies:

> No, Jew. We take particularly thine
> To save the ruin of a multitude,
> And better one want for a common good
> Than many perish for a private man.
> I.ii.97–100

Marlowe's allusion in this passage is one which an Elizabethan would almost certainly hear. Ferneze chooses words similar to those of the Jewish high-priest Caiaphas (John 11:50) in order to 'justify' his treatment of Barabas: 'Nor yet do you consider that it is expedient for vs, that one man dye for the people, and that the whole nacion perish not.' He thereby aligns Barabas with Christ as victim and redeemer. Marlowe is showing us how antichrists like Barabas are born.

Ferneze may have been trying to trap the Jews of Malta in a dilemma. His strategy bears comparison with the use of 'horned argument', defined by the rhetorician Blundeville in terms which provide an interesting parallel to Marlowe's allusive scene: 'The horned Argument is, when by some subtile and craftie manner of questioning, we seeke to have such an answere, as we may take vantage therof, as the Pharises did, when they questioned with Christ touching the payment of Tribute to Caesar.'[15] But when Pharisee answers Pharisee, Marlowe's audience will find it particularly difficult to grapple with the problems of righteousness and retribution being raised. The furious energy with which Barabas and Ferneze both justify themselves might deflect full recognition of how persistently they distort Scripture. When the First Knight attempts to buttress Ferneze's 'Caiaphas' argument by reasoning that all Jews must suffer from a 'first curse', anyway, Barabas retorts, 'What, bring you Scripture to confirm your wrongs?' (i.ii.111). But then he immediately proceeds to mix wisely foolish distortions of Scripture into a profession which powerfully confirms his wrongs or crimes.

J. B. Steane has shown how the strength of the Jew's next line, 'Preach me not out of my possessions' is promptly weakened by a 'piece of straight-and-crooked thinking'.[16] 'Some Jews are wicked, as all Christians are.' Barabas goes on to question the First Knight's assumption that he must be damned with all his tribe. G. K. Hunter feels that there was some contemporary support for the Jew's appeal to an idea of individual accountability, in the Geneva Bible's gloss on Romans 11, which holds that the Jews are not cast out 'in particular'.[17] Of course, the particular Jew who would be saved must still confess that Jesus is Lord. 'For, with the heart man beleueth vnto righteousnes, and withe the mouth man confesseth to saluation' (Romans 10:10).

Marlowe's point may be that Barabas neither believes not confesses, for all the noise he makes with his mouth. 'The man that dealeth righteously shall live', the Jew asserts (i.ii.117). His assertion has been glossed with several Biblical texts.[18] Perhaps even closer than the parallels already suggested are those in Habakkuk

2:4, Galatians 3:11, and Hebrews 10:38: 'Beholde, he that lifteth vp him self, his minde is not vpright in him, but the iuste shal liue by his faith'; 'And that no man is iustified by the law in the sight of God, it is euident: for the iust shal liue by faith'; 'Now the iust shal liue by faith: but if anie withdrawe him self, my soule shal haue no pleasure in him.' Barabas says that the just man shall live, leaving out of his formulation the all-important phrase, 'by faith'.[19] His final challenge to the Christians, 'which of you can charge me otherwise?' may echo, as Sims has pointed out, the question of Christ to the Pharisees in John 8:46: 'Which of you can rebuke me of sinne?'[20] Christ there explicitly contests the Jewish profession, 'Abraham is our father.'

Scholars who have emphasized the Pharisaical and legalistic dependence of Barabas upon Abraham throughout the play have restored Marlowe's work to its historical context.[21] But this context should include more awareness of how learned fooling might affect an audience. The aggressive question, 'Which of you can charge me otherwise?', in itself a probable alteration of John 8:46, is a highly elliptical way of referring even a theologically sophisticated audience to Scriptural distinctions between the Old Law and the New. Ferneze seems to understand the nature of the game which he and Barabas are playing with one another:

> Out, wretched Barabas!
> Sham'st thou not thus to justify thy self,
> As if we knew not thy profession?
>
> I.ii.119–21

But his subsequent reassurance to Barabas, that by patiently relying on righteousness he will increase his wealth again, suggests that Christian and Jew understand righteousness in the same materialistic, self-deceived way. Ferneze's following outburst attributing the 'monstrous sin' of covetousness to excessive wealth simply does not follow from his materialistic interpretation of righteousness. Barabas quickly punctures the Governor's perversely arbitrary proverb with a bit of his own devilish wisdom: 'But theft is worse.' The Ten Commandments do distinguish stealing from coveting. As we have seen, however, in Malta most distinctions collapse into chop-logical nonsense.

'There would be less harm in being frankly Jew or Turk than a Christian hypocrite', wrote Erasmus in one of his best known

adages, 'Dulce bellum inexpertis' ('War is sweet to those who are
ignorant of it').[22] In Marlowe's baffling debate, Jew and Christian
exchange doubtful professions, while the Turks, somewhat more
precise at promise-keeping, courteously grant Ferneze time to find
the 'ten years' tribute'. The situation tends to frustrate any inclination an audience might have to choose sides. In *The Merchant of
Venice* Shakespeare will prepare a confrontation between his two
merchants, Antonio and Shylock, by defining, at least for the
moment, an impersonal standard of justice:

> The Duke cannot deny the course of law;
> For the commodity that strangers have
> With us in Venice, if it be denied,
> Will much impeach the justice of the state,
> Since that the trade and profit of the city
> Consisteth of all nations.
>
> III.iii.26–31

Laws like this one must be at least as old as the judgment given on
Sinai: 'Moreouer, thou shalt not do iniurie to a stranger, nether
oppresse him: for ye were strangers in the land of Egypt' (Exodus
22:21). But Ferneze has no such scruples; in Malta justice depends
upon self-interest.

All that finally keeps the contest between Barabas and Ferneze
from slipping into a chaos of relativism are the insistent, if crooked,
references to righteousness. Righteousness without faith is the
negative Judaism Paul and Christ repeatedly condemned. Marlowe
may have been encouraging his audience to wonder which is more of
a Jew, the knight or the merchant? 'For he is not a Iewe, which is one
outwarde: nether is that circumcision, which is outwarde in the flesh',
wrote Paul (Romans 2:28). It is actually the Christian, Ferneze, who
introduces (with little faith or understanding) that very alliance of
patience and righteousness which will ultimately differentiate the
wicked fool Barabas from his prototype, Job. Marlowe's 'foundation',
his old story of Job, is already in place. He gives his audience a taste
of life as a 'warfare' and as the 'days of a hireling' well before his
First Jew counsels Barabas:

> O yet be patient, gentle Barabas.
>
> I.ii.170
>
> Yet, brother Barabas, remember Job.
>
> I.ii.181

If the audience also remembers Job at this point, it might recall his strong distaste for self-righteous professions.[23] The Zwinglian preacher Henry Bullinger argues that the naturally corrupt man who must depend on God for his salvation should follow Job in refusing to justify himself.[24] The text he has in mind is Job 9:15: 'For though I were iuste, yet colde I not answer, *but* I wolde make supplication to my Iudge.' Richard Hooker also recalls this aspect of Job's righteousness, when, near the conclusion of the Preface to his *Laws of Ecclesiastical Polity*, he appeals for peace with the Puritan brethren. Hooker praises Augustine for confessing that Job, only by saying, 'Behold, I will lay mine hand on my mouth' (40:4), achieved the 'glory of an ingenuous mind'.[25]

Barabas, of course, rarely lays *his* hand on *his* mouth. By congratulating himself upon his ingenuity, he too achieves a kind of 'glory' – the kind stigmatized by St Paul as boasting and rejoicing according to the flesh.[26] Marlowe's dark irony is integral to his meaning. His Jew's worldly plausibility parodies Job's pious reticence. As the play begins, Barabas seems to commend himself for that Proverbial virtue, prudence. He discriminates quickly between the 'needy groom' who would 'make a miracle' of his heaps of coin, and those 'men of judgment' who convert such wealth into precious stones. Both of the long soliloquies in which Barabas describes his wealth and success are soberly reflective in tone; the second (I.i.101ff) includes a number of cautious phrases suggesting his aptitude for learning from experience: 'I can see', 'methinks', 'I cannot tell', 'I must confess', 'Oft have I heard tell'. After the Jews have come to him for counsel, Barabas resorts to his reason: 'Now search this secret out. Summon thy senses; call thy wits together' (I.i.175–6). He decides to 'intercept the worst' – a course of action for which he praises himself after interviews with the Christians and with his fellow Jews, all of whom he has deceived with his ecstatic rages:

> No, Barabas is born to better chance
> And framed of finer mold than common men
> That measure nought but by the present time.
> A reaching thought will search his deepest wits
> And cast with cunning for the time to come,
> For evils are apt to happen every day.
>
> I.ii.219–24

Even when he learns from Abigail that his house has been seized, he maintains a posture of defiant rational competence:

> No, I will live; nor loathe I this my life.
> And since you leave me in the ocean thus
> To sink or swim, and put me to my shifts,
> I'll rouse my senses and awake myself.
>
> I.ii.266–9

Given the hero's emphatic and plausible references to his own wisdom, it is natural that some readers and spectators have found a noble streak in Barabas, and that a great many others have commended his honesty and cleverness.[27] Throughout the play he continually mentions his plots and policies, circumspectly anticipating injuries and 'dispraysing' the wit of his opponents. Eventually the Jew's participation in farce might intimate that he has only been praising his own folly all along. But we must give Barabas (and Marlowe) credit for having done it so persuasively.

Skilful folly-praising is what renders the Jew's opening soliloquies so dark. These speeches do contain a number of allusions, but most of them are woven smoothly into the fabric of the subdued and measured discourse. Some of these allusions attract others as the action develops, creating densities of meaning which are emphasized in spectacular ways. But so early in the play, neither allusions nor spectacle seem capable of deeply qualifying the Jew's strong plausibility. No doubt, the discovery of Barabas seated in his counting house can insinuate suspicions of false value, but Barabas does not venerate his hoard in the way that Volpone will do later. As spectators we would probably note his pragmatic shrewdness, not his sinful avarice, as he tells over his wealth with scarcely a trace of enthusiasm.[28] Even when he begins to describe the stones of great price in which he invests his coin, there is little reduction in his hard-bitten professionalism. The merchant who complains 'what a trouble 'tis to count this trash!' prudently regards his more precious stones as potentially useful for ransom 'in peril of calamity'. Although the Jew's great red nose might look ridiculous enough, Barabas need not be regarded as a fool and a monster from the outset of the play.

Neither, I think, should the 'Prologue' Machiavel who introduces him. Marlowe's Machiavel seems to derive from the Machiavel who describes himself in an earlier epigram by Gabriel Harvey. Both Machiavels announce their own wisdom. Harvey's tells us, 'I alone am wise, I alone live and triumph for myself. / Who knows not the rest? Deceit is my greatest virtue; / Next comes violence. I know no other Gods.'[29] Marlowe makes his Machiavel more appealing than Harvey's by having him attribute this very deceit and violence to hypocritical followers who will not admit that they actually follow him. He disguises what is in Harvey an obnoxious pretence to total wisdom by letting it take the form of a plausible impatience with formulas and superstitions. References to Draco and Phalaris, along with a preference for being envied, not pitied, might have warned a few listeners that Marlowe is assimilating his Machiavel to the older stock type of the selfish tyrant – for Marlowe another variety of wicked fool.[30] While the realist Machiavelli admits in the famous seventeenth chapter of *The Prince*, 'It is far better to be feared than loved if you cannot be both', he also points out that a prince should at least try to make himself feared in such a way that he avoids being hated.[31] Marlowe's tyrants – Barabas, Mortimer and the Guise – brashly opt for hatred.

Just when an audience might begin to have doubts about this clever Machiavel who calls murders 'fooleries', he laughs at himself for giving a lecture in Britain, and presents the 'tragedy of a Jew':

> I crave but this: grace him as he deserves,
> And let him not be entertained the worse
> Because he favors me.

The respect in which Barabas particularly favours Machiavel is his skill at knavish–foolish sophistry.

The second soliloquy is an outstanding example of this skill. Barabas has been busy questioning his merchant assistants and calculating the course of his vessels. Left alone on stage once again, he rejoices:

> Thus trowls our fortune in by land and sea,
> And thus are we on every side enriched.
> These are the blessings promised to the Jews,
> And herein was old Abram's happiness.
>
> I.i.101–4

G. K. Hunter has provided a gloss on this first allusion in the play to Abraham, suggesting that in Christian terms the Jews had no right to congratulate themselves on being his children.[32] To keep them from glorying in their descent from Abraham, he points out, Luther

in his *Commentary on Galatians* cited against the Jews the teachings
of Paul in Romans 9 and Galatians 3. In both epistles Paul moves
from Abraham into discussions of righteousness and the Mosaic law.
Because this complex of concepts regularly surfaces in the action of
the play, it seems all the more probable that Marlowe himself had
the Pauline texts as clearly in mind when he wrote this soliloquy as
when he contrived the debate between Barabas and Ferneze. Whether
his spectators also had them in mind – or could be expected to keep
them there while attending to Barabas – is more doubtful.

Barabas proceeds from the blinding confidence of the assertion
that 'old Abram's happiness' lay in wealth, to an encomium of
wealthy Jews and their prudential shrewdness. First come a series of
direct questions, none of which really can be answered in the terms
Barabas poses:

> What more may heaven do for earthly man
> Than thus to pour out plenty in their laps,
> Ripping the bowels of the earth for them,
> Making the sea their servants, and the winds
> To drive their substance with successful blasts?
>
> I.i.105–9

The idea that Heaven so obligingly rips earth represents a complete
inversion of the values implied when Guyon describes covetousness
to Mammon in *The Faerie Queene* (1590):

> Then gan a cursed hand the quiet wombe
> Of his great grandmother with steele to wound,
> And the hid treasures in her sacred tombe
> With sacriledge to dig.
>
> Bk. II, canto vii, stanza 17

More to the point, it seems to me, is the fact that the 'pathetic'
rhetorical question asked by Barabas almost persuades us of his
assumptions; we tend to agree that Heaven is indeed generous before
noting that his question is premised on the most outrageous materialism. By that time Barabas has moved on to other questions: 'Who
hateth me but for my happiness? / Or who is honored now but for his
wealth?' A discourse knit together out of such subversive queries,
wise saws and modern instances can seduce an audience. Although
this 'unseen hypocrite' may not be fully aware of it, he is surely one
of those who, in Sidney's words, can 'stay the braine from a through
[sic] beholding the worthines of the subject'. He boggles his own

brain, those of other characters, and, finally, the brains of the audience as well.

*The Praise of Folly* makes use of comparable challenges to the wisdom and good faith of the reader. 'What harm is it if everybody hisses you, so long as you applaud yourself?' Folly inquires.[33] Or: 'In your judgment, what difference is there between those who in Plato's cave look admiringly at the shadows and simulacra of various things, desiring nothing, quite well satisfied with themselves, as against the wise man who emerges from the cave and sees realities?' (p. 64). Erasmus subtly exposes the foolishness of his speaker by implying that she often fails to see such differences. In principle she knows what Abigail will discover through grief, that 'all human affairs, like the Sileni of Alcibiades, have two aspects, each quite different from the other' (p. 36). In practice she muddles vital distinctions as thoroughly as Barabas does. But whenever her distorted perspective coincides with the actual follies of this world, her observations acquire point. We forget that she is still in the cave. 'Who is honored now but for his wealth?' asks Barabas, and we begin to applaud him as a satirist. In the rest of his soliloquy folly and wordly wisdom become inseparable. For example, Barabas is moved by his assumption that religious faith can be measured through financial success, to make the following comment on Christians:

> For I can see no fruits in all their faith,
> But malice, falsehood, and excessive pride,
> Which methinks fits not their profession.

I.i.114–16

Five lines later Barabas claims that the Jews are wealthier than those who 'brag of faith', implying that the only fruits he regards are strictly monetary ones.[34] He proceeds quickly with a resonant catalogue of Jewish merchants and a group of political maxims borrowed from *The Prince*. If the audience can get past the thoroughly dubious proposition that Christian rule guarantees Jewish peace, there is little to draw it up short until the outrageous sentiment with which the soliloquy concludes:

> I have no charge, nor many children,
> But one sole daughter, whom I hold as dear
> As Agamemnon did his Iphigen.

I.i.134–6

Once we understand how Marlowe tricks us with the rhetoric of the paradoxical encomium in these opening soliloquies, it becomes probable that he must always have been anticipating the villainous farce towards which his play suddenly turns. It also becomes obvious that a tension between large hero and small plot, long recognized by commentators on *The Jew of Malta*, may be explained as an effect of the Jew's charming unseen hypocrisy. *The Jew of Malta* and *Doctor Faustus* focus on what should be to a Christian the most essential expressions of pride conceivable – avarice, and the denial of God.[35] But it must not therefore be supposed that the heroes of these plays are themselves simple types of pride. Instead of saying, as Eric Rothstein does, that Barabas is 'tropologically totally simple', one might say that it is his destiny to *become* merely a trope, an empty habitation for those interchangeable shadows – the Avaricious Spiritual Jew, the Anti-Job, the Antichrist.[36] As long as he energetically commends himself, Barabas remains dynamic, open, unpredictable. The motives he continually justifies invite close examination, as those of malignant morality vices generally do not. Our sense that Barabas may be too large or complex for the morality convention should warn us that Marlowe is using the convention critically and self-reflexively. The emergence of farce when Barabas takes to his shifts dramatizes the fallibility and futility of prudent self-justification in an evil world. Farce makes the dark and subtle folly of wickedness more visible.

### Concentrating and generalizing power

Barabas advises the audience in his first soliloquy that men of judgment should always attempt to invest their money in precious jewels,

> And as their wealth increaseth, so enclose
> Infinite riches in a little room.
>
> I.i.36–7

In the twenty-eighth book of Job, Job offers, like Barabas, a catalogue of precious metals and stones. But Job has been posing the question, 'Whence then cometh wisdom? And where is the place of understanding?' Job tells his listeners that precious objects cannot match the value of wisdom. God's reply to his question is, according to Job, 'Beholde, the feare of the Lord is wisdome, and to departe from euil is vnderstanding.'[37]

Although the Biblical Wisdom books frequently compare wisdom to hidden or buried treasure, they insist that wisdom is better than silver and gold, and that the character of a miser does not befit a wise man. Just as important, where *The Jew of Malta* is concerned, they regularly express their own riches in the little rooms of proverb and parable. Although it is uneven in its effects, *The Jew of Malta* is a close-knit, highly concentrated piece of dramatic workmanship. We have already seen how Barabas and Ferneze resemble each other, pot and kettle fashion, in their early debate. Throughout the play Marlowe maintains a thematic relationship between these two characters, while bringing in additional connections between both Jews and Christians, and a third group, the Turks. Harry Levin has argued that although the play has three plots – an over, an under, and a main – all of the characters are on the same moral level.[38] But an audience need not recognize this moral equivalence until the end of the play. Its mirrors are veiled, its connections oblique. Retrospectively one can see that the foolish vengefulness of Barabas is indeed precisely comparable to the foolish political opportunism of Ferneze. Machiavelli himself would have smiled at both of them. That Marlowe's own political theory was far sounder than that of his characters is implied by the way his characters act out a vicious circle of mutually destructive enslavements.

Shifty Barabas will have to be our guide through this confining labyrinth. Like the Guise in *The Massacre at Paris*, he brings the other characters within the focus of a satiric view.[39] His actions provoke reflection and rationalization – his own and that of other characters. Moreover he is often the occasion of wickedly disruptive behaviour on the part of other characters. These are of course the traditional functions of a morality vice. But Marlowe complicates the vice's role by accenting the reduction of policy to desperate gambling, the failure of knavery to control time and chance.

Barabas carries off the first of his shifty schemes successfully at the beginning of Act II, when Abigail recovers his money from the nunnery:

> But stay! What star shines yonder in the east?
> The lodestar of my life, if Abigail.
> Who's there?
>
> II.i.41–3

By putting the Wise Men's question into the mouth of a character who can call his treasure 'my soul's sole hope', Marlowe presents avarice as a ridiculous distortion of basic Christian aspirations.[40] Distortions continue as Barabas enters the slave market two scenes later and announces his intention of revenging himself on Ferneze and Ferneze's son Lodowick. Marlowe emphasizes the Jew's hypocrisy and the arbitrary, wilful character of his vengefulness throughout the scene:

> I am not of the tribe of Levi, I,
> That can so soon forget an injury.
>
> II.iii.18–19

As he sets Lodowick and Mathias, the two lovers of Abigail, against one another, and boasts of his villainy to his new slave, Ithamore, Barabas resembles the wicked fools of Proverbs:

*It is* a mans honour to cease from strife: but euery foole will be medling.   (20:3)

*It is* as a passe time to a foole to do wickedly: but wisdome *is* vnderstanding to a man.   (10:23)

His vengeful scheme against Lodowick quickly succeeds, following the prediction and matching the description of the foolish Ithamore:

> Well, I have delivered the challenge in such sort,
> As meet they will and fighting die – brave sport.
>
> III.i.28–9

The exuberant, sporting villainy of *The Jew of Malta* has much in common with 'true prudence' as defined by the Folly of Erasmus:

The fool arrives at true prudence, if I am not deceived, by addressing himself at once to the business and taking his chances...There are two great obstacles to developing a knowledge of affairs – shame, which throws a smoke over the understanding, and fear, which once danger has been sighted, dissuades from going through with an exploit. Folly, with a grand gesture, frees us from both. Never to feel shame, to dare anything – few mortals know to what further blessings these will carry us.

(p. 36)

But while his characters stab, strangle and poison one another, Marlowe is seriously concerned with the righteousness of vengeance. Abigail, the only character in the play capable of addressing herself disinterestedly to other persons and problems focuses on this issue immediately before she enters the convent:

> Hard-hearted father, unkind Barabas,
> Was this the pursuit of thy policy,

> To make me show them favor severally,
> That by my favor they should both be slain?
> Admit thou lov'dst not Lodowick for his sire,
> Yet Don Mathias ne'er offended thee.
> But thou wert set upon extreme revenge
> Because the sire dispossessed thee once.
>
> iii.iii.36–43

Barabas has learned his vengeful policy from Ferneze. 'Your extreme right does me exceeding wrong,' he told the Governor (i.ii.154). Marlowe's frequent use of scourges, massacres, punishments, and vengeances suggests that he may have been concerned with the moral confusions created by righteous wrong-doing. Once again Erasmus may help us to see the serious foundation beneath the superficial fooling. Attacking the destructions of war in a letter written to the Abbot of St Bertin (1514), Erasmus wrote:

But you will say, that the rights of sovereigns must be maintained. It is not for me to speak inadvisedly about the acts of princes. I only know this, that *summum jus*, extreme right, is often *summa injuria*, extreme wrong; there are princes who first decide what they want and then look out for a title with which to cloak their proceedings.[41]

Barabas applies an extreme right not only when he destroys the suitors, but also when he poisons a whole nunnery to punish his erring daughter, and when he arranges to blow up a host of Turks feasting in a monastery. But these later vengeances are no part of his original scheme to get even with Ferneze. Whenever he plans one stratagem, he reckons without those eventualities which will require him to devise still another – Abigail's alienation and conversion to Christianity after Mathias has been slain, her dying confession and the blackmail of the friars, the confession of Ithamore to his Lady Vanity, and the poison which does not work fast enough on Ithamore, Bellamira, and Pilia-Borza:

> One dram of powder more had made all sure.
> What damned slave was I!
>
> v.i.22–3

At least in Abigail's case, the Jew's extreme measures bring about the very thing he seeks to avoid. The dying Abigail only reveals how her father has handled her suitors to obtain absolution from the Friar. Such inept and haphazard vengeances do not come up to the standard announced in the eighth chapter of *The Prince*:

We can say that cruelty is used well (if it is permissable to talk in this way of what is evil) when it is employed once for all, and one's safety depends on it, and then it is not persisted in but as far as possible turned to the good of one's subjects. Cruelty badly used is that which, although infrequent to start with, as time goes on, rather than disappearing, becomes more evident.[42]

Machiavelli could also have warned Barabas against choosing the wronged Ferneze as his ally after he becomes Governor of Malta in Act v. Chapter 7 of *The Prince* concludes, 'Whoever believes that with great men new services wipe out old injuries deceives himself.'[43] The Jew's many mistakes do not prevent him from boasting of his policy and circumspection. But by the time he contrives his final scheme, the audience may have been conditioned to expect loose ends. When, in his last address to the audience, Barabas halts his devilish carpentry and asks,

> Now tell me, worldlings, underneath the sun
> If greater falsehood ever has been done?
>
> v.v.49–50

the audience might say to itself, 'Not yet.'

Ferneze's turn is still to come. He plays his part by cutting the cable which supports the gallery where Barabas stands, dumping Barabas into the boiling cauldron which he has prepared for his guest, the Turkish ruler Calymath. This wickedly foolish disaster has strongly 'Proverbial' overtones: 'He that diggeth a pit, shal fall therein, and he that rolleth a stone, it shal returne vnto him' (Proverbs 26:27); 'his owne iniquities shal take the wicked him self, and he shalbe holden with the cordes of his own sinne' (5:22). In Marlowe's dramatic proverb, Ferneze has only to sever the rope. Marlowe concentrates and generalizes the traditional wisdom that the wicked punish themselves, by making the wicked punish the wicked. Ferneze is the one clearly responsible for carrying out the Jew's scheme to its bitter end – the obliteration of the monastery where all the Turkish knights are dining. Surely the spirit of farce, released by all the cords, hinges, cranes and pulleys in the Jew's flamboyant dumping machine, is still at large when Ferneze explains to Calymath the 'Jew's courtesy' to these Turkish knights:

> For he that did by treason work our fall
> By treason hath delivered thee to us.
>
> v.v.109–10

When Ferneze repays Barabas and the Turks with extreme right, the audience might feel that it was back where it began, without being fully aware of just how Marlowe has structured his viciously circular plot. Until the catastrophe, the mirrors which reflect Barabas and Ferneze in one another are dimmed and darkened. Nevertheless Marlowe has developed a series of parallels between the private revenger and the political opportunist. In his second soliloquy Barabas says: 'Give us a peaceful rule; make Christians kings, / That thirst so much for principality' (I.i.132–3). We soon find out that on Malta such expectations are fatuous; neutrality has a very high price. But because the play is written with more political realism than any of its characters can muster, we also find that Ferneze's general situation resembles that of Barabas. The few Jewish brethren whom Barabas terms a 'multitude', may be a group scarcely smaller than Ferneze's 'multitude' of Knights. 'We take particularly thine / To save the ruin of a multitude', Ferneze claims. But when he must explain to Del Bosco why his crusading Knights are ignobly allied to their supposed enemies, the Turks, he gives as an excuse, 'our force is small' (II.ii.34). Like the Jews, it seems that the Knights themselves are 'strangers', deprived by circumstances of a real choice between freedom and dependency. In constructing this political dilemma, Marlowe may owe something to Machiavelli. If the Knights choose peace with tribute, a course Machiavelli viewed as temporizing, they debase themselves through subjection to the Turks. If they choose war with the Turks they require the support of stronger and equally selfish allies, the Spaniards.[44] Perhaps this is why the harlot Bellamira, crying out in the streets, refers to a state of siege before a shot is fired (III.i.1).

Ferneze's political folly is not always as comic as the Jew's tricksy vengeances, and it is further obscured by 'unseen hypocrisy'. But anyone who assumes that Barabas monopolizes the farce in the play should scrutinize Ferneze's political shifts. The conditions on which he agrees to a sale of Turkish slaves, captured by the Spaniard Del Bosco, are thoroughly muddled. Del Bosco assures Ferneze that the Spanish King means to expel the Knights from Malta – and that he will help them win freedom from the Turks! Del Bosco may be wise in criticizing the Knights for buying their league with the Turks, but just how wise is he in commending to Ferneze the example of the knights besieged by Turks on Rhodes?

For when their hideous force environed Rhodes,
Small though the number was that kept the town,
They fought it out, and not a man survived
To bring the hapless news to Christendom.

II.ii.48–51

Ferneze heroically welcomes the freedom to be exterminated and concludes with a flourish: 'Honor is bought with blood and not with gold.' 'Who is honored now but for his wealth?' Barabas had asked. Where but on Malta could such wisdom be at all convincing?

Ferneze commits similar heroics when he later defies the Turkish Bashaw with a furious vow to demolish his own city (III.v.13). 'You shall not need to trouble yourselves so far', the Bashaw replies. In the meantime other connections have been suggested between Ferneze and Barabas. Barabas has contrived the death of the Governor's son, a suitor for his daughter Abigail, and has 'sauced' the porridge which will kill Abigail too. Ferneze gives promise of matching Barabas as a meddling and extreme revenger if he ever has a chance. The scene in which Katherine, the mother of Mathias, and Ferneze discover their dead children brings vengeance close to parody. Ferneze appears to grieve 'most of all' because he doesn't know whom to blame; he regrets that the Turks didn't kill Lodowick (III.ii.14). While Ferneze is exchanging Turkish for Spanish masters, Barabas has been enslaving his daughter Abigail and adopting his slave Ithamore 'for mine only heir' (III.iv.40).

A fast-paced and fluid manner of staging which uses a few simple emblematic devices could probably insinuate some of the more startling connections in what Alfred Harbage has termed a 'panto-mimic action upon a universalized platform'.[45] For example, the Jew, the religious orders, and Bellamira all require 'houses' and might have to share with one another, while the more public central playing space would have to accommodate both seat of government and slave market. Turkish slaves stand on stage for almost ninety lines in response to Ferneze's order: 'Go, officers, and set them straight in show' (II.ii.43). They provide a stage-emblem for the wicked conceits which are acted out before them during the third scene of Act II. Barabas confesses his vengefulness and double-talks about his 'diamond', Abigail, with the Governor's son. He assures Lodowick, 'no price shall make us part', and is then ready to turn to other business: 'But now I must be gone to buy a slave.' His words to

the slave and to Lodowick after he completes his purchase implicitly
link Ithamore with Abigail:

> Come, sirrah, you are mine.
> As for the diamond, it shall be yours.
>
> II.iii.133-4

Mathias, the other suitor for Abigail, comes with his mother to buy
a slave just before they are taken away. Barabas then interviews
Ithamore and has him stand by while he deceives both suitors. Surely
Marlowe is pressing here toward dramatic allegory, reinforcing
through spectacle his play's fundamental sense of human life as 'the
days of a hireling'.

But only by detaching ourselves from the play's dark spell can we
recognize how thoroughly the metaphor of enslavement has shaped
dramatic structure.[46] At first the Jew, who has a Turkish slave, is
subject to a Christian, and the Christian pays tribute to the Turk.
Barabas is eventually mastered by his slave and betrayed into the
hands of his Christian master Ferneze. But by venturing desperately
he escapes Ferneze and, following the pattern Ithamore has established, betrays Ferneze into the hands of Ferneze's enemy, and
former superior, the Turk Calymath. 'I hope to see the governor a
slave', says Barabas (v.i.65). And so the power hierarchy revolves on
its vicious way. In the beginning, we see Turk and Christian siding
against Jew. Jew and Turk join forces against Christian as Barabas,
aided by Ithamore, executes his vengeances and then traps Ferneze.
Briefly Jew and Christian plot against Turk until the Christian turns
the tables on the Jew with the Turk watching. Such a pattern can
hardly be accidental. As Abigail perceived, 'there is no love on earth'
(III.iii.47). Religious distinctions disappear when the Turk Ithamore
plays the 'morality' role of the prodigal son, when a Jew, Barabas,
rises from the dead and tempts a Turk, Calymath, with a pearl of
great price (v.iii.27), and when Calymath's followers are dined and
destroyed in a Catholic monastery.

Ferneze seems to have the advantage at the end, but with Calymath his prisoner he is still in a precarious spot. 'To keep me here
will nought advantage you', Calymath warns Ferneze. The Knights
who guard such a prisoner against 'all the world' will risk becoming
prisoners to *him*. This is a lesson which Elizabeth's custody of Mary
Queen of Scots could have taught the *Jew*'s first audience.[47] How

wise would Elizabeth have been to have captured Philip II of Spain? There can be little substance in Ferneze's demand of war damages, because Calymath has already 'caused the ruins to be new-repaired' (v.iii.2). Calymath has also admired the impregnability of Malta's site and wondered 'how it could be conquered thus' (v.iii.12). By this time the audience may have become more adept at answering such rhetorical questions. Malta can easily be conquered as long as it is peopled by grasping 'multitudes' who know its 'common channels' and can burrow from within. As Douglas Cole points out, the Governor, Ferneze, 'Has helped to restore order only by adopting Barabas' own principles of treachery and deceit. Barabas may be dead, but his vice lives on.'[48]

## Density of meaning

When Barabas says that of his wealth there 'rests no more/But bare remembrance, like a soldier's scar' (II.i.9–10), he repeats an image he uses first on meeting Ferneze, 'Alas, my lord, we are no soldiers' (I.ii.50), and then again to his fellow Jews:

> But give him liberty at least to mourn,
> That in a field amidst his enemies
> Doth see his soldiers slain, himself disarmed,
> And knows no means of his recovery.
> I.ii.203–6

Just why Barabas, who is 'no soldier', should describe himself in this way might be explained by referring to the underlying analogy between Barabas and Job. By repeating the image of the soldier, Marlowe may be alluding obscurely to the saying of Job already cited: 'The life of man upon earth is a warfare, and his days are like the days of a hireling' (7:1). This phrasing from the Douai Old Testament (1609) preserves the military quality of the Vulgate itself.[49] Erasmus had developed this same source in beginning the second chapter of his *Enchiridion*:

In the first place, you should continually bear in mind that mortal life is nothing but a kind of perpetual warfare – as Job testifies, a soldier both widely experienced and consistently invincible – and very much deceived are the general run of men, whose minds this mountebank of a world captivates with alluring pleasures, who take unseasonable furloughs as if the fighting were already over and they were not living in a most hazardous peace.[50]

When he says, 'Give us a peaceful rule; make Christians kings' (I.i.132), Barabas is taking an 'unseasonable furlough'.

The old story of how the wise and patient Job struggled through a life of warfare and slavery with the weapons of faith gave Marlowe the foundation for his play. This foundation itself supports a number of other stories or parts of stories. As the dark history of Barabas unfolds, other figures and personalities enhance his dimensions with theirs – Father Abraham, the Pharisees, Christ, the thief Barrabas, the magician Simon Magus, Machiavelli and Machiavels, a few wealthy Renaissance Jews.[51] But Barabas is joined by shadowy types as well as by historical ghosts – by the wicked fools of the Bible, and by the morality vices. Each of these figures helps to moralize the central happening in the play. The patterns of their experience twine in and out around the tragedy of the Jew like the ivy on Walter Benjamin's proverb-ruin. Some of these figures remain with Barabas for most of his journey. As Barabas turns into a monstrous villain, his shadowy and symbolic companions grow more noticeable than his historical ones. Marlowe ends his tragedy by confounding all of his Jew's identities in an apocalyptic non-identity – that of Antichrist.

Richard Hooker points out in 'A Learned Sermon of the Nature of Pride' that the minds of the proud are in fact 'turned upside down'.[52] Malta's self-righteous citizens reveal their pride by inverting traditional wisdom. Barabas begins by experiencing, like Job, the destruction of his prosperity. But when he argues that his material loss is greater than Job's total loss, he begins to invert Job's experience. The distance between Job and Barabas widens as Barabas praises his own wisdom and discovers righteous professions with which to justify his cruel vengeances. The final measure of his wicked folly and impatience is provided by his death in the 'furnace of humiliation' he has prepared for his enemy. At the play's end, Job and Barabas have become anti-types. In contrast to Barabas, Job knew that wisdom really meant the fear of the Lord, and he refused to justify himself.

Lacking this wisdom, men do not keep their promises. By alluding to Abraham and his heirs, Marlowe enriches his allegory of spiritual disorder based on Job. For Christians, God's promise to Abraham meant salvation through faith, not through the law. Christ said that the Jews who relied on law were fathered by the devil, not by

Abraham. Both Christ and Paul identify the law with slavery and sin, faith with truth and freedom. Barabas relies slavishly upon the law in his debate with Ferneze. This legalism motivates his remark to Lodowick –

> 'Tis a custom held with us
> That when we speak with Gentiles like to you,
> We turn into the air to purge ourselves,
> For unto us the promise doth belong.
>
> II.iii.44–7

In his famous colloquy 'The Godly Feast', Erasmus uses just this 'custom' to characterize the behaviour of the Pharisees who vaunted themselves as 'strict keepers of the law, though they disregarded those commandments on which all the law and the prophets hung'.[53]

Repeated allusions to the promise and to its fruits suggest that Barabas inverts the Christian understanding of God's covenant with Abraham.[54] His second soliloquy may imply that the only fruits of faith he understands are material ones. His criticism of Christians, 'I can see no fruits in all their faith' (I.i.114), might recall the distinction in Galatians 5 between the works of the flesh and the fruits of the spirit freed from the Old Law. His concluding reference to Abigail in this soliloquy, 'all I have is hers', seems to echo in part the description in Galatians 4:1 of how Abraham's offspring, the children of the promise, stood before the coming of Christ: 'Then I say, that the heire as long as he is a childe, differeth nothing from a servant, though he be Lord of all.' In *The Jew of Malta*, Abigail seems at first to resemble the free child of the promise, while Ithamore enters the action as a slave. As he waits for Abigail to find his gold in the nunnery, Barabas prays,

> O Thou that with a fiery pillar led'st
> The sons of Israel through the dismal shades
> Light Abraham's offspring, and direct the hand
> Of Abigail this night...
>
> II.i.12–15

But Barabas ultimately enslaves his daughter and adopts his slave, giving Ithamore prodigal freedom. When Abigail attempts to turn Christian like a true child of the promise, her impious father poisons her. Once again, wicked folly has confounded the terms so elastically identified in a Christian paradox. The child heir 'differeth nothing from a servant' indeed!

As is the case with references to Job, inversions of 'the promise'
work themselves out in a dynamic, progressive fashion. They begin
with the Jew's financial shrewdness and end with the murder of his
two 'children'. The fruits of this Jew's promises are sterility and
death. His materialism leads ultimately to absolute wickedness. In
*The Praise of Folly*, Folly cheerfully admits that 'at a single nod of
Plutus...all things sacred and profane are turned topsy-turvy' (p. 11).
In place of this single nod, Marlowe provides a more complex
transformation in his hero. The Deadly Sin of Avarice does usurp
and destroy all that remains of the parent in Barabas, but not before
Barabas has willed away his moral freedom, step by impatient step.
By avenging himself on children – Ferneze's and his own – Barabas
collapses all vital moral distinctions between Ishmaels and Isaacs,
the law and the promise, the flesh and the spirit. His war against
posterity anticipates the virtual apocalypse at the end of the play,
when he finally admits, 'I would have brought confusion on you all.'

It would be possible to trace out each of the stories which contribute to the dense meanings of Marlowe's proverb play. But when
the tracing had all been done, we would still have to reckon with a
catastrophe which brings down the whole ruinous heap. Several
commentators have recognized that death in a boiling cauldron is
precisely what Barabas – poisoner, devil, and Antichrist – deserves.[55]
Through the cauldron-emblem Marlowe seems to sum up particular
crimes and general apocalyptic disruptions committed by his Jew.
Yet as an emblem for this confusion the spectacular cauldron offers
the audience something more – or less – than poetic justice. It offers
them a glimpse of the magic in Marlowe's own art, the magic which
here, and again in *Doctor Faustus*, can make a great show from the
nothingness of evil.

When Barabas finally emerges as a pure type of evil, he loses his
typological companions. They take with them that density of ironic
reference to Marlowe's Jew which has enriched and humanized his
character. The cauldron is in a number of ways an 'image sensible'
which finally reduces the 'conceit intellectual'. It symbolizes the
apocalyptic chaos always implicit in the absurdities of knavish wisdom. Dramatically, it reduces the Jew's conceit of his own subtlety
to the broadest and blackest farce. And because 'confusion' outlives
the Jew himself, his deadly-ridiculous cauldron comes to signify the

general condition of Malta. Like the world imagined by John Donne in his melancholy 'First Anniversary', Malta lacks wisdom in the broadest sense. 'Prince, Subject, Father, Sonne, are things forgot.' Spectacle emphasizes the once incredible comparisons of Christians with Turks and Jews. Perhaps all three groups might be regarded as 'spiritual Jews' – defined by Erasmus as people who depend on visible ceremonies and ritual observances ('the credulity of those who prefer to be Jews in outward show rather than inward truth').[56] By enthusiastically exploiting the Jew's cauldron scheme, Ferneze betrays his preference for show over truth. Through Ferneze Marlowe stigmatizes all Christian societies enslaved by their own wicked folly.

Which societies were supposed to perceive their own images in Malta? Marlowe's dark proverbial style would probably deflect immediate recognitions. His pervasive allusions to the Wisdom books of the Bible suggest that he was more concerned with the common genesis of spiritual perversion than with specific, historical breakdowns of social confidence. Although greedy merchants, hypocritical politicians, Mediterranean Catholics, and insular nations all receive some touch of this 'rayler's' scorn, he seems to have been more interested in wicked fools.

Marlowe's most emphatic allusions to wisdom have already been mentioned. To list all parallels probable and possible between *The Jew of Malta* and the books of Proverbs, Job, Ecclesiasticus and Wisdom would be a learned folly. Suffice it to say that these parallels range from the treasure and treasure house at the beginning of the play to the cauldron at its end. Both Ecclesiasticus and Wisdom refer to the crucible in which man's righteousness is tried.[57] The Wisdom books advise prudence in the choice of friends, and warn against trusting an enemy. 'He that walketh with the wise, shalbe wise: but a companion of fooles shalbe afflicted' (Proverbs 13:20). Is this not the fate of Barabas, whose slave's name can be taken to mean, 'Begone, fool'?[58] Ithamore may derive some of his traits from the graphic hypocrisy of morality vices. But when he meets the pandar Pilia-Borza 'within forty foot of the gallows' and speaks 'not a wise word', he resembles the young man 'destitute of understanding' who met the harlot in Proverbs 7:22 and 'followed her straightwaies, as an oxe that goeth to the slaughter, & as a foole to the stockes for correction'. Perhaps the references to Abigail as a diamond owe something to the Proverbial question, 'Who shal finde a vertuous woman? for her price *is* far aboue the pearles' (31:10).

My primary purpose in approaching *The Jew of Malta* as a dramatic wisdom proverb has been to gauge the temper of Marlowe's learned fooling. The Wisdom books which he echoes insist that folly is evil, however entertaining it may be to fools. 'The foole maketh a mocke of sinne' (Proverbs 14:9). These wicked Biblical fools already know how to praise their own wits. The sinner of Ecclesiasticus 32:18 'findeth out excuses according to his wil'. 'As is an house that is destroyed, so is wisdome unto a foole, and the knowledge of the vnwise is as wordes without order' (Ecclesiasticus 21:18; cf. the Douai translation, 'takes refuge in wise talk as a man takes shelter in a ruin'). 'The way of a foole *is* right in his owne eyes' (Proverbs 12:15). But the wicked fool generally gives himself away. 'A wise sentence loseth grace when it cometh out of a fooles mouthe: for he speaketh not in due season' (Ecclesiasticus 20:19). Such fools finally destroy themselves. 'The euil man is snared by the wickednes of *his* lippes' (Proverbs 12:13). 'In the mouth of the foolish *is* the rodde of pride: but the lippes of the wise preserue them' (Proverbs 14:3).

The writers of the Wisdom books clearly had little patience with human folly. Neither, when he created *The Jew of Malta*, had Marlowe. Throughout the play he uses folly to reveal the effects of bad faith upon reason and speech. His dark dramatic proverb emphasizes the confounding of serpent and dove, wisdom and simplicity. Shakespeare's *The Merchant of Venice* will restore Christ's paradox to its proper equilibrium by associating simplicity and innocence with good faith, as well as with bad. Although the follies of Malta are both plausible and amusing, these qualities are probably calculated to remind the audience of its *own* folly. The moral good of the audience 'lies hid in the neereness of the euill' represented on stage. Erasmus remarks in his *Enchiridion* that 'the flesh has its value in that, by a kind of gradual process, it draws our weakness toward spirituality'.[59] A willingness to educate, using the flesh of his characters to draw the weakness of his audience, is what gives Marlowe's style in this play its fundamentally pessimistic temper. His Jew fools us so boisterously because we are assumed to suffer fools gladly. We need – and deserve – the drastic reductions of the Jew's catastrophe because we so easily forget that our world is as dark as his.

# 4

## The tragic folly of Doctor Faustus

*Doctor Faustus* joins the proverbial style of *The Jew of Malta* to a moving 'tragicall history'. Blinded by avarice and bad faith, Barabas dies as a shadow, a symbol of anarchy. Faustus, however, dies as an individual who has achieved a measure of self-awareness. Both as a learned fool and spiritual Jew, Faustus often resembles Barabas. His magic, like the Jew's impatient righteousness, inverts genuine wisdom, turning it into wicked pastime or sport. But in *Doctor Faustus*, wisdom itself has become brighter, more accessible to worldly minds. Malta, as we have seen, is a 'fatal labyrinth of misbelief'. The one potentially wise character, Abigail, attempts to escape from the follies of this world altogether. Christian ideals distorted by the inhabitants of Malta rarely emerge in explicit statement and action. The audience must watch a series of scenes from life under the Old Law – 'hatred, debate, emulacions, wrath, contentions, sedicions, heresies, Enuie, murthers, dronkenness, glottonie, and suche like' (Galatians 5:20–1). Malta may well appear as it did to M. M. Mahood, to be a 'world which has cut itself off entirely from the transcendent'.[1] Like Ithamore in his foolish song to Bellamira, Marlowe seems to have chosen Dis, god of Hades, as his muse. Throughout the play this demonic spirit vexes the guilty worldlings, providing much laughter but little delight.

In *Doctor Faustus*, on the other hand, Dis baits both hero and audience with the pleasures of the imagination. Because these pleasures more obviously distort or invert Christian ideals, the 'transcendent' does influence the world of the play. Whenever Faustus celebrates his inversions, he reaffirms the power and splendour of the ideals themselves. Consequently, his folly has an heroic dimension well beyond the reach of Barabas. Barabas, deceived by his own pretence to wisdom, constantly makes a fool of himself. Faustus, however, is at least wise enough to question devils, manipulate popes, please emperors and maintain friendships – all with appealing energy. As a magician and would-be demi-god he may only parody Christ's genuine miracles, but his magic is still far more powerful and plausible than the Jew's vengeful shifts.

This power and plausibility have caused a number of critics to suspect that Marlowe felt more sympathy for his proud, blasphemous hero than for the values he distorts. Many have found the attractive hero difficult to reconcile with the play's rigorously moral dramatic structure.[2] Augustine's theology of damnation thoroughly informs this structure.[3] Why, then, does the hero's fervid search for beauty, power and fame not seem more sinful? I have already suggested that disproportions between character and dramatic action create instability in all of Marlowe's plays. One can 'explain away' this disproportion in *The Jew of Malta* by demonstrating that 'unseen hypocrisy' makes the Jew appealingly persuasive when he praises his own wit. Where *Doctor Faustus* is concerned, this explanation remains useful, but must be carefully qualified. For when Faustus commends *his* wit, he is praising a quality which is not only transcendent, but has positive value in men's lives as well. Marlowe may adhere to Augustine's psychology of sin. I doubt that he can fully have shared Augustine's – or St Paul's – anti-intellectual bias.[4] Whether he finds that men's wisdom is foolish in God's eyes may depend on how men use their wisdom.

We will see that both Faustus and Tamburlaine address their mistresses in language which recalls the encomium of divine wisdom in Wisdom 7:29.[5] In this same chapter the 'wise' speaker boasts rapturously of Wisdom's gifts: 'For he hathe giué me the true knowledge of the things that are, so that I knowe how the worlde was made, and the powers of the elements' (17). 'And all things bothe secret and knowen do I knowe: for wisdome the worker of all things, hathe taught me it' (21). When Faustus turns from divinity to magic he too adopts an exhilarated tone:

> O, what a world of profit and delight,
> Of power, of honour, of omnipotence
> Is promised to the studious artisan!
>
> I.i54–6

His mistress, Helen, is, of course, a demonic phantom, his magic, a curious collection of tricks, dumb-shows, and sight-seeing expeditions. The central irony of Marlowe's play may be that wisdom is available to Faustus before he tries to be a demi-god, not after. By perverting doctrine and presuming to Christ's deity, he loses the 'fruitful plot of scholarism graced' and the 'golden gifts' of learning to which the Prologue refers. He destroys 'Apollo's laurel bough' which, says the Epilogue, 'sometime grew within this learned man'. These losses can only be tragic ones if the learning itself has dignity and value on earth. Proverbs 8 and Ecclesiasticus 39 promise the scholar that he will be able to understand and hand on traditions, serve great men, travel widely, and win renown. Erasmus and Vives, humanists who accomplished all of these things, actually adopted the ancient Stoic attitude towards human wisdom. For the Stoics, 'sapientia' included a knowledge of things human as well as divine. For Augustine, on the other hand, sapientia could be directed only to things divine.[6] St Paul, too, preferred incorruptible crowns to the all-too-corruptible laurel boughs of ancient triumphs (First Corinthians 9:25).

More important than allusions as evidence of the play's more humane and tragic temper is the extraordinary freedom of the hero himself. The Prologue presents Faustus as being 'swoll'n with cunning of a self-conceit'. Here Marlowe seems to allude to Proverbs 26:12: 'Seest thou a man wise in his owne conceite? more hope *is* of a foole then of him.' 'What can be hoped of those that thrust *Elisium* into hell', wrote Nashe in his Preface to Greene's *Menaphon* (1589).[7] Marlowe may be raising at the outset the possibility that Faustus has been cut off from grace – the essential wisdom of the heart which is given to men by God. Yet Marlowe also supplies Faustus with many occasions to repent. After nearly five Acts and twenty-four years have passed by, the Old Man can observe that Faustus still has an 'amiable soul'.

The theology of this play may be as fundamentally amiable as its hero is superficially appealing. 'Be of good comfort', wrote Richard Hooker in a sermon entitled, 'A Learned Discourse of Justification, Works, and How the Foundation of Faith is Overthrown' (1585): 'We have to do with a merciful God, ready to make the best of a little which we hold well, and not with a captious sophister, which

gathereth the worst out of everything wherein we err.'[8] Faustus himself is a captious sophister who brings the severity of damnation
down upon himself.[9] But only at the last possible moment. His
career has a paradoxical momentum and direction perhaps not fully
recognized by those who have viewed it as a process of degeneration.[10]
His achievements may indeed grow trivial, even as his sins become
more serious. But at the same time Faustus follows a spiritual path
which moves upward in three fairly definite stages. These three
stages provide the framework for the following discussion of his
tragic history. At first, through learned folly, Faustus proudly denies
God. In mid-career, he becomes the folk-hero of Faust-books and
popular legends, the best actor on a great stage of fools. Finally he
reaches an intellectual understanding of the good he once denied.
Because he partly realizes his great loss, he rises towards tragic
stature.

## The learned fool

The traditional symbols of the Prologue to *Doctor Faustus* anticipate
with astonishing precision the hero's attainments, sin, and destiny.
'The fruitful plot of scholarism graced', Marlowe's elaborate peri-
phrasis for the study of theology, may derive from the praise of wisdom in Ecclesiasticus: 'As the vine haue I broght forthe frute of
swete sauour' (24:19); 'The feare of the Lord is a pleasant garden of
blessing' (40:27). Perhaps the 'golden gifts' of learning on which
Faustus becomes 'glutted' also allude to the nature of true wisdom.
'Riches', wrote John Donne, 'is the Metaphor in which the Holy
Ghost hath delight to expresse God and Heaven to us.'[11] Joan Web-
ber has indicated in her study of Donne's sermons, *Contrary Music*,
that the use of indigestion to signify over-intellectualism ultimately
comes from Saint Bernard's homilies on *The Song of Songs*.[12]
Digestion, on the other hand, signifies the assimilation of wisdom.
By referring to glutting, surfeiting and appetite throughout *Doctor
Faustus*, Marlowe suggests that Faustus has abused his mind.

Douglas Cole and Helen Gardner remind us in their studies of
this play that abuse of the intellect is caused by aberration of the
will.[13] Will is vital to an understanding of the psychology behind
Faustus's fall because through his will a man was believed to change

himself into what he loved. Particularly important is the fact that Christian thinkers viewed the disposition or will to move towards and love God as a gift, rather than as part of innate human wisdom. 'The advent of Christ in the mind is through grace, producing grace.'[14] Whether the selfish and conceited Faustus is susceptible to grace or not will remain a mystery. Like the play itself, the Prologue emphasizes the lively processes of misdirection and destruction:

> swoll'n with cunning of a self-conceit,
> His waxen wings did mount above his reach,
> And melting, heavens conspired his overthrow;
> I.Prol. 20–2

The resolute Faustus who will destroy himself through his artful conjuring resembles the Icarus who, in Golding's *Metamorphoses*, was the victim of his father's 'hurtfull Art' through his own 'frolicke courage'.[15] In *Nosce Teipsum* Sir John Davies associated Icarus with Phaeton as an abuser of wisdom.[16] Marlowe concentrates such suggestions within a short space. The wings (not natural, but waxen) which mount, then melt, correspond exactly to the hero's restless, conceited fantasy and learned foolishness. The Prologue not only anticipates the hero's misdirection of mind, the corruption which ensues, and his great loss; it intimates that Faustus has begun to injure his mind before his dramatic journey even begins. By writing 'mount above his reach', Marlowe is not undermining his argument with a subversive image suggestive of man's great capacities, here limited by jealous gods. He is actually preparing us for a foolish hero who confounds Heaven in necromancy, and thrusts Elysium into Hell. Faustus himself may fall, but his pretensions do mount, and his devilish exercises become an inversion of religious experience. An Icarian contradiction underlies the hero's own nature and may partly explain an important aspect of the play's general effect. While its language mirrors the glories of divinity, its action often seems flat and farcical.

The Prologue is only the first of many choral figures in *Doctor Faustus*. These figures comment repeatedly on the hero's choices, but they say little about his disposition. Even at the end of the play they do not come directly to terms with the individual character of the sinner. Generally speaking, the choruses and choral figures simplify the hero's damnable career. Because Faustus can present his own errors far more eloquently than these commentators present their plain truths, they sometimes appear extraneous, alien to the spirit of the play. Only when we realize that Faustus practises sophistical, fallacious rhetoric can we see that Marlowe may have been tempting his audience to reject the 'choral' style of the Good Angel and the Old Man as simple, plain, and out-of-date. Simple, plain truths are just what the clever Faustus can neither see nor hear. Were he himself less of an 'unseen hypocrite' and his soliloquies less persuasive, the choral commentaries might have been unnecessary.[17]

The first great soliloquy in *Doctor Faustus* is a masterful praise of folly. Barabas has more ambiguous motives than Faustus, but less verve. Warned by the Prologue that he prefers magic 'before his chiefest bliss', we soon learn that Faustus has no orthodox estimate of what his 'chiefest bliss' may be. For him, magic, like Tamburlaine's wars, 'illustrates gods', and he wants a god's powers. 'Affords this art no greater miracle' than to dispute well?, he complains, dismissing logic. This is the first of many unanswered and assertive questions in the play, and it could perhaps be answered, 'Yes. Disputing well is a scholastic perversion of logic, whose real end should be to seek truth.'[18] But Faustus is not making the kind of speech that encourages such reflections. Medicine is quickly rejected on the same grounds as logic:

> Couldst thou make man to live eternally,
> Or, being dead, raise them to live again,
> Then this profession were to be esteemed.
>
> i.i.24–6

Faustus, like Barabas, praises his own 'wit'. 'Is not thy common talk sound aphorisms?' (i.i.19). His hasty survey of the four professions might seem to have little of the 'depth' he promises to 'sound', but it does carry enough conviction to sweep doubts behind it. When this searching spirit discovers that human learning is vain, when he rejects the fetters of divinity and turns towards magic, he takes many readers and spectators along with him.

There are no obviously outrageous distortions of learning and tradition in this speech, just as there are none in the opening soliloquy of *The Jew of Malta*. The speech does contain some striking omissions – striking, that is, if the audience knows its Bible well. Douglas

Cole has argued that when Faustus comes to a stop after translating from his Vulgate 1 John 8, Elizabethan spectators, familiar
with this text from the second of the official sermons and homilies,
would have realized that he should have kept on.[19] Presumably they
would also have noticed that the passage Faustus takes for the major
premise of his syllogism on sin and death is another selective quotation: 'For the wages of sinne is death; but the gifte of God *is* eternal
life through Iesus Christ our Lord' (Romans 6:23).[20] Out of these
texts from Romans and 1 John, which he appears to come upon as if
by chance, Faustus constructs his syllogism:

> The reward of sin is death...
> Belike we must sin...
> And so consequently die.

When scrutinized, this syllogism is of course almost ludicrously un-
subtle. Nevertheless it has often been considered powerful enough
to gravel the hero, who sees in the harshness of divinity inevitable
reprobation and desperately chooses magic instead.[21]

On this interpretation, Faustus, who is at least trying to escape
human fallibility and weakness, becomes sympathetic. His behaviour
will seem plausible even if one argues that faith should dispense with
logic or that *his* logic perverts both faith and right reason. After all,
if we are damned anyway, why not have some excitement first? And
so we do not pause to examine the doctrine which Faustus sweeps
behind him. If we did, we might have realized that Faustus has
certainly understood St Paul's 'wages of sin' less well than those who
have sympathized with his desperation or judged it in a Calvinistic
context. Faustus may be 'graced with doctor's name', but he apparently believes that 'wages of sin' refers to the death of the body,
not the soul; his 'everlasting death' implies an afterlife without
resurrection or judgment. How, he speculates, can anything so un-
avoidable as death be regarded as a punishment or consequence?
Why dignify with the name of doctrine a description of sheer necessity? 'What will be, shall be!' Faustus does not believe in the prior
necessity ('will be') of reprobation in Paul's terms, although Marlowe
might be railing at Calvinist severity on just this point. Instead,
Marlowe presents Faustus as failing to see that by 'death' Paul
means eternal damnation, the only alternative to the eternal life
promised in his next sentence.[22] Because 'divinity' appears to labour

the obvious, Faustus finds it beneath his contempt, and he passes on
to magic which, with its many volumes and fascinating symbols,
seems more philosophically respectable. Later Faustus will deny
Hell and the Pauline understanding of spiritual death much more
explicitly:

> This word 'damnation' terrifies not me,
> For I confound hell in Elysium.
> My ghost be with the old philosophers!
> I.iii.59–61

To a bold spirit like this one, the souls of men are only 'vain trifles'.[23]

How should we regard a 'divine in show' who holds such views and
seems to be reading St Paul for the first time? Marlowe laughs con-
temptuously at his hero, but that fact is well disguised by the style of
his hero's soliloquy. Faustus commends himself in belittling the professions – an indication that Marlowe wished to 'appassionate' the
brains of his audience, not convince them that human learning is
vain. As Faustus wrestles with Paul's 'hard' saying he slips into the
role of the wise man who must con proverbs and parables, but he is
not rewarded with the spirit of discernment. James Sims has suggested that Marlowe may be alluding here to the response of those
disciples who could not understand Christ when he claimed to be
the bread of life (John 6:60, 66).[24] Christ's admonition to his mur-
muring disciples might also apply to Faustus: 'It is the spirit that
quickeneth: the flesh profiteth nothing: the wordes that I speake
vnto you, are spirit and life' (John 6:64). Ironically Faustus rejects
law as 'external trash' only to founder on the externals of the Bible.
He strips a famous Christian commonplace to its bare letter.

Faustus's boasted excellence in syllogism and disputation makes
him comparable to the Scotists of *The Praise of Folly*. These learned
fools have not enough time 'to open a gospel or the epistles of Paul'.[25]
They 'deem that they are holding up the universal church . . . by the
props of their syllogisms' (p. 83). They proceed to 'shape and reshape the Holy Scriptures as if they were made of wax' (p. 83).
Often they will 'accommodate to their own purpose four or five
little words plucked out from here and there, even depraving the
sense of them, if need be; although the words which precede and
follow these are nothing at all to the point or even go against it' (pp.
110–11). 'Knowing nothing in general, they profess to know all

things in particular', says Stultitia, and she treats them like charlatan sorcerors, criticizing their learned symbols in terms remarkably close to those which Faustus himself will use to praise the 'metaphysics of magicians' (1.i.50):

When they especially disdain the vulgar crowd is when they bring out their triangles, quadrangles, circles, and mathematical pictures of the sort, lay one upon the other, intertwine them into a maze, then deploy some letters as if in line of battle, and presently do it over in reverse order – and all to involve the uninitiated in darkness.

(p. 77)

Faustus yearns after the 'lines, circles, signs, letters and characters' of magic (1.i.52). Later he boasts to Cornelius and Valdes of his subtlety in syllogisms, and plans to 'canvass every quiddity' of magic with them (1.i.165).

There are more serious analogues for the behaviour of Faustus in the *Enchiridion* of Erasmus. Indeed it may be helpful to regard the early part of this volume as a reliable commentary on the desires and actions of Marlowe's hero in scene i. In his second chapter, Erasmus refers to those men who go over to the adversary *after* being ransomed by Christ's blood, and thereby risk not a physical death only but the death of the soul as well.[26] Erasmus has no doubt that this is what Paul meant by the 'wages of sin' (p. 41). He points out that those who are neither 'deterred by fear' nor 'prevented by love' of Christ 'make a show of his name' (p. 40). Physicians can relieve sickness, holy men may even restore dead bodies, but 'only God... revives a dead soul through His singular grace and power' (pp. 44–5). Erasmus also argues that a distaste for Scripture is the surest sign of a sick soul: 'If the soul does not retain the Word, if it does not pass on into its inner parts digested food for meditation, you have a clear sign of its disease' (p. 43). In the following chapter, Erasmus uses the term 'manna' as a symbol of God's 'secret law':

Only those who had tasted merely this shell of the manna said, 'This is a hard saying; who can hear it?' But dig out the spiritual meaning and nothing is sweeter, nothing more nourishing. Moreover, in the Hebrew tongue manna means 'what is this?' and this meaning neatly applies to the Holy Scripture, which has nothing irrelevant in it, not even a jot or a tittle, nothing unworthy of close study or of being pondered over, nothing incompatible with the question, 'what is this?'

(p. 49)

'What doctrine call you this?' scoffs Faustus, referring to his own literal deductions from Scripture.

Once we understand how thoroughly Faustus has simplified Scripture, the disquieting simplicities in his review of the professions become more intelligible. Commentators and editors have had their reservations about the arts which Faustus describes. As well they might; a divine so ill at ease with theology, the 'Queen of Sciences', could well be expected to distort the ends of other branches of learning partly dependent upon it.[27] Step by step, Faustus surveys and rejects philosophy, medicine, law and divinity. 'Bid *On cay mae on* farewell; Galen, come', he says, moving from philosophy to medicine in search of greater miracles. Although his procedure seems reasonable, another comparison with *The Praise of Folly* is in order here:

It has seemed well, you note, to imitate the rhetoricians of our time, who believe themselves absolutely to be gods if they can show themselves bilingual (like a horse-leech), and account it a famous feat if they can weave a few Greekish words, like inlay work, ever and anon into their Latin orations, even if at the moment there is no place for them. Then, if they want exotic touches, they dig four or five obsolete words out of decaying manuscripts, by which they spread darkness over the reader.

(pp. 10–11)

This is what Marlowe's carefully articulated nonsense generally does. After his Greekish inlay, Faustus immediately continues,

> Seeing *ubi desinit philosophus ibi incipit medicus*,
> Be a physician, Faustus; heap up gold,
> And be eternized for some wondrous cure.
> *Summum bonum medicinae sanitas.*

Both Erasmus and Rabelais had already used the four professions to exemplify learned folly. Although the accounts in *The Praise of Folly* and *The Third Book of the Heroic Deeds and Sayings of the Good Pantagruel* differ from one another as well as from that in *Doctor Faustus*, in all three cases the professions are tried, found wanting, and the way to folly is consequently left open.[28] Stultitia prefers Nature to the art of learned disciplines: 'Nature hates counterfeits; and that which is innocent of art gets along far the more prosperously' (p. 45). Faustus, on the other hand, seems to want even more art and method than he can find in the professions.

Wilful ignorance and its companion vice, dependence on literal appearances, stand out more conspicuously when Faustus begins his interviews with Mephistophilis two scenes later. Confident about his new art, Faustus is determined to be 'resolute'. He describes the ceremonies he has performed and concludes with a lengthy Latin charm. But all these elaborate preparations only serve to summon devils '*per accidens*'. Mephistophilis quickly begins to give Faustus lessons in theology, explaining that:

> When we hear one rack the name of God,
> Abjure the Scriptures and his Savior Christ,
> We fly in hope to get his glorious soul;
> Nor will we come unless he use such means
> Whereby he is in danger to be damned.
> Therefore the shortest cut for conjuring
> Is stoutly to abjure the Trinity
> And pray devoutly to the prince of hell.
>
> I.iii.47–54

The devils appear to have overheard the first soliloquy. If they are present throughout scene iii on an upper level, as the 1616 text indicates, spectators will note that magic art has little substantive power. Faustus himself delights in devilish ceremonies and shows, but is blind to all appearances which are true.[29] He not only questions Mephistophilis about Hell, terrifying the devil with his frivolous ignorance. He persists in denying Hell and damnation, even when a real devil stands before him. That Faustus is a bold scoffer or mocker is never clearer than when he carps and counsels:

> What, is great Mephistophilis so passionate
> For being deprivèd of the joys of heaven?
> Learn thou of Faustus manly fortitude,
> And scorn those joys thou never shalt possess.
>
> I.iii.83–6

This ridiculous blindness continues when Faustus signs away his immortal soul with his blood in Act II, scene i. The ceremony of the deed of gift, arranged by Mephistophilis, inverts, as has often been noted, the sacraments of communion and baptism. Now indeed Faustus does go over to the enemy from whom Christ's blood has already redeemed him. Both participants in the ceremony make frequent appeals to the eye. Faustus stabs his arm: 'View here this blood that trickles from mine arm' (II.i.56). Mephistophilis brings a chafer to warm the congealed blood. 'See Faustus, here is fire. Set it on' (II.i.69). After Faustus signs the bill, an inscription, '*homo fuge*', appears on his arm:

> My senses are deceived; here's nothing writ.
> O yes, I see it plain. Even here is writ
> *Homo fuge!* Yet shall not Faustus fly.
>
> II.i.78–80

Because Faustus wants to believe that the genuinely miraculous inscription deceives his senses, he does not heed its meaning. But he immediately seeks the meaning of the following dance of devils, which, Mephostophilis quite honestly tells him, is 'Nothing...but to delight thy mind' (II.i.83). Later he permits another devilish show and some fireworks to dissuade him from marriage.

It is in the context provided by so much sight and so little discernment that several particularly emphatic allusions occur. As his first step towards understanding the wages of sin, Faustus has begun to feel doubts and to speak of despair and damnation. At first he attempts to strengthen his resolution by promising to serve his own god of appetite, and sacrifice infants to Beelzebub (II.i.11–14). Sims has noticed that this god of appetite parallels the 'false brethren' of Romans 16:18 who 'serue not the Lord Iesus Christ, but their owne bellies, and with faire speache & flattering deceiue the hearts of the simple'.[30] Belly language is what we hear when Faustus signs the deed of gift and quips, '*Consummatum est*; this bill is ended.' He recalls, of course, Christ's dying words on the cross (John 19:30). Ironically, the implicit pun on digestion also suggests that he has gorged himself on the wrong kind of wisdom. In an outrageously comic treatment of learned folly, Rabelais has Pantagruel remark to Panurge that '*Consummatum est*...is what Thomas Aquinas said when he had eaten the whole of his lamprey.'[31] In *Doctor Faustus* such theological punning can provide a ghoulish premonition of the hero's fate.

Through brisk rhetorical questions in response to the guidance of his angels and to the inscription on his arm, Faustus betrays his 'unseen hypocrisy'. 'When Mephostophilis shall stand by me, / What power can hurt me?' (II.i.24–5) ironically affirms that the merciful God of Romans 8:31 is his adversary. Erasmus cites this text in his *Enchiridion* in order to prove that 'In this business no one has ever failed to win except the fellow who did not want to' (p. 45). Faustus's second question, 'Whither should I fly' (II.i.76), reveals the same kind of wilful self-deception. Sims has suggested that Marlowe is alluding through Faustus's reaction to the *Homo fuge!* on his arm, to Psalm 139:7–10:[32]

Whether shal I go from thy Spirit? or whether shal I flee from thy presence?
If I ascend into heauen, thou art there: if I lie downe in hel, thou art there.
Let me take the wings of the morning, & dwell in the vttermost partes of the sea:
Yet thether shal thine hand lead me, & thy right hand holde me.

For the joyful psalmist, God is everywhere. In order to express his hope of escape, Faustus has chosen words which point to an inevitable reunion with God.

Faustus is not the only character who can employ the deceptive 'rhetoric of the belly'. What Faustus accomplishes through unseen hypocrisy and wilful ignorance, Mephistophilis and the Bad Angel accomplish for the purpose of destroying Faustus. So long as Mephistophilis speaks to Faustus on subjects which are 'not against our kingdom' – Lucifer and Hell – he is truthful and frank. But whenever it becomes necessary to tempt Faustus or mislead him, he resorts to those familiar distortions which hold the brain at bay. It would have been in character for Machiavel to scoff, as Mephistophilis scoffs, at marriage as a 'ceremonial toy' (II.i.149). Mephistophilis follows up this taunt by stirring the hero's affections for 1) himself, 2) women, and 3) sweet books. The devil cites the logic of Scripture, if not its words, when he 'proves' that Faustus is better than Heaven (II.ii.6–9). After all, Christ had argued that both woman and the sabbath were made for men. If Heaven was also made for man, he must be superior to it. Faustus brushes this quiet mockery aside, but throughout the play he remains persuaded that his contract with the devil is absolutely binding. Mephistophilis has only to arouse his credulous trust in shows and appearance:

> *Faustus:*  Why, dost thou think that Faustus shall be damned?
> *Mephistophilis:* Ay, of necessity, for here's the scroll
> In which thou hast given thy soul to Lucifer.
> II.i.127–9

Such damnation is a continuing mockery of the redemptive process. Mephistophilis tricks Faustus by transferring spiritual responsibility from Faustus to the scroll. When he tacitly assents to so literal a version of necessity, Faustus briefly re-enacts his initial damnation. Such re-enactments will occur several times. Perhaps the audience can begin to sense, if Faustus does not, the vital difference between the rules of the game Faustus plays with Mephistophilis, and the laws of the tragedy (or near-tragedy) which he actually lives.

The Bad Angel is another of Marlowe's convincing, witty rogues, the kind of spokesman presupposed by Marlowe's own 'Atheist Lecture'. In order to discourage Faustus from repenting, he carps at 'contrition, prayer, repentance' as 'illusions, fruits of lunacy, / That make men foolish that do use them most' (II.i.19–20). Sidney had remarked: 'Sith there is nothing of so sacred a maiestie but that an itching tongue may rubbe it selfe vpon it, so deserue they no other answer, but, instead of laughing at the iest, to laugh at the iester.'[33] Yet neither the audience nor Faustus laughs at this Angel, whose view of penitents so neatly approximates Marlowe's implicit view of clever magicians. He is more eloquent than the Good Angel, and Faustus heeds him. Perhaps the hero's one-sided hearing where the Angels are concerned may be related to his enthusiasm for devilish shows. His condition is analogous to that of the dead soul described by Erasmus in the *Enchiridion*: 'If your spiritual eyes are so clouded that you do not see even the brightest light of truth, if your inward ear can not understand the voice of God, if you are utterly deficient in every spiritual awareness, do you think your soul is alive?' (p. 43).

A dead soul or a living one? Even in this early, foolish phase of his hero's career, Marlowe allows the operations of grace to remain mysterious. Faustus therefore seems to participate in a dynamic and unpredictable process. After signing the bond, he experiences further spiritual development. By the time that he reflects upon his hardened heart in Act II, scene ii, his despair is no longer the exuberant blasphemy of the preceding scene: 'Despair in God, and trust in Beelzebub.' The word 'damnation' has finally begun to terrify him. He swings between 'deep despair' and the security which he finds through 'sweet pleasures'.[34] Approached in doctrinal terms alone, these behavioural extremes may signify only the same false pride. But dramatically speaking, these oscillations between despair and pleasure might discourage an audience from responding to Faustus as a hopeless sinner.[35] How could they regard him as a hardened case of conscience when he himself seems scarcely aware of what his sin is? His fearful despair grows out of intimations; it comes from looking on the heavens or hearing noises in his ears, but not from sure knowledge. It is expressed through changes of mood, rather than through conviction of sin. When he asks Mephistophilis who made the world (II.ii.67), Faustus may be evincing an attitude of unseen hypocrisy, not merely assuming ignorance to bait the devil. What makes this attitude so puzzling, as was shown in the case of Barabas, is that the hypocrisy or deception remains partly unseen by the hypocrite himself. Like more self-knowledgeable sinners, Faustus does contemplate suicide, an illogical short-cut to the very damnation which frightens him. Tempted by pleasure, he continues to go the long way around to the same goal.

Susceptibility to pleasure and pastime condemns Faustus just as surely as do his pride and blasphemy. Through the hero's response to the things he sees, Marlowe suggests the weakness of his reason, preparing his audience for a final damnation exactly adapted to the hero's flaw. But as spectator and showman, Faustus begins to take on a character more human and amiable than that of the learned fool expressed through soliloquy and argument, or of the generic sinner presented in choral commentary. These are characteristics which spectators can readily identify with. Had they not also been susceptible to pleasure and pastime they would never have paid the price of admission. And unless they are well entertained with magic 'sport' they will never understand how Faustus can have lost his soul for it.

I believe that we inevitably lose much of our susceptibility when, as readers, we have become thoroughly familiar with the text of *Doctor Faustus*. The triviality at the centre of the play becomes unmistakeable. Like Will Summers in *Summer's Last Will and Testament*, we tend to say, in effect, 'Nay, 'tis no play, neither, but a show.' Some of the triviality may even be deliberate. For his pageant of the Seven Deadly Sins (II.ii.110), Marlowe (or Nashe) seems to have transposed one folk-tradition into another, reducing the genuinely terrifying monsters of the *Faustbook* into a conventional masque or mumming, replete with pipers. Such pastime would certainly be out of place in the pagan Elysium which Faustus confounds in Hell, but ironically, it does smack of the Old Wives Tales he professes to disbelieve. Even if Nashe, as Paul Kocher has suggested, wrote this 'fit of mirth', its spirit is in harmony with the general approach to Faustus as a learned fool.[36] His anticipated and actual responses appear ridiculously exaggerated. 'That sight will be as pleasant to me as Paradise was to Adam the first day of his creation' (II.ii.106). 'O, how this sight doth delight my soul' (II.ii.163). These responses resemble earlier outbursts like 'make me blessed with your sage conference' (to Valdes and Cornelius, I.i.100) and foreshadow his delight with tawdry spectacles in Acts III and IV.

How can the audience possibly share his enthusiasm for magic or be entertained by any pleasure other than the critical one of watching Faustus watch the devil's bad actors? We must remember that audiences too can be baited or hooked with pleasures. A little will hold out the promise of more to come, especially when the hero's terrible fate is commonly known and cannot provide much suspense. Moreover, conventional amateur pastimes often exert an almost hypnotic fascination. Their transparent, open contrivances can disarm even a sophisticated audience of its scepticism, affecting it as a group with a sense of powers and presences which, as individuals reading and criticizing, it would question. Significantly, Faustus himself suddenly moves from the solitude of his study to the more public spaces of the third and fourth Acts. Most of the earlier shows had been given by devils. Now Faustus emerges from his apprenticeship and takes control of the entertainment. As a Presenter his relation to the audience – especially when he is invisible to characters on stage – becomes more intimate. When we watch a former acquaintance participate in an entertainment, we readily grant him the benefit of our doubts. Marlowe knew how to use such benefits. He turns Faustus into a folk-hero and lets him beguile the audience with his jests. Old Wives Tales they may be, but as Sidney said, a simple tale 'holdeth children from play, and old men from the chimney corner'.

### The great stage of fools

The choruses which introduce the third and fourth Acts seem to be almost wholly preoccupied with the glories that Faustus achieves through magic. They report the adventures of the hero, his skill in

astrology, and his growing fame. Although this positive attitude may
seem almost impertinent, given the fooling which soon follows, it
does mark a new phase in the hero's development. His role continues
to parody the ideal role of the scholar in Ecclesiasticus 39:

He kepeth the sayings of famous men, & entreth in also
to the secrets of darke sentences. (2)
   He seketh out the mysterie of graue sentences, and
exerciseth him self in darke parables. (3)
   He shal serue among great men and appeare before the prince:
he shal traueil through strange countreis: for he hathe
tryed the good and the euil among men. (4)
   When the great Lord wil, he shalbe filled with the Spirit
of vnderstanding, that he may powre out wise sentences,
& giue thankes vnto the Lord in his praier. (6)
   He shal shewe forthe his sciéce and learning. (8)
   Manie shal commend his vnderstanding, and his memorie
shal neuer be put out, nor departe away: but his name
shal continue from generacion to generacion. (9)

These are the rewards which Faustus might have achieved without
magic. Guided by the devil, he serves great men at their weakest,
pandering to their self-righteousness and to their curious conceits.
He also earns the approbation of the credulous drunken idiots who
marvel at his stunts. But the facts that high as well as low characters appear foolish and that Faustus enjoys an advantage over both
groups makes his own foolishness all the more difficult to condemn.
As Marlowe generalizes the scene of folly, he resorts to presentational
techniques as fast-paced and highly concentrated as those used in
*The Jew of Malta*. Oblique mirrors built into the structure of incidents focus their meanings but discourage us from comparing
Faustus too readily with other characters.

   The hero's resemblance to the clowns and fools is a case in point.
In the first two acts the comic episodes would have a stronger influence upon an audience's responses to the main plot. They immediately follow the more serious scenes, and consequently appear
to criticize them. The servant Wagner who appears in the second
scene has enough learning to over-complicate a simple problem:
'Where is thy master?' We might expect therefore that when Wagner
takes up magic, he would adopt the metaphysical flourishes which
delight Faustus. This is just what he does not do. Faustus is instructed by Valdes and Cornelius to carry a small library to his con-

juring grove, but the magic practised by Wagner and the clowns comes out of an old hand-book. Indeed, when Robin enters with a book in Act II, scene iii, Faustus has just left with a book which tells him how to change his shape. Shape-changing is a recurrent motif in the play, supplying magic's closest approximations to the effects of genuine miracle. Faustus has already 'turned' Mephistophilis into a friar, and in the scene following, Wagner has threatened to change Robin's lice into familiars.

In the third and fourth Acts the relation between actions involving Faustus and those involving comics becomes more indirect. Marlowe achieves this indirection by multiplying the reflections in his satiric mirrors. For example, when Robin and Dick steal a cup from the tavern, they resemble Faustus and Mephistophilis who have been snatching both cups and dishes at the Pope's banquet (III.ii). But, in addition, the Vintner who loses the cup might parallel the Pope who has lost banquet, Bruno, and his triple tiara. What the clowns do has begun to reflect not only upon Faustus but also upon the mighty worldlings he befools. Mephistophilis arrives to frighten off the imperious, cursing Vintner, and he too resembles the infuriated Pope. The Pope complains of indignities from Lollards, the devil of vexation by villains. Mephistophilis uses magic to 'purge the rashness of this cursed deed', much as Pope Adrian had used the commination ceremony to punish Faustus.

During Act IV, the clowns emphasize the hero's fame in a way which might have surprised Valdes and Cornelius – the two savants who promised Faustus more prestige than the Delphic Oracle in Act I. Perhaps Marlowe wished to mock at the creation of a folk-hero, satirizing a process already dramatized more seriously in the *Tamburlaine* plays. The cozening of the Horse-Courser who pulls off Faustus's leg is presented in scene v and recounted in scene vi. This procedure has seemed dull to everyone but the clowns who relish the story: 'O monstrous! Eat a whole load of hay!' (27); 'O brave doctor!' (41) This comedy of stupidity grows still more redundant as the knowing clowns try to tease Faustus with questions about his lost leg in scene vii. Nothing could be more welcome than the trick with which Faustus finally charms them all dumb. But it hardly deserves the glowing praise of the Duchess of Vanholt: 'My lord, / We are much beholding to this learned man' (IV.vii.108–9). The genuine wonder of the yokels in these scenes tends to mirror the idle curiosity of the pleasure-seeking courtiers so enormously gratified by a few conjuring tricks.

By extending the range of his satire, Marlowe mutes the full ironic force of the identity between protagonist and analogous figures. Differences within a general resemblance between Faustus and the clowns retain importance. While the clowns mimic the shallow art of magic, they neither invert heavenly wisdom nor presume upon deity. Their magic is a worldly means without damnable ends, zany, relatively harmless, and not very exciting. Although the comic and serious plots of *Doctor Faustus* seem to converge in Act IV, Faustus retains much of his energy and plausibility. Voluptuous and shallow Faustus may be, but in Act V the Old Man will address his injunctions to a 'gentle' Faustus who is still not entirely habituated to sin.

Comparison with *The Praise of Folly* can help to explain why Faustus gains in stature when the action becomes overtly trivial. The persona of Folly makes a similar progress. She begins with many of the characteristics of wicked fools. Like faithless Barabas she collapses the Christian paradox of wisdom and simplicity, serpent and dove, into mere knavish folly. But as her lecture proceeds, she begins to score many palpable hits on a foolish world. The range and accuracy of the satire augments the authority of the critic. This is what happens to Faustus after he asks Mephistophilis:

> Then in this show let me an actor be,
> That this proud Pope may Faustus' cunning see.
>
> III.i.76–7

The visual Epicurean who delights in shows becomes capable of exposing in others a preference for disguise and false appearances. Magic tricks are just what his victims deserve. The devil who helps Faustus was thought to be incapable of performing transformations beyond the power of nature; he could only 'work on man's imagination' or alter appearances by clothing 'any corporeal thing with any corporeal form'.[37] In other words, the devil has just enough skill to bring off a mumming or dumb show before people whose imaginations or 'conceits' are weak.

At first Faustus and Mephistophilis look on as Pope Adrian triumphs over his rival, Bruno:

> Sound trumpets then, for thus Saint Peter's heir
> From Bruno's back ascends Saint Peter's chair.
>
> III.i.97–8

Bruno does not say much but he is at least wise enough to expose Adrian; he calls him 'proud Lucifer' and points out that his predecessor, Pope Julius, had promised that all popes would obey the Emperor. As for Adrian, he appears to judge himself when he accuses the Emperor of growing 'too proud in his authority'. He also indulges in lame parables, praising himself with a 'golden sentence' which few of Marlowe's conceited fools could have bettered:

> 'That Peter's heirs should tread on emperors
> And walk upon the dreadful adder's back,
> Treading the lion and the dragon down
> And fearless spurn the killing basilisk.'
>
> III.i.140–3

Crooked thinking enters too when he argues:

> Pope Julius did abuse the church's rites,
> And therefore none of his decrees can stand.
> Is not all power on earth bestowed on us?
> And therefore, though we would, we cannot err.
>
> 150–4

But Julius erred. Adrian adds, as the last of his seven-fold powers from Heaven, 'whatso pleaseth us'. This wilful, avenging tyrant, who uses his enemy as a foot-stool, is a satiric version of Tamburlaine – a frolicsome Machiavel. When Faustus and Mephistophilis disrupt his banquet, his folly becomes more obvious, but the spectacle of one Pope climbing on another, similarly dressed, could scarcely have been solemn. Adrian quite prudently orders Bruno's triple tiara sent to his papal treasury – an example of Marlowe's fondness for passing crowns around the stage whenever he wants to hint at folly.

Pope Adrian's banquet is a mockery of ceremonious behaviour and the 'church's rites'. So too is his commination service preached against the 'invisible' spirits guilty of snatching away his cups and dishes. Broad anti-papal satire is surely one element of this episode. Marlowe readily appeals to anti-Catholic prejudice in all of his plays. His political and religious hypocrites are explicitly Catholic; so, at least implicitly, is his magician when he exchanges Wittenburg and the garden of wisdom for scholastic necromancy and the prospects of 'canonization'. But the foreign Catholicism of such butts may only be a blind which permits Marlowe to rail at English Protestants. When Adrian curses his cardinals for losing Bruno and the crown with 'By Peter, you shall die / Unless you bring them forth immediately', Reformation burlesque probably includes criticism of all Christians who behave in un-Christian ways. One passage from the worldly, central section of *The Praise of Folly* seems especially close in both temper and content to Marlowe's scene:

There remain only those weapons and sweet benedictions of which Paul speaks, and the popes are generous enough with these: interdictions, excommunications, anathematizations, pictured damnations, and the terrific lightning-bolt of the bull, which by its mere flicker sinks the souls of men below the floor of hell. And these most holy fathers in Christ, and vicars of Christ, launch it against no one with more spirit than against those who, at the instigation of the devil, try to impair or to subtract from the patrimony of Peter.

(p. 100)

Aided by Mephistophilis, Faustus not only 'subtracts' Bruno and the 'rich triple crown' intended for the treasury, but a number of cups and dishes as well.

During his visit to the German imperial court in Act IV Faustus acquires a more critical spectator. To the enthusiasm of his fellows for furies and rare exploits, Benvolio replies, 'What of this?' 'Has not the Pope enough of conjuring yet?' He looks on from above as Faustus enters in triumph, and his mocking detachment could help an audience glimpse some disparities between the pleasures of sight and their sources. The hero of the *Faustbook* had at least raised 'such spirits as haue seene *Alexander* and his Paramour aliue'.[38] Faustus must explain that *his* spirits merely 'present the royal shapes', and urges that they be greeted in 'dumb silence'. Could this dumb-show have caused the Emperor, Carolus, to forget that 'These are but shadows, not substantial', if he had not been especially prone to 'surfeits' of conceit? Carolus explains that his thoughts have been 'ravished' by the 'sight of this renowned emperor', and a glance at the wart on the paramour's neck sends him into raptures:

> Faustus, I see it plain,
> And in this sight thou better pleasest me
> Than if I gained another monarchy.
> 
> IV.ii.65–7

His extravagant enjoyment of the 'sport' when Faustus puts antlers on the doubting Benvolio anticipates the reactions of the Duke of

Vanholt: 'Nothing in the world could please me more' (IV.vii.4);
'His artful sport drives all sad thoughts away' (IV.vii.112).

Benvolio gets his first set of horns for scoffing at the shows of the
magician. When he complains that he can 'see nothing', Faustus
replies, 'I'll make you feel something anon, if my art fail me not'
(IV.ii.42). Faustus punishes Benvolio for refusing to share in his
visions. We will see that Tamburlaine punishes and eventually
murders his scoffing son Calyphas because he refuses to share Tamburlaine's 'conceits' of war. He threatens the kings who have refused to 'see' his strength, with 'Now, you shall feel the strength of
Tamburlaine.' Although the incidents in *Doctor Faustus* are farcical,
the farce has serious undertones. By building suggestions from the
*Faustbook* into a version of the Actaeon myth, Marlowe hints that
Faustus uses his power unjustly. Because Benvolio himself responds
so vengefully to the conjuror's first horn joke, he may seem to deserve a second set even more. As Faustus orders the devils to torment
the knights, balked in their 'just revenge', he exclaims:

> The world shall see their misery,
> And hell shall after plague their treachery.
>
> IV.iii.82–3

But because this misery is dramatically emphasized in the ensuing
scene (IV.iv), Benvolio's punishment, like that of Calyphas, seems
particularly harsh. 'Sporting' though the magic of false heads and
horns may be, these scenes nevertheless reflect Marlowe's abiding
concern with extreme rights and exceeding wrongs which originate
in 'conceit'.

### The tragedy of mind

The entertaining interlude in Acts III and IV contains only one direct
suggestion that the hero's pursuit of pleasure expresses his desperate
attitude towards damnation. After he has cozened the Horse-
Courser into purchasing a straw-horse, Faustus pauses to reflect:

> What art thou, Faustus, but a man condemned to die?
> Thy fatal time draws to a final end.
> Despair doth drive distrust into thy thoughts.
> Confound these passions with a quiet sleep.
> Tush! Christ did call the thief upon the cross;
> Then rest thee, Faustus, quiet in conceit.
>
> IV.v.33–8

Faustus is leaving behind some of his wilful ignorance about the wages of sin. By comparing himself with the thief (who called on Christ), he at least recognizes the possibilities of penance and the amendment of life. It is significant that this knowledge appears to make his danger all the greater. With his 'fatal time' approaching, Faustus prefers to rest 'quiet in conceit'. The angry Horse-Courser who returns and pulls off his leg while he sleeps in his chair fore-shadows the devils who dismember him at the end of Act v. Know-ledge, even exact theological knowledge, will not be powerful enough to save Faustus from Lucifer.

In a play by Marlowe, knowledge *can* give the hero near-tragic stature. The stature of Faustus is precarious, however, for Benvolios in the audience may not have succumbed to the magical seductions of rhetoric and show. Potentially the audience always has greater awareness than the hero and can recognize his limits even as he faces imminent destruction. 'Until you understand a writer's ignorance, presume yourself ignorant of his understanding', said Coleridge. The fifth Act of *Doctor Faustus* is calculated, I think to acquaint the audience with the fatal ignorance which abides within the hero's knowledge. Whether the tragic responses, terror and pity, can overcome or at least moderate the effects of this awareness depends on two things. It depends upon the continuing power of the ideals which Faustus so energetically pursues in the wrong direction. It also depends upon Marlowe's success in creating the illusion that Faustus is more sinned against than sinning. Had *Doctor Faustus* ended, as it began, in the mode of oblique satire, Marlowe could have followed a doom scenario similar to the one Erasmus describes in his *Enchiridion*: 'Will not the mocker be mocked? He that lives in heaven will laugh at them in turn; the Lord will jeer at them. In the Book of Wisdom you read that they will see Him and reject Him, but that God will laugh them to scorn' (p. 61). Marlowe, as we shall see, has almost certainly been reading the Book of Wisdom. Never-theless he punishes *his* mocker by allowing him both to see the God he no longer rejects, and to call for his help. Significantly, devils do all the jeering, not the Lord himself. It may well appear that the demonic game has been carried too far, that Marlowe has allowed the Old Law to destroy the wrong man.

The splendid speeches given to Faustus in Act v could strengthen this final sense of contradiction between growing character and shrinking plot. Marlowe's strategy reaches its climax when Faustus takes Helen of Troy as his paramour. Or perhaps we should say that his dark irony here rises to new depths of power and plausibility. Ever since Sir Walter Greg argued that Helen of Troy is a demonic phantom or succuba, the serious doctrinal intention of the scene has been widely accepted.[39] By rejecting the counsels of the Old Man, signing another bond for Mephistophilis, and loving Helen, Faustus damns himself – perhaps irrevocably. He reveals that he is a hardened sinner incapable of the penitence which would rescue him from violent revolutions of abject terror and Epicurean delight. What has not so far been understood is why Marlowe should give his damned hero such extraordinarily fine lines with which to celebrate Helen:

> O, thou art fairer than the evening's air,
> Clad in the beauty of a thousand stars.
> Brighter art thou than flaming Jupiter
> When he appeared to hapless Semele,
> More lovely than the monarch of the sky
> In wanton Arethusa's azured arms,
> And none but thou shalt be my paramour.
>
> v.i.112–18

The eloquence of Faustus becomes more intelligible once we recognize that Marlowe is alluding to the encomium of divine wisdom in Wisdom 7. As usual, Marlowe transforms the original text, which says:

For she is the brightness of the euerlasting light, the vndefiled mirroure of the maiestie of God, and the image of his goodnes. (26)

For she is more beautiful than the sunne, and is aboue all the order of the starres, and the light is not to be compared vnto her.

For night cometh upon it, but wickednes can not ouercome wisdome. (29–30)

But if wisdom cannot be overcome, she can still be parodied by Magus-figures like Faustus and Tamburlaine who identify their mistresses with her.[40] This allusion goes far to suggest the nature of the hero's basic flaw. He praises Helen, historically a destructive wanton, and dramatically a demonic phantom, in terms appropriate for the female wisdom figure, retained in Christian theology as a created analogue for Christ, the second person of the Trinity. In order to explain Donne's extravagant compliments to Elizabeth Drury in his *Anniversaries*, Frank Manley has shown that in the

Renaissance, this figure could still be used to symbolize 'sapientia creata'– a 'participation in the uncreated Wisdom of God'.[41] Although she had Greek origins as well, she retained many of her Hebraic attributes, and was probably more useful to poets than to theologians. She tended to represent 'the subconscious, intuitive feminine intelligence of the heart as opposed to the active, conscious, masculine intelligence of the mind'. Such wisdom included 'direction of life' and 'inclination of the heart', as well as an 'intellectual perception of God'.[42] Marlowe's hero is finally damned because he lacks the wisdom of the heart, a will to love goodness.

Through this allusion to the divine wisdom which Faustus inverts, Marlowe ironically fulfils the earlier promise by Mephistophilis to bring Faustus concubines 'As wise as Saba, or as beautiful / As was bright Lucifer before his fall' (II.i.155–6). Marlowe could have read in the *Faustbook* that Lucifer 'surpassed the brightnes of the Sunne and all other Starres'.[43] The star metaphor has a theological tradition behind it. According to Aquinas, 'Gregory says that the chief angel who sinned, being set over all the hosts of angels, surpassed them in brightness, and was by comparison the most illustrious among them.'[44] By combining in Helen the attributes of Lucifer and of Solomon's ideal bride, Marlowe symbolizes the devilish wisdom of St James with astonishing exactitude. But even more astonishing is his achievement in obscuring this exactitude. There can be few stronger testimonies to the seductions of rhetoric. Once we recognize the allusions to wisdom, we discover that Marlowe was putting a mock-encomium into the mouth of his unsuspecting hero. Like its predecessor in the same vein, Gorgias's praise of Helen, the speech has almost always persuaded readers and spectators far too well.[45]

We can surmise, I think, that Marlowe deliberately sought to gain sympathy for Faustus by means of a speech which subtly exposes him. In general this is the way his prophetic style works where all of his more tragic figures are concerned. Tamburlaine's speeches have the power to shake the Christian–classical norms by which Marlowe invites us to judge him. In *Doctor Faustus* the foundation implied through Biblical allusions stands firm. Even so, the hero's praise of Helen encourages the reader or spectator to use his imagination. Helen, the object of praise, is worthless, but the derivative language of this praise invokes the elemental creative energies of the universe. Winged by apprehension of these energies, our minds take flight, imitating the brief, vain flight of Faustus himself. Reading or listening, we pass quickly over the disconcerting comparisons between Helen and Faustus, Jupiter and Semele in the remaining portion of the speech. That the nymph Arethusa was probably too chaste ever to entertain the 'monarch of the sky', Apollo, in any myth, does not give us pause. We move on past this symbolic reduction of energy to lust, and past the Old Man's ominous last warning to Faustus, arriving at the final scene prepared to experience its confining, trapping mechanism in an immediate, very painful way.

So does Faustus. Once again I must emphasize the hero's freedom and the playwright's humanism – a humanism more expansive and less Erasmian than that of *The Jew of Malta*. Erasmus himself defined the course of wisdom 'alien to God' with no less rigour than Luther did:[46]

That, as James says, is a brutish, a devilish wisdom alien to God. Its end is death, and attending to it always is its pernicious handmaiden, presumption, with blindness of heart following presumption, tyranny of passions following blindness, plus the license to sin as much as you like. After that license comes habit, and following habit the most luckless insensibility of mind, whereby is lost all awareness of evil.

(*Enchiridion*, p. 61)

Faustus does follow this path from presumption to licence, but at its end he is far from sinking into 'the most luckless insensibility of mind'. Although he may lack the wisdom of the heart which would incline him towards the love of God, he has still managed to achieve an intellectual perception of God. Marlowe fills the last great soliloquy with an almost unbearable tension between the foolish heart and the knowing intellect of this doomed scholar.

To some critics the hero's knowledge has looked like penitence itself. Santayana, for example, wrote: 'This excellent Faustus is damned by accident or by predestination; he is brow-beaten by the devil and forbidden to repent when he has really repented.'[47] Other critics might feel that this knowledge merely reflects the self-descriptive 'convention' which allows Elizabethan dramatic sinners to understand their own sins. But in this case, knowledge is a psychological as well as a technical necessity. It characterizes the man who has acquired it and cannot be saved by it. As Hooker pointed out in

'A Learned Discourse of Justification, Works, and How the Foundation of Faith is Overthrown' (1585): 'Devils know the same things which we believe, and the minds of the most ungodly may be fully persuaded of the truth; which knowledge in the one and persuasion in the other, is sometimes termed faith, but equivocally, being indeed no such faith as that whereby a Christian man is justified.'[48] The final soliloquy by Faustus indicates that he has as much theology as does Mephistophilis, which is not to say that he has faith. He now knows that by the wages of sin as 'death' Paul meant the eternal damnation of the soul:

> O God,
> If thou wilt not have mercy on my soul,
> Yet for Christ's sake, whose blood hath ransomed me,
> Impose some end to my incessant pain.
> Let Faustus live in hell a thousand years,
> A hundred thousand, and at last be saved.
> O, no end is limited to damned souls.
> Why wert thou not a creature wanting soul?
> Or why is this immortal that thou hast?
> v.ii.162–70

By learning to understand Paul's hard saying, Faustus has at last reached genuine theological despair. He will never really understand the other half of the saying: 'The gift of God is eternal life.' For, as Hooker goes on to point out in his 'Learned Discourse', faithful men apprehend things believed 'not only as true, but also as good'. Ungodly men can recognize truth but not goodness. Hence they react differently to it: 'The Christian man the more he increaseth in faith, the more his joy and comfort aboundeth: but they, the more sure they are of the truth, the more they quake and tremble at it. This begetteth another effect, wherein the hearts of the one sort have a different disposition from the other' (p. 515). This different disposition in the hearts of evil men is such that: 'Being conscious what they are to look for, [they] do rather wish that they might, than think that they shall, cease to be, when they cease to live; because they hold it better that death should consume them into nothing, than God revive them unto punishment' (p. 515).

Hooker might have been describing the disposition of Marlowe's Faustus. It is Faustus himself who has what Harry Levin, referring to his creator, calls 'the conviction of sin without the belief in sal-

vation'.[49] Without doubt the cries of the terrified Faustus can terrify
an audience too, but as Erasmus observes in the *Enchiridion*, 'Not
the outcry of the mouth but the burning desire of the spirit gets, like
some very penetrating voice, a hearing from God' (p. 48). These
cries are still those of the proud magician. Phrases like 'Stand still,
you ever-moving spheres of heaven', 'Earth gape', 'O soul, be changed
to little water drops', ironically echo the imperative charms spoken
twenty-four years and four Acts earlier. His quotation from Ovid's
*Amores*, 'O lente, lente currite noctis equi!' not only caps his use of
inappropriate learned references. As J. P. Brockbank has pointed
out, the words 'sound like a last attempt to cast a spell'.[50]

The change of shape which Faustus now wishes to bring about
requires the dissolution of his soul, as well as the metamorphosis of
his body:

> Ah, Pythagoras' *metempsychosis*, were that true,
> This soul should fly from me and I be changed
> Into some brutish beast.
>
> v.ii.171–3

Such an escape from his own soul would require a miraculous alteration of nature itself. But only Christ, as distinct from devils and
magicians, has the power to change the order of nature. Against the
vain spells and distracted cries of the magician, Marlowe sets actual
miracles which Faustus perforce observes: 'See, see, where Christ's
blood streams in the firmament.' 'And see where God / Stretcheth
out his arm and bends his ireful brows!' Faustus expresses his desire
to escape punishment in traditional apocalyptic images:

> Mountains and hills, come, come, and fall on me,
> And hide me from the heavy wrath of God.
> No, no!
> Then will I headlong run into the earth.
> Earth, gape! O no, it will not harbor me!
>
> v.ii.149–53

For Faustus, his last hour *is* his judgment day, and the apocalyptic
mood is just as appropriate for his death as it is for that of Barabas.
Faustus, too, has been an Antichrist. By adopting magic in order to
become a demi-god, Faustus has presumed upon Christ's power to
alter nature, and denied its author.

Lacking faith, Faustus cannot be saved. He exhausts his learning in the search for a third path, but in his Christian world there are only two ways out. Marlowe might have shared Arthur Golding's attitude towards the kind of Pythagorean metempsychosis Faustus yearns for:

> But for to deeme or say
> Our noble soule (which is divine and permanent for ay)
> Is common to us with the beasts, I think it nothing lesse
> Than for to bee a poynt of him that wisdome dooth professe.
> Of this I am ryght well assurde, there is no Christen wyght
> That can by fondness be so farre seduced from the ryght.[51]
>
> p.406 ll. 49–54

Such 'wisdome', employed only to secure his own destruction, is what the final chorus of *Doctor Faustus* warns the audience against:

> Regard his hellish fall,
> Whose fiendful fortune may exhort the wise
> Only to wonder at unlawful things,
> Whose deepness doth entice such forward wits
> To practice more than heavenly power permits.

To the very end, Faustus is a 'forward wit', learned but foolish. As the devils carry him away, he superstitiously offers to burn his books. The devils have already shown just how little regard they have for the books and the 'metaphysics of magicians'. Because Faustus still mistakes the letter for the spirit, he must yield to the severity of the Old Law and be punished with Mosaic harshness.

Tamburlaine almost turns his death-scene into a triumph of the human imagination, but, as Hell yawns, Faustus finds that his learned conceits have lost all their strength. At the beginning of the last scene, Lucifer and his devils enter above the stage to observe Faustus. They probably remain there while Faustus takes his leave of true friends and false, watches the angels display Heaven and Hell, and speaks his final soliloquy. Faustus is forced to participate in a show of the sort he has relished most. Erasmus, who carefully warns the readers of his *Enchiridion* never to live as if Heaven and Hell were old wives' tales or bugaboos, counsels them: 'Like Virgil's Aeneas you should shrug off as nothing all the bogey men and fantasies which assail you, so to speak, in the very jaws of hell' (p. 90). How thoroughly Marlowe must have controlled his material in order to end his tragic 'praise of folly' in these same jaws. With almost sardonic economy he seems to have fulfilled Folly's promise that fools 'go straight to the Elysian fields' (p. 50) by confusing this Elysium with the picture-book Hell Faustus earlier refused to take seriously. His old wives' tales come true before his eyes. As he watches the Good and Bad Angels 'present' Heaven and Hell, these ever-curious eyes grow sated for the first time:

> Bad Angel: But yet all these are nothing; thou shalt see
> Ten thousand tortures that more horrid be.
> Faustus: O, I have seen enough to torture me.
>
> v.ii.123–5

The Bad Angel's reply, 'Nay, thou must feel them taste the smart of all', recalls the punishment of Benvolio, made to 'feel' torment by spirits he would not 'see'. Because Faustus has regularly preferred letter to spirit, the knavish Bad Angel assails him with a kind of emblematic pun.

The essential trick of pessimistic ironists who value absolute ideals is to expand the spirit by reducing the letter. In order to symbolize infinite riches they employ very little rooms. Trapped within one of these reductive, ironic mechanisms, the hero's own spirit may seem to have grown in a way out of all proportion to its actual change. R. B. Sewall says of Faustus that 'Like Job in the agony of his suffering, he has visions never vouchsafed in his days of prosperity.'[52] This is high praise for a foolish wit, but it does testify to the dynamic effect of placing an energetic, imaginative character in an extremely limiting context. Marlowe has reserved his most provoking ironies for the last. Even if Faustus is initially reprobate, he has spent an exciting stage-life, surrounded by friends and admirers, as well as by other fools more trivial than he is. Benvolio and the Old Man excepted, he has done little harm to anyone but himself. The wisdom which he misdirects has given his speeches great strength and beauty. He has gained a knowledge of God, as well as some awareness of his responsibility. And his lack of saving wisdom may be a lack scarcely presentable by dramatic methods. Certainly his desperate schemes for escape are far more moving than the shows presented by angels and devils. Faustus will always appear too large for the hell-mouth he deserves.

The death of Faustus should be regarded as a tragic illusion, rather than a tragedy. The final tragic effect depends more upon the

deceptive rhetoric which has amplified Faustus and upon the freedom he has hitherto enjoyed, than upon his intrinsic worth or stature.
Not the least disturbing aspect of this satiric-tragedy is its power to
make us doubt the very means we must use in responding to it.
Throughout the play, Faustus has inverted a form of wisdom more
humane and worldly than that defined by St Paul or Augustine. But
his apocalyptic death seems to remove wisdom beyond the reach of
the human mind. The problem is this: If the audience is fully to
grasp the hero's responsibility for his own destruction, it must be
made acquainted with the ideal wisdom parodied by his folly. It
must be convinced on some level that his preference for show over
substance merits punishment. But how can the audience feel confident of its capacity for understanding, when the play itself dramatizes the vanity of all reason not informed by wisdom and grace?
Those who have most thoroughly understood Faustus are the foolish,
faithless devils who tear him apart.

At the end of *Doctor Faustus* we may mock with the devils in bad
faith, or dream on about wisdom in good, but we are prevented from
finally answering the central question of the play. Who damns
Faustus? Like Faustus himself, we never know:

> Cursed be the parents that engendered me!
> No, Faustus, curse thyself, curse Lucifer
> That hath deprived thee of the joys of heaven.
>                                    v.ii.177–9

Marlowe has deprived his audience of the satirist's and the wise
man's special prerogative – 'true knowledge of the things that are'.
He has checked our 'forward wits', reminding us of our blindness
and leaving us in a fallen world of shows. Religious literature has
often called in question the means by which it communicates;
satires manage to tell us that satires lie; tragedies remind us of how
limited our reasoning abilities are. All move conflicts between faith
and reason right into the minds of the audience itself. Why, then, does
the sense of mystery created by *Doctor Faustus* seem religious and
satiric, rather than fully tragic? Because the play always implies that
given a vertical advantage, such as devils and angels enjoy, we could
shake off the tragic illusion and solve the paradox. A tragedy like
*Tamburlaine*, Part Two or *Edward II* checks the wit in quite a different fashion. Although these plays lead us to suspect that man

depends on shows, they ultimately tolerate that dependence. More-over they deny to characters and audience any privileged over-sight or vertical advantage. They offer a definite alternative to blindness because they create memory, thereby compelling us to dream about visible rather than invisible worlds.

# 5

# Mirrors for foolish princes

*The Massacre at Paris* is the most topical of Marlowe's plays. As Paul Kocher has carefully demonstrated, Marlowe often relies on current sources – anti-Catholic pamphlets and histories designed to arouse the indignation of English Protestants.[1] We might expect that because his play encourages this indignation, it would be less ironic than *The Jew of Malta* or *Doctor Faustus*, dark satires which betray the follies of the audience as well as those of the mocking heroes. Yet irony pervades *The Massacre at Paris*, an irony dependent less upon 'hard' allusions, more upon dramatic structure and implicit ideas.

Because Marlowe's irony functions so obliquely in *The Massacre at Paris*, it is easy to understand why J. B. Steane dismissed his own inclination to regard the play as a satire: 'One would like to think that Marlowe was intending, or at least sensing, an irony; that with all the noise and savagery, a satire existed safe in the knowledge that a knavish speech sleeps safe in a foolish ear.'[2] Although knavish speeches abound in *The Massacre at Paris*, they never achieve the plausibility we have observed in the soliloquies of Barabas and Faustus. Had he so wished, Marlowe could have glorified knavery and created a relationship with an audience like that established in *The Jew of Malta*.[3] He could have exaggerated French bloodshed as a means of saying, 'My show is aimed at foolish hypocrites who criticize the Catholics, but not themselves.'[4] While his text will support such an interpretation of his purpose, we should not stress the guilty spectator at the expense of the guilty Frenchmen. The plausibility so lacking in the characters of *The Massacre at Paris* may be recognized instead in its plot. Marlowe has not merely woven an old wives' tale out of Catholic ghoulishness. His 'show' emphasizes follies which have been warranted by recent events.

This is an important point to bear in mind when attempting to judge the general effect of *The Massacre at Paris*. Later in this chapter I will suggest that the play can be approached as a *speculum principis*, or mirror for princes, which has been deliberately turned upside down. Its princes resemble those misguided rulers discussed by Erasmus in *The Praise of Folly*, *The Education of a Christian Prince*, 'Julius exclusus', and a number of adages and colloquies which deal with warfare and religious hypocrisy.[5] If we compare Marlowe's Guise with Pope Julius II in the dialogue 'Julius Exclusus', we will recognize strong similarities in presentation.[6] Both portraits are caricatures of proud and wilful tyrants who brag about their likeness to Julius Caesar. Erasmus makes the moral condemnation of Pope Julius overt, criticizing him through the other spokesmen in the dialogue, Julius's companion 'Genius' and St Peter, who refuses to admit Julius to Heaven. As satire, 'Julius exclusus' parts company with *The Praise of Folly* in two respects; Erasmus attacks particular, rather than general vices, and he uses a direct method calculated to instruct the reader, not involve him in explorations of his own folly.

*The Massacre at Paris* also attacks particular vices, but without providing overt and reliable criticism like St Peter's. Consequently, the main guide to the audience on how it should respond to this play becomes the order and emphasis created by the arrangement of events. We must attend closely to the unfolding history, as we do when we consider the fortunes of Tamburlaine or of Edward II. We can find, I think, that these worldly plays tend to employ more recondite classical allusions and that all portray violations of cosmic 'degree'. But such discoveries may be more useful as indications of Marlowe's own attitudes than as evidence about the responses of his popular audiences. With surprising objectivity, given his subject matter, he avoids imposing judgment.

In order to describe the arrangement of its action, I will have to examine closely a play assumed to be so corrupt that it 'precludes any close analysis'.[7] Inferences about the soundness of the text will be secondary to the main hypothesis in this chapter: that a play which so stresses the interlocking destinies of its characters and the precise nature of their catastrophes is unlikely to have been purely sensational Protestant propaganda. Because outrage succeeds out-

rage in a remorseless and predictable fashion, we may miss the sense
of mounting intensity which provides one measure of Tamburlaine's
ambitions. But we can find another measure in the treatment of
different groups fatally knit together through comparable motive and
mutual recrimination.

The fact that *The Massacre at Paris* occupies a central position in
this study does not mean that it is central to my argument about
Marlowe's ironic style. I discuss it here because of its similarity to the
darker satires. Marlowe's slightest and shortest play benefits greatly
from supporting references to stronger and richer texts. When surrounded by such texts, its authenticity becomes much more apparent. For example, like *The Jew of Malta* and *Edward II*, *The
Massacre at Paris* seems to be preoccupied with the moral confusions
introduced through justified revenge and righteous wrong-doing.
Corruption will not explain all the repetitiousness in the play; the
other two plays also give the terms 'resolution' and 'revenge' to a
number of wilful speakers. All three works insistently associate love
and hate, extreme right and extreme wrong.

Moreover, the evidence of Marlowe's other plays often suggests
that qualities disturbing to us in the *Massacre* provide dramatic
images of moral anarchy rather than symptoms of textual corruption.
As in *Edward II*, characters draw attention to the hastiness of their
actions – a fact which might imply that a rapid pace and a less-than-
adequate set of motivations were intended from the first. Wilbur
Sanders has noticed that the speakers in the play 'sound like ven-
triloquists' dummies for the ghost of the Scythian war-lord', and has
argued that, 'The very act of murder, the strange relationship between agent and patient (cf. Clarence and *his* murderers), is emptied
of all content. There is no sense of interaction.'[8] But we have already
seen how Barabas reduces himself to a mere trope and destroys, with
the 'promise' of his faithful child Abigail, all meaningful social
relationships. By the middle of *Tamburlaine* Part Two, Tamburlaine
himself begins to sound like a ventriloquist. At the outset of *Edward
II*, the King quickly turns his wife and courtiers into shadows by
loving his own shadow, Gaveston.

When he plunged his audience straight into the company of savage
caricatures, Marlowe severed *The Massacre at Paris* from his own
ideals and emotions. If we do not observe his dramatic design with

care, we will regard the play as a pot-boiler, a work which appeals to
naive prejudice, rather than one which presupposes highly critical
prejudice. The difference between these two attitudes is not easy to
recognize when we examine the play itself. By suggesting that Marlowe wrote it as an objective, satiric history and that neither the play
nor its intended audience were naive, I have risked over-rating both.
No other play raises so acutely the issue of Marlowe's own patience
and detachment. Never does the obliqueness of his ironic style
appear more irresponsible. *The Massacre at Paris* badly needs a
Shavian preface. We are closer to Swift's Ireland than to Counter-
Reformation Europe. We would prefer to have more realistic portraits of Medicis and Huguenots. Time has carried this satire far
from its creative origins. But enough of Marlowe's art has survived
to hint that his irony could have been a response to the contradictions of religious warfare, a defence against pain, and an attack
upon the very sources of political disorder.

* * *

I shall consider four aspects of Marlowe's design: the treatment of
the Duke of Guise as a focus and symbol for evil in other characters;
the analogies among different groups of characters; the repetition
of particular motifs; and the use of spectacle to achieve emphasis.
Marlowe's structural analogies function as obscurely here as in
*The Jew of Malta*. By mirroring one powerful group or individual
in another, Marlowe has distributed sympathies and antipathies
more evenly than many commentators have realized. Spectacle
occasionally serves to brighten some of these clouded mirrors, suggesting connections between characters or events by presenting
them in similar visual terms. Many displays and gestures seem to
arise naturally from the fast-paced action. But ceremonies do in-
terrupt this action, and the regular connection of ceremonial with
violent behaviour can scarcely be accidental. Marlowe must have
counted on his audience to note the incongruity some of the time.

Like Barabas, the Guise brings other major characters within the
range of a satiric view; he serves as a 'prop' (xxii.4) for more vil-
lainies than those of his own faction.[9] It is generally in response to
his activity that political issues are exposed and discussed. Moreover
he is often the occasion of wickedly disruptive behaviour on the part

of other characters. All of the soliloquies in the play are either related to or spoken by the Guise. By this device Marlowe calls attention to the qualities of mind and character which produce tyranny.

As early as the second scene of the play, the Guise shares with the audience 'those deep-engendered thoughts' which very soon will 'burst abroad those never-dying flames / Which cannot be extinguished but by blood'. This long soliloquy articulates his own political position, as well as motives and attitudes typical of those in the play who aspire to rule. The speech is a 'profession' marking the speaker as a vengeful meddler of twisted pretensions and practically super-human desires. His pretensions recall those of Barabas in several respects. It is no more likely that Heaven has 'engendered him of earth' (like Adam) to busily wreak havoc than it is that Heaven promised material riches to the offspring of Abraham. Both characters favour the bowel metaphor in describing the sources of their income. Both commend their own cleverness. Both also use the word 'simple' to mean foolish or insignificant, as well as sincere. After the Guise explains that he cloaks his policy in religion to get aid from the Pope and from Spain, he bursts out:

> Religion! *O Diabole!*
> Fie, I am ashamed, however that I seem
> To think a word of such a simple sound
> Of so great a matter should be made the ground.
> ii.66–9

For the Guise, as for other clever scoffers, religion is beneath contempt. Where the Guise differs from his Marlovian predecessors is in the almost abstract purity of will which places resolution above achievement. 'That like I best that flies beyond my reach.' The continuous restlessness of the Guise – his waiting, waking, thirsting, contriving, and imagining – may seem disproportionate to the 'fully executing' of important matters, which, he tells us, none understand. We tend to lose sight here of the French diadem, his ostensible aim.

In general, *The Massacre at Paris* lacks that foundation in Biblical allusions which ironically supports the Judaism of Barabas or the sorcery of Faustus. But the Guise does seem to use one such allusion when he sends the Apothecary to the Queen of Navarre with a pair of poisoned gloves:

> For she is that huge blemish in our eye
> That makes these upstart heresies in France.
>
> ii.23–4

It is easy to suspect here a covert reference to Matthew 7:3, suggested by Oliver, or to Luke 6:42: 'Hypocrite, cast out the beams out of thine owne eye first, & then shalt thou se perfectly, to pul out the mote that is in thy brothers eye.' The Guise appears to be a knowing hypocrite, but like Barabas he sometimes seems to fool himself with his professions. We find him soliloquizing a few lines later about Navarre in terms comparable to those he has applied to the Queen Mother. With a 'rabblement' of heretics, Navarre 'Blinds Europe's eyes and troubleth our estate' (95–6). To understand the Guise, we must 'hear' him the way we 'hear' Pope Adrian when he accuses Bruno of 'pride' in *Doctor Faustus*. The Guise means to praise himself in dispraising others, but many of his charges and comparisons turn back upon himself. Is it Navarre who 'blinds' Europe's eyes, when the Guise wants to 'weary all the world' with his seditions? He concludes his idealized allegorical portrait of himself as monarch (101–8) by saying that those who behold him will 'become / As men that stand and gaze against the sun'. But the play implies that the Guise is an ominous comet, rather than a sun or favourable star. When in scene xviii he vaunts over his fallen enemy Mugeroun as an 'imperfect exhalation' or 'fiery meteor in the firmament' (17, 19), his dispraise again works reflexively. Two scenes later, the Captain of the guard, who prepares for the Guise's assassination, is made to say, 'Now fall the star whose influence governs France' (xx.14).

The most conspicuous allusion in the Guise's long soliloquy is to Julius Caesar, a figure with whom the League propagandists of the day often identified the great Duke:[10]

> As Caesar to his soldiers, so say I:
> Those that hate me will I learn to loathe.
>
> ii.100–1

Is the Guise any more faithful to his prototype than Barabas is to Job? One doubts that the historical Caesar ever said anything of the kind. It is interesting to compare the Guise's brand of Caesarism with the concluding reference to Caesar in a speech by Gargantua. This 'harangue' is addressed to the vanquished subjects of a tyrant,

Picrochole, and it deals with the treatment of enemies:

> I remember also that Julius Caesar, who was so gracious a Commander that Cicero said of him, 'that his Fortune had nothing higher than that he could, and his Temper nothing higher than that he would, save and pardon every one.' Notwithstanding this, he did in certain Instances rigorously punish the Authors of Rebellion.[11]

What the Guise puts into the mouth of a more villainous Caesar is another variant of the stock tyrannic formula, 'Let them hate me, if only they fear me.' Such severity characterizes the Machiavels in Marlowe's other plays. The fact that the Guise is so rashly impolitic, so insensitive to a world of contingencies, suggests that we should view him against the background of the *speculum principis*. In this tradition moral absolutes remained politically viable and wilful tyrants were soundly excoriated. Machiavelli found practical wisdom in encouraging his Prince to keep before him the deeds and actions of some eminent man: 'In this way, it is said, Alexander the Great imitated Achilles; Caesar imitated Alexander; and Scipio, Cyrus.'[12] Perhaps more germane to the spirit of Marlowe's play, crowded as it is with Christian properties and religious hypocrisies, is the attitude of Erasmus in *The Education of a Christian Prince*:

> Now what could be more senseless than for a man who has received the sacraments of the Christian church to set up as an example for himself Alexander, Julius Caesar, or Xerxes, for even the pagan writers would have attacked their lives if any of them had had a little sounder judgement.[13]

In addition to the reference to Caesar, the soliloquy contains other important allusions. Let the French crown be placed on the 'high pyramides', says the Guise:

> I'll either rend it with my nails to naught
> Or mount the top with my aspiring wings,
> Although my downfall be the deepest hell.
>
> ii.45–7

References to wings and Hell may imply the similarity of the Duke's pride to Lucifer's. Marlowe's tyrant also resembles the tyrant whom Erasmus compared to an eagle in his well-known adage, 'Scarabeus aquilam quaerit' ('The beetle searches for the eagle').[14] Erasmus mentions the eagle's headlong force, terrifying appearance and voice, voraciousness, and belligerent singularity, as well as its proverbial ability to stare into the sun. The Guise longs for a look that makes 'pale death' walk on his face, and a 'hand that with a grasp may gripe the world' – attributes of power that can only be seen with the mind's eye. Guise wants to be a sun himself, dazzling the men who gaze upon him. In a passage of 'Scarabeus' Erasmus wrote: 'It [the eagle] nests not in the plain but among rugged and lofty rocks, sometimes in trees, and only in the tallest, like a tyrant muttering to himself, "let them hate me as long as they fear."' [15]

Marlowe has so structured his play that two other major characters, Henry King of France and Henry of Navarre, mirror the attitudes of the Guise. By shifting rapidly among these characters, Marlowe's plot may encourage us to compare their seemingly disparate actions. As in *The Jew of Malta*, Marlowe sometimes throws more light upon his mirrors by emphatically repeating particular motifs. In the absence of conspicuous allusions, however, the righteous self-justifications offered by his characters become harder to assess. In order to recognize them as 'unseen hypocrisies', a fully capable spectator would have to note incongruities between earlier and later professions or between professions and the deeds they refer to. Perhaps an exaggerated style of delivery would have given the original spectators some guidance. Modern scholars who insist on the pro-Protestant spirit of play and audience have had to minimize these incongruities. [16] Righteous professions did not trouble Marlowe's age, they maintain. Yet they surely troubled the playwright who put such a variety of religious professions into the *Tamburlaine* plays and *The Jew of Malta*.

Marlowe's 'dark' treatment of righteous hypocrisy may best be studied in his handling of the Protestant champion, Henry of Navarre. Even while he remains at the French court, the activities of this hero tend to raise disturbing questions. It would be risky to make much of his reactions to his mother's sudden death, although his shift from smug reproof for her incautiousness to ecstatic despair over her death resembles the shifts of Barabas when he loses his house. Why, we might speculate, does Navarre abandon his tutors to the mercies of the Guise and Anjou? (Why, for that matter, do these diehards who have sworn to spare neither king nor emperor (iv.33) spare their primary enemy?) Marlowe collapses history in order to suggest that the death of the young King Charles makes

Navarre begin to fear for his own safety.[17] He recognizes from the outset that the Guise party regards his marriage as a dynastic threat, yet reposes his confidence in God's justice. When he leaves the court, Navarre's faith in his own righteousness grows ever more strident. Thereafter Marlowe manages to tar him with the same brush that has whisked over Ferneze.

Navarre regards the 'broils' at the court (Charles's sudden demise) as an 'opportunity' for him to steal away and muster up an army, anticipating that the Guise will block his 'enterprise' (xii.30). On a first hearing, his explanation may seem plausible enough, but just what is this enterprise? Ostensibly Navarre feels threatened as the next heir to the throne, but because France already has a king, and because he is a king himself, we can only wonder at the 'truth' that he discovers in Pleshé's suggestion that his triumphant army will crown him in Pampelonia. A few lines earlier he has been concerned about the French crown, 'my due by just succession'. He concludes by vowing to 'labor for the truth / And true profession of his holy word'. We can of course explain away the confusing mixture of crowns and motives by assuming that Navarre's anticipation of opponents and policies gives the playwright an economical way of summarizing future events, and that it does not therefore reflect upon his character. But would a playwright or even a memorial reconstructor have accidentally permitted Navarre to refer to truth three times in his last four lines? Or have let him employ twelve self-references in his first twelve lines, concluding with the pious hope that God will 'preserve us still'? Such repetitions would seem to require some effort on the writer's part. The whole emphasis of the conversation between Navarre and Pleshé falls on opportunistic 'enterprise' rather than on the excuse of seeking 'safety' with which it begins. When Navarre later returns to help Henry against rebellious Paris and the Guise, it is because his adviser Bartus points out his 'fit opportunity / To show your love unto the king of France' (xix.4–5).

Scenes presenting Navarre and his advisers in the field interweave through the middle of the play with scenes presenting a variety of more personal court broils, which in fact stretched from 1581–8.[18] When Navarre reappears in scene xv, he seems capable of a still more jumbled group of motives. He immediately justifies his 'quarrel' against those 'proud disturbers of the faith', meaning, he adds, the

Guise, the Pope, and the King of Spain. We can compare his sentiments with those in the Guise's earlier reference to the heretical
Navarre who 'troubleth our estate'. Navarre goes on to say that this
just quarrel is purely preventive; its purpose is 'to defend their
strange inventions / Which they will put us to with fire and sword'
(xv.8–9). He adds two other reasons – 'honor of our God and country's
good'. An audience might not remember it, but the playwright could
hardly have forgotten that a comparable mixture of motives preceded
the great massacre itself nine scenes earlier. Anjou had argued that
the 'wisest' will 'rather seek to scourge their enemies / Than be
themselves base subjects to the whip' (iv.15–16). Guise had backed
up Anjou by advising King Charles 'rather choose to seek your
country's good / Than pity or relieve these upstart heretics' (iv.19–
20).

News that the French army is approaching provokes the following
valiant outburst from Navarre:

> In God's name, let them come!
> This is the Guise that hath incensed the king
> To levy arms and make these civil broils.
>
> xv.31–3

Guise is indeed raising an army, for use against Navarre and the
Bourbons, according to the Cardinal (xiii.57), but for use against the
King, according to the Guise (xviii.27). Besides, the first one to levy
arms seems to have been 'rebellious King Navarre', as Henry III
calls him in the following scene. Rebels and heretics become difficult to distinguish. Three scenes later, questioned by King Henry
about the host he has raised, the Guise replies with an argument of
the Protestant stamp:

> Why, I am no traitor to the crown of France.
> What I have done, 'tis for the Gospel's sake.
>
> xviii.35–6

Throughout this muddle of professions, the one clear value is the
power signified by the French crown, the 'chiefest mark' which all
'level' at. As soon as Navarre learns (scene xix) that the Guise and
King Henry have each other by the ears, his own rebellion, always
dependent on, if not provoked by, the acts of the Guise, comes to an
end. The butt of his zealous hostility is no longer Catholicism generally but the Guise specifically. In rebellious victory against the

King's troops Navarre had proclaimed a general onslaught on popery
and 'relics' (xvii.16–17). Now, however, he fathoms the Guise's
motives well enough to disclose something of his own:

> For his aspiring thoughts aim at the crown,
> And takes his vantage on religion.
>
> xix.24–5

There is no way of being fully confident that Marlowe means such
judgments to fall back upon those who make them. Kocher suggested
that 'Not enough is made, in the drama, of Guise's references to the
Protestants as "heretics" to produce an effect of relativity comparable
to that achieved by more emphatic measures in *The Jew of Malta*.'[19]
Had the professions of the Guise and Navarre met head on, as do
those of Barabas and Ferneze, their 'unseen hypocrisies' and self-
deceptions would perhaps be easier to recognize.

The other major character developed through his relation to the
Guise is King Henry III. Together Henry and the Guise lead
the Paris massacre. When, as Anjou, Henry provisionally accepts the
Polish diadem, he betrays his wilfulness. To the Polish ambassadors
he boasts of being:

> Such a king whom practice long hath taught
> To please himself with manage of the wars,
> The greatest wars within our Christian bounds.
>
> ix.8–10

Henry also reveals his strong will when he is crowned King of France
(xiii.14) and when he discharges his council, resolving to trust only
his own 'head' and to be 'ruled' by his minion Epernoun
(xviii.95–6).[20] Like the Guise, Henry is similar to the princes described in the pages of *The Praise of Folly*:

Fashion me now a man such as princes commonly are, a man ignorant of the laws,
almost an enemy of the public welfare, intent upon private gain, addicted to
pleasure, a hater of learning, a hater, too, of liberty and truth, thinking about any
thing except the safety of the state, and measuring all things by his own desire
and profit.[21]

Henry does not, like the Guise, constantly seek out respectable titles
with which to cloak his proceedings. He emerges as a scheming
politician, who, as he boasts to the Poles, 'hath sufficient counsel in
himself / To lighten doubts and frustrate subtle foes' (ix.6–7).
'T'were hard with me if I should doubt my kin', he reassures the

Guise, whom he has lured into a trap. His doubts will prove much harder on the Guise. Only in this scene, with its insistence on false friendship, does the Proverbial language of wicked folly rise to the surface of the dialogue. 'Come, Guise', vaunts Henry –

> And see thy traitorous guile outreached,
> And perish in the pit thou mad'st for me.
>
> xx.32–3

Somewhat more obvious than the analogies among tyrants is the repetition of particular motifs in a variety of situations. Marlowe used this technique for ordering plot when in *The Jew of Malta* he emphasized the terms 'simplicity' and 'profession'. One word especially reiterated in *The Massacre at Paris* is 'resolution'. In Marlowe's plays this term is often 'sicklied o'er'. Faustus conjures resolutely, Barabas schemes resolutely, the barons resolutely make head against Edward. No one is more 'resolute' than Lightborn. Repetition of the word in *The Massacre at Paris* suggests that Marlowe considers seemingly distinct actions as variants on the theme of pure will articulated by the Guise. For the Guise, 'resolution' is 'honor's fairest aim' (ii.39). 'Then thou remainest resolute?' he questions the Apothecary whom he sends to the old Queen of Navarre with the poisoned gloves (ii.18). He tells his assistants in the massacre that if they will be as resolute as he, 'There shall not a Huguenot breathe in France' (v.50). Navarre's just quarrel seems almost to involve a parody of this attitude when he exclaims, 'We must with resolute minds resolve to fight' (xv.10). It is carried to its furthest extreme by the murderers who await the Guise in the palace at Blois:

> *Second Murderer :* O, that his heart were leaping in my hand.
> *Third Murderer :* But when will he come, that we may murder him?
> *Cossin :* Well, then, I see you are resolute.
>
> xx.6–8

Another motif with which Marlowe weaves patterns in his history is vengeance or punishment. The cutting off of the Admiral's head and hands as a present for the Pope, documented by Marlowe's source, is, Anjou declares, a 'just revenge' (v.45). Still more extravagant is the speech of Navarre in scene xv which begins:

> The power of vengeance now encamps itself
> Upon the haughty mountains of my breast...
>
> 20–1

Navarre says nothing about the massacre; presumably he is avenging himself on the 'proud disturbers' who have not yet raised an army to oppose his. Punishments are also extravagant. In scene xiii Mugeroun cuts an ear off the Cutpurse who has taken his gold button. Three scenes later, King Henry 'makes horns at the Guise', and implies (what we already know) that the Guise's wife is attracted to the King's minion, Mugeroun. In reply to Henry, the Guise swears 'by all the saints in heaven' (xvi) that Mugeroun,

> That villain for whom I bear this deep disgrace,
> Even for your words that have incensed me so,
> Shall buy that strumpet's favor with his blood.
> Whether he have dishonored me or no,
> *Par la mort de Dieu, il mourra.*
>
> 24–8

Through his oath, Christ's passion is juxtaposed with the foolish violence of the play.

The motif of revenge begins to degenerate into black farce as the dying Guise and Queen Catherine scream out their furious and historically unwarranted curses in scene xx. These are not the curses of Shakespeare's Margaret, which in *Richard III* do make the hair stand on end and have uncanny power over a wide sweep of history. In quick succession the Cardinal and Duke Dumaine follow them up by swearing vengeance upon King Henry. Marlowe's sources might have suggested their attitudes, but the tight sequence may well be his. As the play draws to a close, Henry slays his assassin, leaving the minion Epernoun to wish that the murdered Friar were still alive for further punishment. Henry then vows (twice) to 'ruinate that wicked church of Rome / That hatcheth up such bloody practices' (xxiii.64–5). Finally Navarre vows to avenge the King's death on Rome and on 'popish prelates' (xxiii.107). Marlowe's sources had included Henry's vengefulness, but they also included his confession to a priest.[22] It is difficult to believe that a pirate left this confession out, for the characters of this play tend to be desperately singleminded. What would a Henry who recommends the slicing of 'Catholics' have to confess?

The impression of great speed which the play makes on us must have been intended by Marlowe. Among the most commonly recurring statements and phrases are those urging 'Begone', 'Away,

then', 'Dispatch', 'Delay no time.' This technique is most apparent
in scene xii when, as soon as the soul of King Charles is 'fled', his
mother Catherine hastens to recall Henry from Poland, and Navarre
rushes away, promising to muster his army 'speedily'. In the preceding scene the impetuous Catherine urges the Guise to slaughter
the hundred Huguenots who pray in the woods. 'Let us delay no
time.' 'Be gone. Delay no time, sweet Guise.' 'Madam', replies the
Guise, 'I go as whirlwinds rage before a storm' (x.29–30). Like
Tamburlaine's, the actions of the Guise present in an inverted way
the traditional commonplace of the wise ruler piloting the ship of
state. Guise is the storm, not the pilot, just as he is the predatory
eagle rather than the sun he gazes upon.

Through spectacle Marlowe accentuates hypocrisy and further
orders his whirlwind plot. He stresses hypocrisy by frequent conjunctions of ceremony with violence. For an audience which may
learn to see better than any character, these violent shows could
point up differences between fact and pretence. They might also lead
the audience to ponder the deeds of princes obsessed with forms and
appearances. Particularly important as evidence that Marlowe uses
spectacle to create dramatic order is the fact that he lingers over four
groups of incidents, all of which rely on display. These include: 1)
the preparations for the massacre, with its 'entrance', the murder
of the Admiral; 2) the coronation of Henry III; 3) the inception of
Henry's plot against the Guise and its fulfilment, and 4) the death of
Henry himself.

In the first episode, Guise reveals his characteristic concern with
show by insisting on the ritual nature of the massacre he is planning.[23]
The 'actors' who are to participate are to be costumed with white
crosses and white scarfs. Their garb is surely stressed when in the
following scene these actors swear on their crosses to kill heretics
and to be unmerciful.[24] 'I am disguised', says Anjou, 'And therefore
mean to murder all I meet' (v.5–6). Perhaps the Cardinal, strangled
in scene xxi, or the Friar who assassinates Henry III for conscience
sake are also 'disguised' by their religious habits. The massacre is to
begin with a 'peal of ordnance' and continue as long as a bell rings.
The Guise reminds his actors of these procedural rules again after
the murder of the Admiral. At the massacre's finish, three scenes
later, he gives an order to 'stay / That bell that to the devil's matins

rings' (viii.86–7). The massacre itself, for all its violent disruptive-
ness, resembles a short play composed of several brief scenes and a
slightly more detailed induction.

It is the ceremoniousness of the Catholic actors which makes their
violent murder of the Admiral particularly shocking. His assassins
stab him with the words, 'Then pray unto our Lady; kiss this cross'
(v.29). Again in scenes vii and xi, victims are killed in postures of
prayer. The 'crucifixion' of the Huguenot Admiral is first referred to
when Anjou vows that,

> Unto Mount Faucon will we drag his corpse;
> And he that living hated so the cross
> Shall, being dead, be hanged thereon in chains.
>
> v.46–8

What to do with the body of the Admiral becomes matter for a series
of grim jests in scene x. 'First Man' and 'Second Man' end by hanging the body in a tree after all, where it is admired by the Guise and
by Queen Catherine. This crucifixion 'show' provides a speaking
picture of un-Christian Christianity.[25]

Ceremony and violence are also linked in the second spectacular
sequence, the 'holy feast' of King Henry's coronation. Catherine
welcomes her newly crowned son home from Poland with an idealized
description of the France he will rule:

> Here hast thou a country void of fears,
> A warlike people to maintain thy right,
> A watchful senate for ordaining laws,
> A loving mother to preserve thy state.
>
> xiii.4–7

Well before she curses Henry in scene xx, indeed at the conclusion
of the same scene, Catherine threatens to 'dispatch him with his
brother presently' (xiii.64). The warlike people of Paris will shortly
prefer the Guise to their King, and the King will dispense with his
'false' senate. Navarre has already mustered a rebellious army. How
fitting it is then that this 'holy feast' be 'profaned', not only by the
activities of a cutpurse, but also by the harshness of his judges.
Among the pretexts for war Erasmus criticized in his adage 'Dulce
bellum inexpertis' was the excuse that it is comparable to punishing
a felon or criminal. But, he objects, even a criminal must first be
legally prosecuted.[26] Marlowe seems to use his felon, and the mock

justice of Mugeroun who summarily cuts off an ear with the King's approval, to imply royal lawlessness within a formally religious setting. Mugeroun's act could recall the incident which occurred in Gethsemane when Christ was arrested. A disciple (Peter, according to St John) cut off the ear of one of the high priest's servants, provoking Christ's admonition (Matthew 26:52): 'All that take the sworde, shal perishe with the sworde.'

In *The Massacre at Paris*, almost all ceremonies and tableaux modulate into violence or mingle with it. The 'union and religious league' just achieved through marriage as the play begins seems to be breaking up quickly when the bride must leave her husband to hear a mass. In an aside the Queen Mother vows to dissolve 'this solemnity' (the marriage of Navarre) 'with blood and cruelty' (i.25–6). The Guise, introduced in the following scene, not only arranges to poison the Queen of Navarre with gloves, but also stations an assassin to shoot at the Admiral: 'Now come thou forth and play thy tragic part' (ii.28). No sooner does the Admiral give order to see the body of the poisoned Queen 'honored with just solemnity' than the Guise's hired assassin shoots at him (iii.30). The dignified parting between Henry and his general Duke Joyeaux gives way to furious oaths as soon as the King makes horns at the Guise (xvi). Assassins mix murder with civility. 'You are welcome sir. Have at you', says the soldier with a musket who shoots Mugeroun (xviii.14). The 'Third Murderer' addresses the Guise as 'good, my lord', and actually asks his pardon for being sent to murder him (xx.60).[27]

In the 'death of the Duke of Guise', his third spectacular sequence, Marlowe sketches a tragedy of conceit resembling that of Barabas. The fact that Henry, its contriver, refers to his own 'tragical' humour two scenes earlier (xviii.105) and later applauds his 'device' suggests that Marlowe, the satirist, wants his audience to cast a critical eye upon Henry's play. Henry views his tragedy as a punitive trap:

> Then come, proud Guise, and here disgorge thy breast,
> Surcharged with surfeit of ambitious thoughts.
> Breathe out that life wherein my death was hid,
> And end thy endless treasons with thy death.
> xx.22–5

The 'belly' metaphor, suggestive, as in *Doctor Faustus*, of folly and self-deceit, has made its timely appearance in scene xviii; there the

Guise announced that his soul had been hot enough to 'work' the King's 'just digestion', even before the King incensed him. Later in this scene Epernoun, who had entered with Henry, accuses the Guise of living 'by foreign exhibition'. According to Henry, the Pope and the King of Spain 'feed him with their gold' (xviii.56).

Characteristically, the Guise himself decides to view Henry's trap as a tragedy. In a moment of splendid confidence immediately before his fall, he vows to triumph over Henry 'As ancient Romans o'er their captive lords' (xx.52). Such Caesarism seems essential to his character as originally conceived, rather than an accident of textual corruption. He refers to Caesar in his first long speech (ii.100), and in scene xviii Henry ironically tells him:

> Guise, wear our crown, and be thou king of France,
> And as dictator, make or war or peace,
> Whilst I cry *placet* like a senator.
>
> 70–2

Faced with death, the Guise sustains this Roman posture:

> Yet Caesar shall go forth.
> Let mean conceits and baser men fear death.
> Tut, they are peasants; I am Duke of Guise,
> And princes with their looks engender fear.
>
> xx.67–70

He finds, as Tamburlaine did not, that his emblematic appearance cannot help him. 'To die by peasants, what a grief is this', he admits, but goes on to identify his fate with Caesar's anyway, ending his life with more than just one 'vain Thrasonical brag':

> Ah, Sixtus, be revenged upon the king!
> Philip and Parma, I am slain for you!
> Pope excommunicate, Philip depose
> The wicked branch of cursed Valois his line.
> *Vive la messe!* Perish Huguenots!
> Thus Caesar did go forth, and thus he died.[28]
>
> xx.82–7

No amount of corruption could account for the special effects of this furiously muddled outcry. The whole speech is a masterpiece of tragic farce, followed immediately by Cossin's blunt question to the assassins: 'What, have you done?' Marlowe's Guise bears a remarkably strong resemblance to Pope Julius in the 'Julius exclusus' a proud churchman whose desire to imitate Caesar made him a satiric butt.[29] The Guise's assassination has been contrived in a spirit analogous to that of *The Praise of Folly*. Folly had suggested that if a bad prince were ever to compare his emblematic props of power with his life, 'He would have the grace to be ashamed of his finery. He would be afraid some nosy satirist might turn the whole spectacle, suited as it is for high tragedy, into laughter and derision.'[30] As usual, the more sardonic Marlowe darkens his satiric spectacle, creating a more provocative mixture of tragedy and game.

The tragedy of the Guise is rounded off in a spirit of grim raillery as the gleeful Henry rejoices in the 'sweet sight' of the corpse, loads it (as Navarre had done earlier) with the sins of its age, and points it out to other observers – the Guise's son and the Queen Mother, Catherine. Marlowe has here added little of importance to his sources, except for the Queen Mother's response to Henry and her vindictive cursing.[31] Catherine cuts immediately through to the folly of Henry's *post facto* rationalization: 'I slew the Guise because I would be King.' 'King!' she exclaims, 'Why so thou wert before!' In the economy of the play, the death of the Guise provides a structural balance for the earlier massacre sequence. The two sequences parallel one another both as animal hunts and as theatrical performances. As for the 'Massacre at Paris' which the play's title claims to present, does it not include both the indiscriminate public slaughter and the more clandestine dynastic murders? Marlowe implies that the infamous massacre itself was, like other religious gestures in his play, only a means of promoting secular ambitions, and spends only four of his twenty-three scenes upon it.

The last 'show' of all, Henry's assassination, is not as spectacular as the death of the Guise. Significantly Henry dies because he is deceived by the false appearance of a 'holy' friar. Just why this Jacobin Friar would consider it 'meritorious' for him to kill a Catholic king (xxii.27) we are not told, but the situation does permit an ironic handling of a commonplace object of Reformation criticism, the 'treasury of merit'. Henry, although unwittingly, speaks to the point when he assures Epernoun that such friars 'will not offer violence to their king for all the wealth and treasure of the world' (xxiii.24–5). Marlowe's violent Jacobin is seeking the grace of the next world. Can it be merely a coincidence or a corruption that 'Sancte Jacobe' is twice invoked in the play, once by a massacring Catholic who stabs his victim for calling directly on Christ (vi.13), and again by the King's assassin? One suspects that Marlowe's 'saint', the patron of the Parisian Jacobin (or Dominican) friars, may be Antichrist in a Jesuit's dress, or another phantom incarnation of that restless spirit, Machiavel. The last scene of *The Massacre at Paris* has more than just a hint of Machiavellian frolicking. Henry turns the tables on his assassin by stabbing him with his own knife. The King then vows in apocalyptic style to attack the anti-Christian papistry. He insists on making his fate into a warning mirror for the English queen, to whom he refers no less than four times.

After his treatment of his 'sweet coz' the Guise, the Guise's brothers, and his own mother, Catherine, there is at least cause to speculate on what kind of 'faithful friend' (103) Henry would have been to England or to his 'sister' Elizabeth. Henry's France has little brotherhood in it. By focusing on Christian brotherhood – and Christian garments – throughout his play, Marlowe has suggested the incongruity of warfare waged among Christians. One scene, which presents the Guise slaughtering five or six Protestants who kneel with their books, seems to have been his invention.[32] He also turns a 'Leranne', merely mentioned by François Hotman in his account of the massacre, into a preacher (vi).[33] Guise, wearing a white cross upon his burgonet, stabs this preacher with the words '"Dearly beloved brother" – thus 'tis written', and two scenes later we come upon the following significant exchange:

> *Gonzago :*   Who goes there?
> *Retes :*   'Tis Taleus, Ramus' bedfellow.
> *Gonzago :*   What art thou?
> *Taleus :*   I am, as Ramus is, a Christian.
> *Retes :*   O, let him go; he is a Catholic.
> viii.11–15

The play contains numerous references to unbrotherly behaviour. A particularly striking example is that of the Queen Mother, Catherine, who longs to 'build religion' and is so willing to 'dispatch' her sons.

We can hardly doubt that *The Massacre at Paris* contains anti-Catholic polemic. Marlowe emphasizes the idolatrous and un-Christian nature of the faith his Catholics profess. They are worshippers of show and appearance who repeatedly break their closest bonds and highest vows. That Marlowe could have viewed such wicked fools as an imminent threat to England seems doubtful. Queen Elizabeth was indeed endangered by a small group of dis-loyal Catholic agitators whose actions alarmed both her official and her self-appointed advisers. Marlowe was willing enough to frighten his audience with the spectre of international Catholicism. But behind his appeal to their fears may lie the suggestion that their true enemy is politic religion in general. Their best defence against such an enemy would be, for a start, a disposition to suspect keenly partisan attitudes, to respond sceptically when vengeful Henry refers in his dying words to his 'friend' Queen Elizabeth. The equivocating Machiavel who has flown over the Alps to destroy Henry may all too easily navigate the English Channel and destroy Protestant Elizabeth as well.

Marlowe's play contains ample evidence that he conceived of his Catholics as monstrous bogey men – the creatures of a political nightmare. He not only finds new, unhistorical crimes for the Guise or Anjou, whose hypocrisy he stresses whenever possible; he implies, as in *The Jew of Malta*, that the deliberate hypocrisy of his villains contains self-deception. The Guise threatens to wake Henry from his 'foolish dream' when Henry 'most reposeth on my faith' (xviii. 29–30). Instead, Henry 'wakes' the Guise, and the Friar wakes Henry, instantly converting him to extreme Protestantism. All three seem to die for 'conceits' or fancies – the Guise trusting in his own frightening looks, Henry trusting the Friar's holy ones, and the Friar counting on his 'merit'. As in *The Jew of Malta*, retributive mechanism clicks along with a justice more farcical than tragic.

But if Marlowe had intended only to reassure and flatter a Pro-testant audience, he would surely have made Navarre a stronger figure; he would not have joined to his anti-Catholic farce the darker suggestion that this Protestant champion is, like his adversaries, a self-willed, pre-emptive warrior who cannot see the beam in his own eye. The play's conclusion would not undermine Protestant righteousness by repetitively associating love with blood. 'He loves me not that sheds most tears, / But he that makes most lavish of his blood', cries the converted Henry (xxiii.98–9). In a breath he wipes away his minion's tears and invites him to whet his sword on 'Sixtus' bones' (95–6). His oath to Navarre includes the promises of ruin to Rome and 'eternal love to thee' (63–6). As we have seen, such associations of love and blood begin with the marriage of Navarre and run throughout the violent ceremonies of the play. The word 'sweet' is invariably yoked with blood and death.

The hypothesis that *The Massacre at Paris* is a satire on the in-human worldliness of Christian rulers would account for its unusual blend of ironic detachment and moral outrage. Chaotic disruption and sacrilege are exaggerated, but nevertheless believable. As in *The Jew of Malta*, the general predicament seems more convincing than the specific figures who cause it. Marlowe has reduced the behaviour of his princes to its first principle, wilfulness. Excess of will, especially where the Guise is concerned, takes the place of more defined and specific political ambitions. Such a motive tends to be depersonalized and transferable. Even Richard III aims at an earthly crown. With the Guise we can never be quite sure. He has few individual traits to distinguish him from the conventional tyrants portrayed by a long line of writers on statecraft. He particularly resembles the type of the 'Platonic' tyrant described by Born in his Introduction to *The Education of a Christian Prince*:

> By contrast with the good prince, Plato shows us the tyrant. He is either the master or slave of the others; he never realizes true freedom or true friendship. This type comes into being when a leader becomes filled with uncontrolled lusts and desires, when his means are insufficient for his supposed needs...The essence of a tyrant's power is disorder; when he has stirred up sufficient confusion and uprising against established government, he appears as the leader of the people...It is the task of the tyrant to seek out and guard against all high-minded, wise, and influential men, for they are his enemies...The tyrant lives furthest removed from true pleasure and the philosophers, while the king is the nearest to them. [34]

Marlowe, the objective satirist, gives us no ideal philosophers or true kings from whom we may derive a set of moral norms. In place of 'high-minded men' we are shown flatterers and pedants. Even Ramus, the King's professor of logic sought out by the Guise, is foolishly illogical. Were the various groups bound less tightly together, were the Guise less singularly wilful or the Christian reference not so insistent, *The Massacre at Paris* might have been another *Tamburlaine*. The apocalyptic imagery of comets, fires, storms, and destruction would then have amplified the Guise, rather than stigmatizing him as a spirit of discord. As it is, however, *The Massacre at Paris* allows us to judge its action as an inverted *speculum principis*

– a kind of judgment which the *Tamburlaine* plays make almost impossible.

One further comparison between Marlowe and Erasmus seems pertinent. I have found no contemporary analogue so close in style and temper to Marlowe's play as a colloquy written some sixty years before it. With wry detachment, 'Charon' considers furious destruction, distrust among families and friends, war begun under 'pretense of religion', and the crowds of slaughtered souls who arrive, as a consequence, in Hell.[35] Tamburlaine had earlier boasted of sending millions to wait for Charon's boat (1:v.ii.400), and Edward will call on 'hags' to 'howl for my death at Charon's shore' (v.i.89). 'Stay/ That bell that to the devil's matins rings', cries the Guise. Some of the souls in 'Charon', those belonging to 'heavy lords, Thrasos, and swashbucklers' who die suddenly, are said to be unusually weighty. The large numbers who arrive in wartime threaten to sink Charon's boat – which has indeed just sunk as the colloquy begins, leaving a number of shades swimming about in the Stygian swamp. Weighting and sinking are two images emphatically associated with the aspiring Guise (ii.57–8; xx.94–5), and his order to shoot at swimmers in the Seine (viii.65) appears to be a bathetic innovation on Marlowe's part. Some of these heavy souls, says Charon, 'come loaded not only with debauchery and gluttony but with bulls, benefices, and many other things', or rather with the 'dreams' of them. The conceited Guise has his 'pension and a dispensation too' (ii.63).

If *The Massacre at Paris* is approached as a satire on un-Christian behaviour, its blatant anti-Catholic propaganda seems rhetorically useful. The official package becomes a means of smuggling in a wider range of meanings. Because he so thoroughly blackens the Catholic hypocrites, Marlowe can risk putting a few spots on the Protestant ones. On the other hand, had he added more than a few, he could scarcely have caught the conscience of an audience favourably disposed towards the Huguenots. The quality of Marlowe's satire may be closely adapted to the needs and attitudes of his audience. We know that the spectators came to the Rose in large numbers. But until we have seen productions of *The Massacre at Paris*, we can only guess how many may have enjoyed the violence, how many may have been turned against it.

As long as there is a possibility that a longer, richer version of the play might appear, interpretations of it are bound to remain speculative. An approach to the play as historical satire does have the merit of restoring some life to a text generally deemed a bad quarto. Taken on such allusive terms as Marlowe provides and closely examined, the extreme variations in length of speech or scene seem functional. Leisurely murders or expositions of haphazard, confused motives scarcely seem called for. Marlowe does treat the central Catholic figures more expansively. Treatment in depth may have been precluded by his awareness of their folly. Folly probably accounts for some, if not all, of the play's mangled verse and confused images. Critics would like to find more lyricism in a genuine Marlowe text. But when historical incident readily provides such illustrations of madness, there may be less need for vainglorious verse. Marlowe's energies go into the making of a fast-paced plot, more complex than that of *The Jew of Malta*. The web of thematic relationships is tightened by the close narrative interdependence of the major characters. Catastrophe and the Jacobin Friar do come rather pat, but not without convincing appropriateness, typically extravagant gesture, and a final surfeit of conceit. Like all satire based on particular vices, *The Massacre at Paris* has dated. But many varieties of 'politic' religion have not. That may be the best reason for hoping that this play will win more approval and attention.

# 6

## Merlin's prophecies

Marlowe's farce in *The Jew of Malta*, in the central section of *Doctor Faustus*, and in *The Massacre at Paris* veils a serious attitude comparable to that of Erasmus in *The Education of a Christian Prince*:

Now, while everyone is looking out for his own interests, while popes and bishops are deeply concerned over power and wealth, while princes are driven headlong by ambition or anger, while all follow after them for the sake of their own gain, it is not surprising that we run straight into a whirlwind of affairs under the guidance of folly.[1]

The whirlwind image used by Erasmus seems to fit the two *Tamburlaine* plays as well. A verbal storm of contradictory attitudes swirls furiously about Tamburlaine himself as he sweeps on from triumph to triumph. Where his affairs differ from those of the princes in the three other plays is in their relation to 'folly'. 'Merlin's prophet' seems to have carefully dislodged the moral and intellectual foundations on which a dark satire might rest. He uses a 'mad and scoffing' style which many readers and spectators, like Robert Greene, have found 'intollerable'. Especially baffling for any persistent student of the *Tamburlaine* plays is their combination of Christian allegory, based upon apocalyptic allusions, with tantalizing references to classical gods, heroes, and monsters. This whirlwind of possibilities rarely touches familiar ground. Instead it devastates a fictive space which we might call 'the land of fortune'.

Sidney, I believe, was thinking of a landscape similar to Marlowe's when he contrasted the activities of the Historian with those of the Poet. The Poet, Sidney wrote, may 'frame his example to that which is most reasonable'. But 'the Historian in his bare *Was* hath many times that which wee call fortune to ouer-rule the best wisedome'. Later Sidney added that the Historian, 'beeing captiued to the trueth of a foolish world, is many times a terror from well dooing, and an incouragement to unbridled wickednes'.[2] Tamburlaine is the Poet who constantly uses his own 'best wisedome' in order to frame himself as an example. Marlowe is the Historian who chronicles the gradual unbridling of wickedness in his warrior-poet and repeatedly hints that Tamburlaine is foolish.

Because these hints are not particularly emphatic, Poetry often over-rules History in the *Tamburlaine* plays. While Marlowe's whirlwind is in progress, audiences might find a 'bare *Was*' difficult to identify. Tamburlaine's actions have an assured energy which judgment can scarcely catch up with. Never does he pause, like Henry V before Harfleur, to discriminate between 'impious war' and the 'cool and temperate wind of grace'. Despite fervid speculation about him, much of it negative, Tamburlaine comes to rest on his laurels at the close of Part One; at the end of Part Two he dies suddenly of a mysterious illness, leaving the audience to wonder whether he is a god, a devil or a man. Repeated verbal patterns and recurring situations may help to direct this wonder, but the burdens of inference and interpretation still fall squarely upon the audience. We must draw our conclusions about Marlowe's insistence on the similarities among monarchs, their pretensions to divine support, their severity to their children, their concern with honour, and their fondness for shows. We must puzzle out the sources of the hero's power, deciding whether he indeed masters the land of fortune or is over-ruled by its ultimate bareness.

> View but his picture in this tragic glass,
> And then applaud his fortunes as you please.

In the following pages I will view both *Tamburlaine* plays as if they provided one picture of Tamburlaine. Because Marlowe's tragic glass is so enigmatic, I will begin with the general landscape through which Tamburlaine moves, and then, as a second step, consider the many princes whom he encounters there. This landscape seems to impinge upon the attitudes of all the characters in the two plays. It provides the broadest of symbolic constructs, a metaphysical frame in which we can place Tamburlaine on the chance of viewing him more distinctly. For the meanings constantly generated by Tamburlaine himself often touch him obliquely and retroactively. Although he is the focus of Marlowe's glass, he is a moving focus – the vortex of the whirlwind, one might say. He attracts and repels hard meanings, much as he either attracts and repels people, in an absolute and magnetic way. A description of the landscape around Tamburlaine will not altogether falsify his immediate dramatic impact; few characters so insistently impose upon us the sense that they are themselves riddles or puzzles. Moreover, unless we first consider the frame of Marlowe's glass, it may be difficult to understand why he termed it 'tragic' in the Prologue to Part One.

Although Tamburlaine never falls from greatness, like a *de casibus* hero, he creates horrible sensations and he dies – two facts which might have made his career sufficiently tragic for a Renaissance audience.[3] Most commentators seem to assume that the 'tragic' properties of the plays require little scrutiny. Like Marlowe's contemporaries, who reacted to the success of *Tamburlaine* Part One by writing moral dramatic histories about the good conqueror Alphonsus and the evil one, Selimus, they have imposed on Marlowe's history the more poetic demands of 'that which is most reasonable'. In other words, they have preferred to interpret the plays by deducing from the contradictory speculation about Tamburlaine a strong preponderance of either positive or negative attitudes towards the hero himself. By approaching the plays as heroic romances rather than moral allegories, Eugene Waith has greatly advanced our understanding of how the *Tamburlaine* plays might affect an audience.[4] His conclusions can also help us to see why it is both difficult – and necessary – to attempt a more precise definition of what Marlowe might have meant by 'tragic'.

Waith tries to accommodate the full range of speculation about Tamburlaine by viewing him as a Herculean figure whose special morality transcends contradictions.[5] He argues that Marlowe's own attitude towards Tamburlaine, 'going beyond simple approval or disapproval, remains constant'.[6] This argument takes the hero on his own aspiring terms, which are as persuasively self-glorifying as those of Barabas or Faustus. It is Tamburlaine's *own* attitude which remains constant in the plays, not the attitudes of the author or of the audience. Because the framing landscape constantly reminds us of limits, we are apt to grow sceptical of Tamburlaine's romantic trust that all the barriers in his world are permeable. Thoroughly as he may dazzle us with his poetry, Tamburlaine cannot finally outrun our perception that his power falls far short of his hopes and that it does enormous damage to other men.

I am not denying that the *Tamburlaine* plays do create a strong impression of constancy. Even in an age of long narrative mirrors and moral histories, most tragic glasses were more sharply focused than Marlowe's. Marlowe often seems to be as interested in anatomizing the world around Tamburlaine as in Tamburlaine himself.[7] He regularly patterns discourse and stage action so that history tends towards paradox – a running riddle on the theme of language and power. Their constancies may prevent readers of the plays from recognizing how deeply they engage the fundamental problem of all tragedy – man's dependence on human relationships within time. If we are really to explore the tragic aspect of the plays, we must consider further how they might affect a theatre audience. At least we must read them through with emphasis on their visual qualities. That is what the third and final section of this chapter will do. The suffering of victims might add more authority to their criticism of Tamburlaine when this criticism concerns shows and gestures which the audience can also observe and assess. No one can 'see' Tamburlaine rival the heavens. But everyone in the playhouse could have seen his footstools, thrones, coloured tents and chariots. As the action turns away from practical politics and physical conflict towards the methods of creating reputation, the theatre audience may note that Tamburlaine is less like Hercules than he himself wishes he were. Through verbal and spectacular images Tamburlaine attempts to make his conquests genuinely heroic, even godlike. But they can be godlike only in an indirect way; they illustrate, but do not embody, the miraculous power he constantly seeks. Tamburlaine rages at other characters who take his emblematic displays for private symbols rather than objective, supernatural signs. 'Villain', he exclaimes to the 'sturdy governor' of Babylon:

> Should I but touch the rusty gates of hell,
> The triple-headed Cerberus would howl
> And make black Jove to crouch and kneel to me;
> But I have sent volleys of shot to you,
> Yet could not enter till the breach was made.
>
> II.v.i.96–100

Success in any one of the labours of Hercules would have brought Tamburlaine the kind of renown he desires. And only such a success could prevent a theatre audience from distinguishing the substance of his shows from the surface he himself imposes upon them.[8]

Tamburlaine's cruelty to the Governor of Babylon occurs near the close of his career. Time itself is a key factor in determining the effect which his stage poetry might have upon an audience. As they mount in intensity, his shows could convey the Erasmain insight that 'every bad thing either finds its way into human life by imperceptible degrees or else insinuates itself under the pretext of good'.[9] Audiences almost certainly admire Tamburlaine's first brave self-righteous gestures. But they could well be appalled by his behaviour at Babylon. How could they then go on to regard the hero's death as a Herculean apotheosis which glorifies the hero? The final scene dramatizes many efforts to make poetry from the 'bare *Was*' which destroys Tamburlaine, and it checks them all. Alterations in Heaven and earth have become all too obviously absent at the end of *Tamburlaine* Part Two. There are no storms, no music under the stage, only the disconsolate friends, unprepossessing heirs, and a chariot drawn by exhausted kings who resemble the hero himself. Pity for the warrior poet who cannot change the course of fortune would mingle with a more critical, ironic attitude. Spectators moved by the failure of his exciting pretensions would still have to notice that the hero himself never becomes thoroughly aware of that failure. Faustus, who tries to deny miracles, seems to meet them everywhere. Tamburlaine, who considers himself a miracle, is answered with a kind of speaking silence.

It is against the silence of any powers above nature and against the problem of shaping recalcitrant nature for 'show' that the audience must assess Tamburlaine's faith in wars which 'illustrate' gods. Men of the Renaissance might believe that the ancient gods had in reality been only great men 'immortalized' by loyal followers.[10] Tamburlaine's own followers play this part readily enough, but he himself goes even further. His repeated efforts to give his magnificent conceits literal existence in a foolish world bring home to an audience the tragic consequences of his great imagination.

### The landscape of fortune

As we read – or listen – to the debate over the character of

Tamburlaine, we notice that the incessant pattern of opposed judgments gradually exposes a distinction in the factual basis of competing views.[11] So long as Tamburlaine is capable of performing what he threatens, his enemies are foolish to discredit his pretensions. By showing that Tamburlaine's enemies are reluctant to alter their ideas about him in conformity with their experience of him, Marlowe gives to fact, event, and experience a large measure of influence in shaping audiences' responses towards his hero.

Tamburlaine's vaunts are at least confirmed by events as long as he measures himself mainly by success in battle. His words do not merely express his power; words well chosen can actually augment power. The fatuous language of Tamburlaine's enemies undermines their vaunts even before events finally prove how empty these vaunts are. For example, when Bajazeth meets with his lieutenant-kings to assess the threat posed by Tamburlaine, the King of Argier dismisses the report that Tamburlaine is already King of Persia. He is judged too weak to challenge Bajazeth, at whose magnificence 'all flesh quakes'. The King of Morocco adds that the 'smothering' Turkish host prevents both rain and sun from reaching the earth, and Bajazeth himself concludes:

> All this is true as holy Mahomet,
> And all the trees are blasted with our breaths.
>
> I:III.i.54-5

Turks, comments Tamburlaine to Bajazeth's emissary, 'menace more than they can well perform' (III.iii.4). When, after defeating Bajazeth, he is cursed by Bajazeth's queen, Zabina, Tamburlaine reasonably observes:

> The pillars that have bolstered up those terms
> Are fall'n in clusters at my conquering feet.
>
> I:III.iii.229-30

Bajazeth does come to admit Tamburlaine's power, and the Governor of Damascus even calls him a 'god of war'. But his next enemy, the Soldan, goes back to the theme on which his early opponents have harped and which even Callapine will echo well on into Part Two – that Tamburlaine is essentially a lucky rogue, 'famous for nothing but for theft and spoil' (I:IV.iii.66). So long as Tamburlaine's enemies rest secure on their own conceits of power, they consistently under-estimate his. We may doubt that Tamburlaine is a god, but his opponents prevent us from doubting that he is a real conqueror. To create his reputation, he must forever be raising up new enemies who deny his myth.

A whole series of denials is woven into the verbal texture of the *Tamburlaine* plays, providing constant tension between the 'best wisedome' of poetry and the 'bare *Was*' of history. Marlowe often organizes his discourse so as to throw weight upon critical statements which undercut or puncture more poetic ones. Particularly memorable are the question and answer following Theridamas's lofty encomium of kingship in Part One, which begins, 'A god is not so glorious as a king':

> *Tamburlaine :*   Why say, Theridamas, wilt thou be a king ?
> *Theridamas :*   Nay; though I praise it, I can live without it.
> 1 :II.v.65–6

Similarly, when Bajazeth and Zabina are cursing Tamburlaine, Bajazeth suddenly checks their hyperboles with:

> Ah, fair Zabina, we may curse his power,
> The heavens may frown, the earth for anger quake,
> But such a star hath influence in his sword
> As rules the skies and countermands the gods
> More than Cimmerian Styx or Destiny.
> 1 :v.ii.167–71

Later, Zenocrate concludes her long and eloquent lament for 'the Turk and his great emperess' with the fear that she and Tamburlaine may be punished for their own lack of pity. Her handmaiden Anippe immediately replies:

> Madam, content yourself, and be resolved,
> Your love hath Fortune so at his command,
> That she shall stay and turn her wheel no more,
> As long as life maintains his mighty arm
> That fights for honor to adorn your head.[12]
> v.ii.309–13

Amidst the lofty arguments and flights of fancy which rationalize events, these dry statements and quiet contradictions remind us of basic truths on which Tamburlaine's history rests – his power over his enemies, the weakness of these enemies, and his own weakness in the face of sickness and death. When Tamburlaine begs his dead wife Zenocrate to 'Come down from heaven, and live with me again!' Theridamas sounds the recurrent factual note:

Ah, good my lord, be patient. She is dead,
And all this raging cannot make her live.
2:II.iv.119–20

Only basic truths like these have ultimate authority in Marlowe's
land of fortune. This authority becomes particularly (and sometimes
painfully) strong whenever characters speculate on the role of the
gods in human affairs. Tamburlaine and all of his generation not only
seek signs. They find them regularly and emphatically. In all ten
Acts of the *Tamburlaine* plays, only one character swears by himself
alone – Almeda, the jailer, 'for that's the style and title I have yet'
(2:I.iii.69).

There are several ways of explaining why everyone calls on God
or gods in the *Tamburlaine* plays. One possibility is that Marlowe is
using his pagans to laugh at human vanity. It was a Renaissance
commonplace that pagans, like Paul's Gentiles, might 'shewe ye
effect of the Law written in their hearts' (Romans 2:15). Hooker
wrote, 'A longing, therefore, to be saved, without understanding the
true way how, hath been the cause of all the superstitions in the
world.'[13] The speed with which Marlowe's characters praise their
gods when events are favourable, and blame them when disaster
strikes does seem to smack of satire. 'Mahomet! O sleepy Mahomet!',
'O cursed Mahomet!' is the response of Bajazeth and Zabina when
Tamburlaine makes them his prisoners (1:III.iii.269–70). Equally
disconcerting are passages in which characters obviously reduce
divinities to poetic embellishments. There is a particularly foolish
sequence of references to Dis between the third and fourth scenes
of Act IV in Part Two. In the first of these, Theridamas, Tamburlaine's chief follower, imagines that 'infernal Dis is courting of my
love Olympia / Inventing masks and stately shows for her' (IV.iii.
93–4). One wonders if the audience is meant to recall that Tamburlaine envisioned a similar reception for the dead Zenocrate in a more
Judaic and angelic Heaven, but that when he actually lost her he
blamed either the Fates in Hell or 'amorous Jove' (III.iv). In the next
Act (IV.iv) we hear Tamburlaine's enemy, the Turk Orcanes, inviting Dis to come, and as he took Proserpina from her 'garden-plot',
pull Tamburlaine 'headlong to the lowest hell'.

Another group of references suggests more serious versions of
pride. In the year of Marlowe's birth the following prayer for the

delivery of Malta invaded by the Turks was read out in 'the City and Diocese of Sarum': 'Suffer not thine enemies to prevail against those, that now call upon thy name, and put their trust in thee, lest the Heathen and Infidels say: Where is now their God?'[14] Whether Marlowe actually heard such prayers or not, he does put a number of them into his play. They not only tell us that the gods are assumed to have an abiding concern in the affairs of men. They also tell us that men see the gods in their own images – as worldly monarchs vain of their reputations. Even Zenocrate, the quiet and conventional mistress of Tamburlaine, imposes such concerns upon the gods above. When she discovers the suicides of Bajazeth and his queen, she exclaims:

> Earth, cast up fountains from thy entrails,
> And wet thy cheeks for their untimely deaths.
> Shake with their weight in sign of fear and grief.
> Blush heaven, that gave them honor at their birth
> And let them die a death so barbarous.
> 1:v.ii.284–8

In Part Two both the Turk Orcanes and Tamburlaine call on God to prove his divinity through miraculous intervention. Before he attacks the Christian traitor, Sigismund, Orcanes ends his appeal to Christ and the moral law with,

> To arms, my lords! On Christ still let us cry.
> If there be Christ, we shall have victory.
> 2:II.ii.63–4

More provocative is Tamburlaine's judgment on Mahomet after Mahomet fails to stop him from burning the Koran:

> Seek out another godhead to adore –
> The God that Sits in heaven, if any god,
> For He is God alone, and none but He.
> 2:v.i.198–200

At the end of Part Two, Tamburlaine's three followers, Theridamas, Techelles, and Usumcasane, attempt to embarrass the gods into overt actions by arguing in their prayers that Heaven cannot afford the loss of fame and glory which will result if Tamburlaine is allowed to die.

While Marlowe is criticizing human pride in these passages, he is also encouraging his audience to ponder the general need for signs and miracles.[15] A spectator who came to a *Tamburlaine* play expecting to discover the nature of divinity from the testimony of the characters would probably be sent home in Sir Walter Ralegh's frame of mind:

> If we will hearken to men's opinions concerning one and the same matter, thinking thereby to come to the knowledge of it, we shall find this to be impossible; for either we must believe what all men say of it, or what some men only say of it. To believe what all men say of one and the same thing is not possible; for then we shall believe contrarities.[16]

For example, although both Sigismund and Orcanes seem to be agreed that a god of vengeance has helped Orcanes to punish Sigismund for his treachery, just which god is left conspicuously in doubt:

> *Orcanes :*  Now lie the Christians bathing in their bloods,
>              And Christ or Mahomet hath been my friend.
>                                      2:II.iii.10–11

Equally doubtful is Sigismund's fate in the afterlife. The dying Sigismund hopes for endless mercy; the pagan Orcanes, on discovering his enemy's body, vividly imagines the endless pain Sigismund will suffer in a strangely ecumenical Hell. Orcanes has called for a miracle when Sigismund attacked him, and Sigismund attributes his defeat directly to God. But the last word may just as well be that of Gazellus, even though it does not discourage Orcanes from honouring Christ. When Orcanes pointedly asks his follower Gazellus whether God's power has not indeed appeared 'as full / As rays of Cynthia to the clearest sight', he replies:

> 'Tis but the fortune of the wars, my lord,
> Whose power is often proved a miracle.
>                           2:II.iii.31–2

In effect miracles, like boasts, can only be proved by brute physical strength. The plays allow us to smile at characters not enlightened or sceptical enough to recognize such limitations. But they also allow us to hear, above the noisy righteousness of men, the fearful silence of the gods. In the *Tamburlaine* plays, Heaven and Hell lack the objective reality Marlowe gives to them in *Doctor Faustus*. They become metaphors for extreme spiritual states keenly experienced here and now. I emphasize this metaphorical 'becoming' because early in *Tamburlaine* Part One the extreme conditions analogous to spiritual states have not yet been created. When Tamburlaine compares himself to Jove or to some other god, he generally implies that the god is great enough to serve as his example, helper, or antagonist. Such comparisons are still rhetorical, a measure of his upward aspiration, rather than a confounding of Heaven and Hell in earth. Existential revaluation of priorities between this world and those to come enters later on. Hell begins to intrude when the dramatic action focuses on Tamburlaine's victims. The most powerful expression of the hellish state is Zabina's

> Gape earth, and let the fiends infernal view
> A hell as hopeless and as full of fear
> As are the blasted banks of Erebus.[17]
>
> 1:V.ii.179–81

Tamburlaine explicitly sets Heaven down on earth when he decides that an 'earthly crown' is the 'perfect bliss and sole felicity' of the aspiring soul (1:II.vii.28), or when he prefers his own court to the 'state and majesty of heaven' (2:I.vi.28). When misery finally comes to Tamburlaine himself, the metaphors of the underworld come with it. It is fair to suggest that while Tamburlaine imagines Zenocrate as going to Heaven, she also takes Heaven – the divinity he always attributes to her – away from *him*. By the time we reach the death of Tamburlaine himself, spiritual conceits can provide the strongest emotional colouring. His faithful friend Theridamas says that the 'woeful change' in Tamburlaine 'daunts our thoughts / More than the ruin of our proper souls' (V.iii.181–2). And Amyras, his son, mounts Tamburlaine's empty chariot with the words,

> Heavens witness me with what a broken heart
> And damned spirit I ascend this seat,
> And send my soul, before my father die,
> His anguish and his burning agony!
>
> 2:V.iii.206–9

This ambiguous speech hints that Tamburlaine may be punished after death; it stresses that he and all his followers are certainly punished before it.

The last scene of *Tamburlaine* Part Two, focused on the hero's dissolution, accentuates the characteristics of the metaphysical landscape I have been describing. When he raves, Tamburlaine's followers simply force him to 'sit still', underlining his physical

weakness and the irrelevance of a mythic combat with Heaven or with
the monster death which he imagines. His physician further deflates
this fanciful view of death by describing it in more materialistic
terms:

> The humidum and calor, which some hold
> Is not a parcel of the elements,
> But of a substance more divine and pure,
> Is almost clean extinguishèd and spent,
> Which, being the cause of life, imports your death.
>
> 2:v.iii.86–90

However much Tamburlaine would like to project his final struggle
as an heroic combat, that satisfaction is denied him. Theridamas
matter-of-factly reminds him that his ringing phrases are only 'impatient words'. Now it is Tamburlaine rather than Bajazeth or
Orcanes who promises what he cannot perform. The ultimate fate of
his spirit is deliberately kept in doubt. The announcement by the
physician that the 'divine substance' is almost extinguished is
followed by Tamburlaine's own intimation of apotheosis. Christian
eschatology joins classical when his followers refer to the last judgment. By the time we reach the final exchange – Tamburlaine's long
advising speech so rich in mythic allusion, and his son's brief
summing up – the very modulation of the dialogue should be familiar. We hear once more the pattern of expansive poetic statement and
deflating counter-statement:

> Meet heaven and earth, and here let all things end,
> For earth hath spent the pride of all her fruit,
> And heaven consumed his choicest living fire.
> Let earth and heaven his timeless death deplore,
> For both their worths will equal him no more.

Such an ending should give us little reason to believe that Tamburlaine will become a god through apotheosis or even that his miserable
successor will be transformed by his spirit.[18] It leaves us with a
heightened sense of antagonism between the best wisdom of imagination and the bare fact of fortune, between a man's longing for signs
and the stillness of the universe.

It is tempting to speculate that a sixteenth-century audience would
have identified Tamburlaine's Asiatic cruelties with the Christian
cruelties of those Renaissance battlefields so convincingly illustrated
in Dürer's series of woodcuts on the Apocalypse. Or that they would

have recognized his world as a carefully contrived order of nature in which some blessings and more cursings, some rights and more wrongs, have been deliberately confounded. Surely Marlowe cannot be defining this nature in a strictly secular spirit.[19] He has made the need for justification too general, the pathos of spiritual isolation too evident. As we draw circles of interpretation more closely around Tamburlaine, the centre of Marlowe's Asiatic mirage, we can begin to recognize additional evidence of a fundamental thematic order. The mirage may obscure the ground, but without this ground there could be no mirage.

### Princes and potentates

The *Tamburlaine* plays have great dialectical vigour. In addition to expressing a pervasive tension between poetry and history, they present a number of more localized debates about divinity, beauty, love, loyalty, wit, education, immortality. Everything, it seems, is arguable in a play whose very plots are organized so as to provide perspectives on a central enigma – the real character of Tamburlaine. The fact that those who argue almost invariably share Tamburlaine's ambitions and pretensions might help us to see that Marlowe actually defines this problem in his usual disciplined way. Instead of getting drawn into the arguments ourselves, we might study Marlowe's concentration on a particular type of arguer. Traditional accounts of greatly powerful rulers or tyrants often tell how they oppress their people, waste the country's wealth on wars and personal vices, stamp out dissent, and rely on flatterers. Marlowe subordinates these dimensions of tyranny, emphasizing instead the ruler's creation of a public image and its function in both his public and private relationships.

Here, then, is an even narrower field in which we may hope to catch glimpses of Tamburlaine himself, but only if we are willing to attend very closely to the aesthetics of Marlowe's analogical structures. In Part One Marlowe develops monarchs like Mycetes or Bajazeth as contrasts to Tamburlaine. In Part Two such analogies become more puzzling. The secondary episodes appear to be linked to Tamburlaine's career by themes and ideas. Once we posit such a connection the episodes do seem to criticize his experience. But because the play keeps these episodes remote in place and usually in time from Tamburlaine's own history, it does not really encourage us to connect the two. Of course, connections that have been at least superficially obscured create a far more powerful satiric resonance than do obvious ones. If we compare the link between Mycetes and Tamburlaine in Part One with the link between Ferneze and Barabas in *The Jew of Malta*, we find that satire and criticism batten on those similarities which are disguised. Obvious resemblances between Mycetes and Tamburlaine have not yet thickened into the misleading masks of role or social status. Mycetes, like other rulers, serves primarily to make Tamburlaine himself more plausible, and his similar pretensions are used at first as a way of establishing Tamburlaine's superiority.

I have already suggested that the many monarchs introduced in Part One serve to indicate the direct relationship between words and power, so important for Tamburlaine's continuing progress. Frequently his enemies witlessly underestimate his power while exaggerating their own. By far the most foolish of these enemies is Mycetes, the first speaker in the play. Through Mycetes, we quickly discover that a strong ruler must be a strong poet as well.[20] In his first extended speech, charging Theridamas to capture Tamburlaine, Mycetes uses mixed metaphors, inappropriate images and ridiculous rhymes in a true 'jigging vein'. He addresses Theridamas as

> The hope of Persia, and the very legs
> Whereon our state doth lean, as on a staff
> That holds us up and foils our neighbor foes.
>
> 1.i.59–61

Even sillier is Mycetes's conclusion, with its ironically inept simile and fatuously expressed moral:

> Go frowning forth, but come thou smiling home,
> As did Sir Paris with the Grecian dame.
> Return with speed; time passeth swift away.
> Our life is frail, and we may die today.
>
> 1.i.65–8

Mycetes assures Theridamas that he will welcome his return, with an image which seems particularly strained:

> I long to see thee back return from thence,
> That I may view these milk-white steeds of mine
> All loaden with the heads of killèd men,

And from their knees even to their hoofs below
Besmeared with blood; that makes a dainty show.
1.i.76–80

The blood-smeared horses perhaps allude to the image of God's winepress in Revelation 14:20.[21] Such language actually anticipates the apocalyptic hyperbole Tamburlaine will use after he vanquishes Bajazeth and after the foolish Mycetes has probably been forgotten by the audience. The dramatically important point being made so early in the action seems to be that Mycetes, like Tamburlaine, relishes a spectacle. But his impertinent image, 'dainty show', suggests that he has little sense of the important political use to which spectacles may be put.

The connection between bad poetry and bad politics is forged most strongly in the scene where Mycetes and Meander prepare to battle with Tamburlaine and Cosroe. We recognize that Meander is giving dubious advice when he suggests that Tamburlaine's men will fight each other for the gold he proposes to strew on the battlefield. It is already clear from the scene introducing Tamburlaine that loyal support means more to him than does gold. Prizes are only 'friends that help to wean my state, /Till men and kingdoms help to strengthen it' (1.ii.29–30). 'Think you I weigh this treasure more than you?' he asks Zenocrate and her attendant lords. 'Not all the gold in India's wealthy arms / Shall buy the meanest soldier of my train.' Meander mistakenly envisions these soldiers as 'cruel brothers of the earth, / Sprung of the teeth of dragons venomous' who will turn on one another. The 'poetic' origin of his military strategem is emphasized:

> *Mycetes :* Was there such brethren, sweet Meander, say,
> That sprung of teeth of dragons venomous ?
> *Meander :* So poets say, my lord.
> *Mycetes :* And 'tis a pretty toy to be a poet.
> Well, well, Meander, thou art deeply read,
> And having thee, I have a jewel sure.
> 11.ii.51–6

But Meander's wit does not make his party the victor, as Mycetes so foolishly hopes. Devices like his are basically unrealistic; Tamburlaine leads a greater and more loyal force. As in *The Jew of Malta* and *Doctor Faustus*, Marlowe alludes to the myth of Jason and the golden fleece ironically. Here it provides an instance of the kind of poetry which 'clownage keeps in pay'.

After Mycetes disappears from the action it becomes more difficult to differentiate between the speeches of Tamburlaine and his opponents where quality is concerned. Once the 'jigging vein' is gone, both sides share poetic splendours and excesses. Poetry is only 'good' when a speaker can employ it to control events. The ineffectual rhetoric of Cosroe, Bajazeth, and the Soldan sets off by contrast Tamburlaine's use of 'high-astounding terms' throughout Part One. At first it is simply 'in conceit' that Tamburlaine's men 'bear empires on our spears'. By Act v, Tamburlaine, secure in military strength and confirmed in his power to use beautiful language for conceits and conquests both, can invite even his enemies to identify his conceits with his fortune.

In Part Two Tamburlaine remains a central figure to whom all other characters refer, but a central figure in a dramatic structure which contains several plot-lines of nearly equal integrity and interest. Tamburlaine does not actually meet his enemies until the final scene of Act III, and only begins to dominate the stage in Act IV. Episodes which are not explicitly related to him need not impose themselves on our judgments with the same kind of urgency present in the connection between Tamburlaine and Mycetes. Perhaps it is the repeated confrontation of Tamburlaine with his adversaries in Part One which, almost as much as anything Tamburlaine does or says, suggests his superiority. Marlowe relies on our fondness for partiality. Part Two baffles this tendency. By the time Tamburlaine's critics and opponents are allowed to challenge him directly, Zenocrate has died and he has become a raging scourge. Everyone uses hyperbole. The effect ascribed to Part One by Alexander Sackton has been created once more: 'The audience is kept at what seems to us an unbearably high tension of feeling.'[22] It has become far more difficult to take sides.

In Part One Tamburlaine can use wit and poetry pragmatically. But in Part Two both Tamburlaine and his fellow monarchs seem to lose control of their own public images. The mythic 'conceit' which the ruler uses to address his world becomes subjected to more impersonal criticism by the agencies of time and distance. Even personal critics tend to be indifferent or to doubt, rather than to deny or contradict. In stressing the role of political myths in Part Two, I am only singling out a variation on the general theme which Dame Helen

Gardner defined as 'the clash between man's desires and his experience'.[23] Throughout this play Marlowe explores the efficacy of the self-conceit as a pledge or commitment – to other members of the social order, and to those women and children, 'hostages to fortune', who must conserve it. Such an exploration is no novelty in Marlowe's work; all of his plays deal with obedience to bonds and promises, false and true.

In the lengthy sequence concerning the treaty between the Christian Sigismund and the Mohammedan Orcanes, Marlowe focuses attention on the oaths the monarchs swear by their respective gods. When Frederick and Baldwin later try to persuade Sigismund to break his oath to Orcanes, their hypocrisy is implied through their references to 'policy' and 'opportunity' (2:II.i.38, 51).[24] These Christians closely resemble Ferneze in *The Jew of Malta*. And like Ferneze they are Catholics, a fact which may have made their un-Christian behaviour more acceptable to an Elizabethan audience.

That at this stage they bear any resemblance to Tamburlaine himself is not particularly obvious, unless one notes that both Tamburlaine and the two Christians seek to justify vengeful behaviour. Lynette and Eveline Feasey have pointed out that the 'Homily against Wilful Rebellion' includes the example of King Saul who was punished by God because he spared the king and the property of the Amalekites, contrary to God's command.[25] This is of course just the example with which Frederick buttresses his argument for scourging paganism and Orcanes. But the argument is immediately undercut when Frederick joins to his mention of Saul (1 Samuel 15:22), Balaam – another example of one who 'would not kill and curse at God's command' (2:II.i.55). In Numbers 22:12, however, God specifically ordered Balaam *not* to curse the Israelites.

In *The Jew of Malta* and *Doctor Faustus* distorted allusions like Frederick's are used to reveal 'unseen hypocrisy'. Its intrusion here, along with the more 'orthodox' reference to Saul, may well suggest some question as to the righteousness of *any* revenging scourge, human or divine, Catholic, Protestant, or pagan. As in *The Jew of Malta*, breach of promise is linked to self-justification and impiety. But if Baldwin and Frederick, the subordinates, are wicked fools, the two kings, Sigismund and Orcanes, are not. And there is a significant difference between Frederick's use of Biblical self-justification and

Tamburlaine's. Tamburlaine often appears to echo the language of
the Biblical prophetic books where these describe God's calamitous
vengeance on the wicked.[26] But he need not distort these violent
texts, for they support rather than contradict his actions.

As we have seen, Marlowe so manages the dialogue in Act II, scene
ii, that we can wonder whether Sigismund's subsequent defeat
represents divine intervention or 'fortunes of the wars'. Sigismund
surely deserves punishment for his politic perjury; Orcanes seems to
be rewarded for his appeal to Christ. Orcanes, like Barabas, can
powerfully criticize the divergence between Christian profession and
practice. Whether he himself is morally superior to Sigismund is less
certain. Orcanes invites Christ to prove himself a 'perfect God' by
being revenged on Sigismund; Sigismund bears witness to Christ's
vengeance upon him, but dies asking for mercy. The contradiction
between his prayer and Orcanes's vindictive insistence on the tor-
ments of Hell might suggest that, although Sigismund deserved his
defeat, Orcanes does not necessarily deserve his reward. Sigismund
recognizes one God of justice and mercy, Orcanes recognizes two
gods of justice, and Gazellus the henchman suspends judgment.

Parallels between the 'exemplary' death of Sigismund and Tamburlaine's final agony should not be over-emphasized. If Sigismund's
prefigures Tamburlaine's downfall, it does so as a kind of 'dreaming
prophecy'. Tamburlaine's challenge to Mahomet and his sudden illness in Act V, scene i, cry out for the kind of explanation Sigismund
and Orcanes would gladly provide, but it never comes. Marlowe
could easily have treated this sequence as the writer of 2 Maccabees
treats a comparable illness in his history. Commenting on how the
tyrant Antiochus was suddenly smitten with a pain in his bowels and
fell from his chariot, he writes: 'And thus he that a little afore thoght
he might commande the floods of the sea (so proude was he beyonde
the condicion of man) & to weigh the hie mountaines in ye balance,
was now cast on the ground, and caried in an horselitter, declaring
vnto all the manifest power of God' (9:8). Marlowe does not give us
such declarations. The fact that Tamburlaine dares Mahomet out of
heaven does not seem to alter his pagan intimation that another and
higher God may exist. To the end, Tamburlaine shares with Orcanes
and Sigismund the confidence that a god made in his image is supporting *him*. His is no 'guilty soul...crushed by its own form of guilt'.[27]

Another secondary episode dealing with the love of Theridamas for Olympia seems to have an even more tenuous relation to Tamburlaine's own affairs.[28] In order to forestall the tortures of the victorious Scythians, Olympia stabs her own son, entreating Mahomet's pardon 'if this be sin'. Extensive stage business follows as she burns two bodies, those of her husband and son, and attempts suicide. It seems quite natural to ask, with Theridamas, 'How now, madam, what are you doing?', if not to agree with Techelles that it was 'bravely done' (III.iv.38). 'Was it not bravely done?' asks Lightborn after the murder of Edward II. Three scenes later Tamburlaine executes a ritualized justice on his own son, Calyphas. Both parents have the best reasons for killing their children, but the righteousness of each act seems problematic, even if there are no disquieting references, as in *The Jew of Malta*, to Iphigenia or Isaac.

An additional disturbing parallel between Olympia and Tamburlaine is suggested by the climax towards which the episode tends, the trick with which Olympia beguiles Theridamas and makes him kill her. Olympia is not at all impressed when Theridamas describes Tamburlaine to her. In response to his splendid verbal portrait (2:III.iv.46) she only repeats her wish to destroy herself. Theridamas, on the other hand, long familiar with the myths used by Tamburlaine to support his power, is far too credulous about the supposedly swordproof ointment with which she later anoints her throat (IV.iii). Is there not some resemblance between his belief in magic and the presumption of all the other monarchs?

Another character who responds negatively to myths of power is Calyphas, the cowardly son of Tamburlaine. Calyphas has not been convinced by his father's promise that at night wounded soldiers may refill their empty veins with wine. By waiting out the battle in his tent, he refuses Tamburlaine's advice to 'run desperate through the thickest throngs, / Dreadless of blows, of bloody wounds, and death' (III.ii.139-40). If this is what Tamburlaine literally expects his sons to do, then perhaps the foolish wisdom of Calyphas almost excuses his cowardice:

> And should I go and do nor harm nor good,
> I might have harm, which all the good I have,
> Joined with my father's crown, would never cure.
>                                         IV.i.56-8

Calyphas is an ignoble figure. But the folly he praises in such plain speech must at least be measured against his father's parody of the Eucharist and his extravagant notions of honour. This fool can expose others as well as himself. When Tamburlaine tells his sons that his throne will be placed in a bloody field and that 'he that means to place himself therein, / Must armed wade up to the chin in blood', Zenocrate cautions,

> My lord, such speeches to our princely sons
> Dismays their minds before they come to prove
> The wounding troubles angry war affords.
>                    I.iv.85–7

As one who has been improperly educated for his task, Calyphas makes us doubt whether Tamburlaine's conceits still have any essential relation to the facts of his military success. The distance between the aging father's claims and the son's performance suggests that the one may be as extreme and distorted as the other.

The subordinate incidents in Part Two offer obliquely critical perspectives on the righteousness of Tamburlaine, without denying his distinctive qualities. Each is linked to him, often not by one idea only but by several. *Tamburlaine* Part Two lacks the final ironies of structure which, in *The Jew of Malta*, accentuate identities among characters and coerce moral judgment. Analogies are left for the audience to infer. The characters themselves are of course unaware that they resemble one another at all; Tamburlaine goes to his necessary death celebrating his uniqueness, and there is no other king or emperor to gainsay his proud contention with a final proud retort. The erstwhile dissenters stand broken in their harness.

If the analogies among rulers portrayed in Part Two do not create satire or moralize history, what should we make of them? *The Education of a Christian Prince* maintains that the good prince 'ought to have the same attitude toward his subjects, as a good *paterfamilias* toward his household'.[29] Is it perhaps significant that Tamburlaine's household so often prompts him to act out his barbaric fantasies? Olympia's treatment of her son gives us another household to reflect on. It can scarcely be accidental that Tamburlaine encounters enemies who justify their use of power with similar conceits. Readers and spectators could grasp the importance of this fact, even if precise thematic connections eluded them. If Tamburlaine repeatedly overcomes figures resembling him, may the audience not eventually surmise that he is struggling against himself? That the vengeful scourge is often tilting at mirrors?

When we look once more at Tamburlaine himself within the two contexts provided so far, we can see that this is probably the case. Both plays use Tamburlaine's reliance on shows, gestures and costumes to explore the paradoxes of controlling oneself and others through visual as well as verbal images. Motifs and allusions ironically stressed through these images hint that Tamburlaine's poetic wisdom increasingly gives way to his poetic madness. The process reaches a climax when Tamburlaine contrives his most spectacular theatrical conceit. By harnessing the rulers he has conquered, Tamburlaine creates an emblem for his own unbridled imagination.

### The warrior poet

The long soliloquies with which Barabas and Faustus introduce themselves are praises of folly. Although we may fail to heed the allusions which betray folly, dramatic action soon casts doubt upon the wit which Barabas and Faustus celebrate. Tamburlaine, too, has a speech in which he praises *his* wit, but Marlowe places it in the fifth Act of Part One, after this wit of Tamburlaine's has brought him great success. This fact alone may suggest that a slippage or discontinuity occurs between the 'superficial part' of the *Tamburlaine* plays and their foundation. Sidney's architectural metaphor remains appropriate; in repeatedly presenting Tamburlaine as a paradox or a problem, Marlowe appears to be guided by concepts which, like foundations, have temporal and logical priority. But these plays are dynamic as well as demonstrative; their 'constancies' verge on becoming tragic laws which inform the development of character and plot.

This dynamic quality may be observed in Marlowe's use of allusions. The dramatic action of *The Jew of Malta* makes a swift and ironic comment upon the Jew's resemblance to patient Job. Faustus speedily illustrates the literalism which makes it impossible for him to con St Paul's hard saying. But in the *Tamburlaine* plays, meanings of allusions tend to emerge in a cumulative, incremental manner. Whether these meanings are grasped at all depends heavily upon the manner in which the audience responds to spectacles and shows. To study this response at all we must constantly bear in mind that the mythical–heroic matter Marlowe alludes to was in common use by poets, painters, and pageant-makers, as well as by dramatists. Rulers who sought immortality through art favoured illustrations of their victims drawn from this matter. As a magnifico who turned to art for visible signs of grace, one could compare Tamburlaine with Henri II of France. This king had the ceiling of his chateau at Tanlay decorated with a picture of his court portrayed as the Olympian gods.[30] Elizabeth herself welcomed identification with Cynthia, Astraea, and the Virgin Mary.[31] In his poem *Elizabetha Triumphans* (1588), describing how the Queen went to meet her land forces awaiting the Armada at Tilbury, James Aske compared her to Mars, Bellona, Zenobia, Hercules, and Dido.[32] Glittering harness on her magnificent coach made planets and earth fear that Phaeton was come again; the smoke of the horses' breath frightened Jove.

Aske can remind us of something that better poets or artists rarely forgot – that to use commonplace matter successfully they must assess the tastes and knowledge of their audiences.[33] Like a pageant-maker, Aske creates a compliment which would be rapidly intelligible to a large, uncritical public. A dramatist like Marlowe makes the task of those who would interpret his use of visual commonplaces far more complex. Not only do his icons tend to appear in ironic disguises. Their meanings also change and grow with the design of the two plays. We can only determine what kind and quality of art Tamburlaine's insistence on his heroic image produces if we observe responses to this image through dramatic time.

The second scene of Part One reveals that even as a novice Tamburlaine knows well how to use spectacle in shaping the attitudes of others. The main spectacle at this early stage of his career is his own appearance. His consciousness of its importance is suggested when he dramatically removes the shepherd's garment hiding his armour:

> Lie here, ye weeds that I disdain to wear!
> This complete armor and this curtle-axe
> Are adjuncts more beseeming Tamburlaine.
>                                     I.ii.41–3

Later, in order to impress Theridamas, Tamburlaine makes a com-

parable use of both his gold wedges and of Zenocrate as evidence of
Jove's favour:

> See how he rains down heaps of gold in showers,
> As if he meant to give my soldiers pay;
> And as a sure and grounded argument
> That I shall be the monarch of the East,
> He sends this Soldan's daughter, rich and brave,
> To be my queen and portly emperess.
>
> I.ii.181–6

In contrast to Mycetes with his 'dainty shows', Tamburlaine can
exploit whatever comes to his hand as a public sign of his success.
His conscious opportunism and his awareness of the impression he
produces distinguish him from morality-play heroes, such as Mag-
nyfycence, All for Money, and Worldly Man, whose fortunes were
dramatically charted by changes of clothing. The morality hero
relies on display because display signifies his generic disposition in
an external, objective manner. Tamburlaine relies on display because
Marlowe is developing a character who attempts to identify his
creative imagination with his use of power.

We should note that the ironies produced by this attempt are
generally weaker when Tamburlaine himself provides the show,
stronger when he composes shows by arranging and interpreting the
actions of other characters. In scene ii, Techelles and Theridamas
give us the first in a series of verbal portraits of Tamburlaine. Techelles compares him to a lion in his armour, and imagines that

> I see kings kneeling at his feet,
> And he with frowning brows and fiery looks
> Spurning their crowns from off their captive heads.
>
> I.ii.55–7

Theridamas, dazzled by the first sight of his future leader, exclaims:

> Tamburlaine! A Scythian shepherd so embellished
> With nature's pride and richest furniture!
> His looks do menace heaven and dare the gods.
> His fiery eyes are fixed upon the earth
> As if he now devised some stratagem,
> Or meant to pierce Avernus' darksome vaults
> To pull the triple-headed dog from hell.
>
> I.ii.154–60

This type of verbal portraiture occurs again and again throughout
the plays. It culminates when Theridamas pictures Tamburlaine to

Olympia in Part Two as a triumphal superman attended by figures
who might have stepped right out of a mythographer's manual –
Death and the Fatal sisters, Rhamnusia bearing a helmet full of
blood, the 'ugly Furies', and, overhead, Fame sounding a trumpet
(2:III.iv.46–66). Such portraits are emblematic; they appear to grow
from an intellectual analysis of Tamburlaine's qualities, and the presentation of these qualities in images is a way of symbolizing his
spirit, not of recording actual physical traits. Although the images
often refer to postures of power which neither the speaker nor the
audience could ever literally see, I doubt that they could produce
a sharp sense of disjunction between the real and the imagined
Tamburlaines.

Edgar Wind has pointed out the effectiveness of painted allegorical
portraits in terms which can help us to understand why the verbal
ones in the *Tamburlaine* plays do not have a particularly strong
ironic impact. Although the portrait of a powerful man begins as a
'fiction' – an artistic representation that makes power visible – such
fictions have the potential of becoming real. He who deliberately
acts the part of a god may eventually be venerated as one.[34] That
Tamburlaine knows how to earn such veneration is suggested by the
verbal portraits which testify to the sentiments of friends and occasional foes. Oddly enough, even the more flamboyant passages do
not strike us as particularly far-fetched. They are one measure of
Tamburlaine's contagious imagination and of that extraordinary
presence which even at the end of his life enables him to frighten away
an army by looking at it. Although emblematic in style, they do presuppose the series of probable impossibilities on which these plays
rest – Tamburlaine's uncanny successes in battle.

Using hindsight, it is possible to surmise that the references to
Tamburlaine's fiery looks and eyes in the portraits by Techelles and
Theridamas allude to the flaming eyes of Christ in Revelation (1:14;
19:12).[35] For after Tamburlaine defeats both Cosroe and Bajazeth,
his pretensions as a divinely appointed scourge do take on an
apocalyptic cast. At the same time the action of Part One shifts away
from physical conflict towards overt myth-making, and the shows
begin to invite a more critical, strongly ironic response. Tamburlaine's pretexts for using spectacle begin to reach beyond the
Machiavellian one of winning esteem.[36] Tamburlaine continues to

fight because, as he tells us in Part Two, the wars 'illustrate gods'.

Immediately after Tamburlaine has brought out his 'footstool',
Bajazeth, and mounted on the Turk's back to his throne, he grants
the universe an opportunity to behold a change in his attitude:

> Now clear the triple region of the air,
> And let the majesty of heaven behold
> Their scourge and terror tread on emperors.
>
> . . . . . .
>
> For I, the chiefest lamp of all the earth,
> First rising in the east with mild aspect,
> But fixèd now in the meridian line,
> Will send up fire to your turning spheres
> And cause the sun to borrow light of you.
>
> IV.ii.30–2; 36–40

He is at work illustrating the myth of his own divinity when he
concludes:

> As was the fame of Clymene's brain-sick son
> That almost brent the axle-tree of heaven,
> So shall our swords, our lances, and our shot
> Fill all the air with fiery meteors.
> Then, when the sky shall wax as red as blood,
> It shall be said I made it red myself,
> To make me think of naught but blood and war.
>
> IV.ii.49–55

This prophecy has the stamp of Merlin upon it. It joins the Biblical
images of divine wrath – shattered cedar trees, darkened air, and
bloody sky – to the Phaeton myth, often read in the Renaissance as
an allegory for temerity or folly.[37] Although such metaphoric riches
could probably inhibit the audience from seeing Tamburlaine himself as a 'brain-sick' over-reacher, they could not prevent it from
recognizing that the 'footstool', Bajazeth, is extremely reluctant to be
used in this show of apocalyptic strength.[38] When Bajazeth is put
back into his cage, Tamburlaine explains:

> The ages that shall talk of Tamburlaine,
> Even from this day to Plato's wondrous year,
> Shall talk how I have handled Bajazeth.
>
> IV.ii.95–7

But in the following scene the Soldan protests that he is not dismayed
at Bajazeth's fate and calls it an 'ignominious wrong'.

Tamburlaine's treatment of Bajazeth becomes much more grotesque in the fourth scene of the Act. His manipulation of spectacular elements has also increased. Scene iv includes a banquet before the walls of Damascus, hung about presumably with 'bloody colors', and a 'course of crowns' for Tamburlaine's three generals, as well as the baiting of Bajazeth, drawn on in a cage.[39] Tamburlaine asks Zenocrate, 'doth not the Turk and his wife make a goodly show at a banquet?' (iv.iv.56–7). 'Yes, my lord,' she replies, but her expression is a sad one, and her attention has been distracted by thoughts of 'my father's town besieged, / The country wasted, where myself was born' (63–4). Although Tamburlaine's three followers join enthusiastically in the cruelty to Bajazeth and Zabina, Theridamas asks, at least half seriously, 'Dost thou think that Mahomet will suffer this?' (51). Because Bajazeth and Zabina so fiercely refuse to accept their humiliation, we cannot ignore their feelings, as we might ignore those of earlier victims. Tamburlaine's ceremonies are becoming more difficult to 'see' only as he himself sees them. Perhaps the pageantry of crowns so prominent in this scene insinuates some doubt about Tamburlaine's wisdom.[40] Earlier Marlowe presented Mycetes in the act of burying his crown on the battlefield by 'a goodly stratagem, / And far from any man that is a fool' (ii.iv.11–12). In *Doctor Faustus* and *Edward II*, crowns get freely handed about when characters become either foolish or mad.

By the last Act of Part One, suggestions of Tamburlaine's own folly have gathered more strength. Now wearing black and looking 'very melancholy', Tamburlaine refuses mercy to the four supplicant virgins sent out by the Governor of Damascus. This incident may allude to the parable of the wise and foolish virgins (Matthew 26), used in the Commination service as a warning to sinners not to delay penitence.[41] Because they are remarkably eloquent and because theirs is not the responsibility for the tardy submission of Damascus, Marlowe's virgins seem more wise than foolish. By contrast, Tamburlaine's insistence upon punishing them in accordance with his established customs appears mad indeed. When he discovers that the 'minds' of the virgins are 'thick and misty' – they cannot 'see' death on the point of his sword or understand what his sequence of white, red, and black furnishings means – he 'shows' them death. Then in soliloquy he eloquently celebrates the relationship of his poetry to his power.

In effect, just as the audience could well be on the point of con-
demning Tamburlaine for his cruelty to the virgins, Marlowe 'stays'
them from beholding their object too closely. He does this by inviting the audience to consider the paradox which seems to animate
his hero. This paradox makes Tamburlaine's folly a virtue as well as
a vice. Speaking about divine and prophetic, as opposed to evil, madness, Socrates told his disciple, Phaedrus, 'He who, having no touch
of the Muses' madness in his soul, comes to the door and thinks that
he will get into the temple by the help of art – he, I say, and his
poetry are not admitted; the sane man disappears and is nowhere
when he enters into rivalry with the madman.'[42] By the end of his
long soliloquy, Tamburlaine has justified his militant conceits and
shows by placing them beyond 'the highest reaches of a human wit'.

Corruption of the text has obscured the fact that, as a poet, Tamburlaine claims the divine power to transform nature. Like Faustus
he has already eulogized his mistress/muse with faint echoes of the
splendid encomium in Wisdom 7:29:

> Zenocrate, lovelier than the love of Jove,
> Brighter than is the silver Rhodope,
> Fairer than whitest snow on Scythian hills...
> 1.ii.87–9

> Zenocrate, the loveliest maid alive,
> Fairer than rocks of pearl and precious stone,
> The only paragon of Tamburlaine,
> Whose eyes were brighter than the lamps of heaven...
> III.iii.117–20

As a number of commentators have recognized, the soliloquy does
expose a conflict between Zenocrate's inspiring beauty and Tamburlaine's military honour.[43] More important, it also exposes Tamburlaine's characteristic method of sublimating an ethical conflict
into an aesthetic programme. He is beginning to transmute the
traditional terms in what might be called the 'warrior's dilemma'
when he exclaims:

> But how unseemly it is for my sex,
> My discipline of arms and chivalry,
> My nature, and the terror of my name,
> To harbor thoughts effeminate and faint!
> V.ii.111–14

He then reconciles beauty and warfare by saying that each man's soul is touched with an instinct for beauty; the warrior must needs have beauty 'beat on his conceits' in order to win fame, valour and victory. His soliloquy garbles to a close with:

> I thus conceiving and subduing both,
> That which hath stopped the tempest of the gods,
> Even from the fiery-spangled veil of heaven,
> To feel the lovely warmth of shepherd's flames
> And march in cottages of strowed weeds,
> Shall give the world to note, for all my birth,
> That virtue solely is the sum of glory,
> And fashions men with true nobility.
>
> v.ii.120–7

The meaning of the speech, and, with it, Marlowe's conception of Tamburlaine, becomes clearer if we realize that the myth alluded to at the end concerns the miraculous power of the gods, not their distracting amours. Tamburlaine is referring to the 'topmost' (alt. 'tempest') of the gods who once visited men in order to test their hospitality.[44] In Act I, scene ii, he adopted as a model for his ambition, Jove, who 'sometimes masked in a shepherd's weed'. Now he refers more explicitly to the occasion for this masking – Ovid's story in the *Metamorphoses* Book VIII of the old couple Baucis and Philemon who graciously cared for their surprise visitors – 'the mightie Jove and Mercurie his sonne in shape of men'.

Both in this speech, and in his final speech at the close of Part Two, Tamburlaine's language resembles the language of the Golding translation.[45] Ovid's gods must duck their heads to enter under the 'low made Wicket'. Significantly, this 'one Cotage' willing to receive the visiting gods is a 'pelting one', 'the roofe . . . thatched all with straw and fennish reede' (804–6). Jove and Mercurie feel what Tamburlaine refers to as the 'lovely warmth of shepherd's flames' when Baucis stirs the embers and blows up the fire (818–21). The gods reward the old couple by preserving them from a general deluge, making them caretakers of a temple, and finally granting Baucis's wish that they be allowed to die together. As they die they are turned by the gods into trees.

What connection does this delightful idyll have with the warrior's beautiful conceits? Ovid introduces the story of Baucis and Philemon with a brief debate between two Greeks who have been listening to the

River god, Achelous. One of them, Pirithous, 'being over hault of mynde', scoffs and says:

> The woords thou spaakst
> Are feyned fancies, Acheloy: and overstrong thou maakst
> The Gods: to say that they can give and take way shapes.
>
> 787–9

Lelex, the other, replies:

> Unmeasurable is the powre of heaven, and it
> Can have none end. And looke what God dooth mynd to bring
> about,
> Must take effect.
>
> 792–4

The story of Baucis and Philemon then follows as support for his argument. Tamburlaine is identifying his use of beauty in 'conceiving and subduing both' with the supernatural power that can 'give and take way shapes'. By implication, therefore, Tamburlaine's stage poetry actually transcends the 'highest reaches of a human wit'. Tamburlaine is not expressing the Renaissance theory that the poet's creating activity is analogous to God's. Instead he is suggesting that the poet, like the hero, competes with God. This poet, the most gifted of Marlowe's self-praisers, has more than just a 'touch of the Muses' madness in his soul'.

Tamburlaine's long soliloquy has immediately followed his command, 'But go, my lords, put the rest of the Virgins to the sword.' After his speech, he turns again to another of his methods for making fame and power quite literally visible:

> Who's within there?
> *(Enter two or three [Attendants].)*
> Hath Bajazeth been fed to-day?
>
> v.ii.128–9

A dramatist so sensitive to the effects of context as Marlowe was must have wanted his audience to experience Tamburlaine's measured lyric meditation as a sudden wrench in the rhythms of his history. The impersonality of the soliloquy is a symptom of character, not of choral detachment.[46] Tamburlaine is still the master of his own revels, indifferent to all other perspectives upon them. But as Part One draws to a close, Marlowe emphasizes alternative ways of seeing.[47]

When Zenocrate enters with her maid Anippe, she describes what she has seen of the destruction of Damascus, especially the beauty of the 'sun-bright' virgins 'subdued' by Tamburlaine. She then notices 'another bloody spectacle' (v.ii.276), the bodies of Bajazeth and Zabina who have brained themselves. 'Behold the Turk and his great emperess!' she exclaims three times in her lament. For Zenocrate, who at least pities them, they represent the danger of pride in 'fickle empery'. For victorious Tamburlaine they are, with the dead King of Arabia,

> All sights of power to grace my victory.
> And such are objects fit for Tamburlaine,
> Wherein, as in a mirror, may be seen
> His honor, that consists in shedding blood
> When men presume to manage arms with him.
>
> v.ii.411–15

As a final stationary tableau he arranges the crowning of Zenocrate while the three dead bodies lie at her feet.

In Part Two, Tamburlaine's efforts to make life into a mirror for his honour produce more obvious contradictions. The human material with which he works becomes recalcitrant. In the third scene he arranges his wife and three sons in a portrait group. Although Zenocrate is as ideally beautiful as ever, the sons disappoint him:

> But yet methinks their looks are amorous,
> Not martial as the sons of Tamburlaine.
>
> 2.I.iv.21–2

So strong is his faith in the surface of the mirror, in the visible attribute, that he doubts their capacity until Zenocrate defends them:

> My gracious lord, they have their mother's looks,
> But when they list, their conquering father's heart.
>
> I.iv.35–6

Tamburlaine also relies on extravagant figures and images in educating his sons. His successor must have the furious appearance we have already noted in the allegorical pictures of Tamburlaine. His throne, he tells the sons, will be set:

> In a field, whose superficies
> Is covered with a liquid purple veil
> And sprinkled with the brains of slaughtered men,
>
> ......

> And he that means to place himself therein,
> Must armed wade up to the chin in blood.
>
> I.iv.79–84

Two of the sons, apparently little dismayed, answer in kind. One will cross this bloody sea on a ship; the second will bridge it with dead bodies. These apocalyptic promises might not boggle the minds of spectators who could observe that they are made by young men who look 'too dainty for the wars'.[48] Perhaps they would even smile at Tamburlaine's exhortations:

> If thou wilt love the wars and follow me,
> Thou shalt be made a king and reign with me,
> Keeping in iron cages emperors.
>
> I.iv.47–9

> When I am old and cannot manage arms
> Be thou the scourge and terror of the world.
>
> I.iv.59–60

After Tamburlaine turns from his family to the kings who offer him their crowns, emblematic language and stage image again function together more convincingly. At the height of his power, the 'sight' of all his friends and kings makes Tamburlaine surfeit 'in conceiving joy'.

When Zenocrate, his symbol of ideal beauty, dies in Act II, scene iv, transformed as she herself recognizes, by 'enforced and necessary change', Tamburlaine has still greater difficulty in mastering life through art. He discovers a number of meanings in her death; in this respect he almost converts it into an exemplary death like that of the treacherous Christian, Sigismund. As we have seen, his followers remind him that it is useless to rage, to blame a god for taking his wife away, or to call upon her to return. Nevertheless, Tamburlaine rapidly hits upon two kinds of show which will permit him to minimize the loss of the real woman:

> Though she be dead, yet let me think she lives
> And feed my mind that dies for want of her.
>
> II.iv.127–8

As far as he can he will control nature by keeping the body embalmed in a sheet of gold; he will subdue it by burning houses to make them 'look as if they mourned' (II.iv.139).

Two scenes later, Tamburlaine and his followers enter, bringing with them Zenocrate's hearse, while the town where she died burns in the background. This episode was inspired, it has been suggested, by 'Furor and Rabies', the forty-fifth of Whitney's *Choice of Emblemes*. This emblem shows Agamemnon standing before the burning city of Troy, and the gloss refers to the fury of tyrants:

> The crewell kinges, that are inflam'de with ire:
> With fier, and sworde, their furious mindes suffise.[49]

By now Tamburlaine has acquired all of the symptoms described by Hooker in his 'Learned Sermon of the Nature of Pride' – appalling looks, oaths, intolerance of any opposition, unappeasable wrath, and insistence on behaviour beyond the common rules. The proud, according to Hooker, 'browbeat all men which do not receive their sentences as oracles, with marvelous applause and approbation'.[50] Marlowe's use of the emblem is consistent with such associations. By letting Tamburlaine organize this tableau himself he emphasizes the hero's need to 'suffise' his furious mind by feeding it with destruction. It seems significant that Alciati, who groups this particular emblem with two others Marlowe may have used (Phaeton, and a horseman who cannot control his wilful steeds), precedes its motto, 'Furor et Rabies', with another, 'Stultitia'.[51] For in this episode Tamburlaine's pretended power to bring about signs becomes linked with the suggestion that his attitude towards Zenocrate is idolatrous. Tamburlaine immediately expands the significance of the town he set out to burn two scenes earlier; its flames are meant to kindle ominous meteors, and he goes beyond that to invoke a series of miraculous disruptions which his 'blazing star' will create. Each son then leaves a memorial explaining the import of the blackened town – a pillar crediting Tamburlaine with the destruction, a streamer with arms revealing Zenocrate's birth and fortune, a table of her virtues. But Tamburlaine is not able to part with his own contribution to the show – a portrait of Zenocrate. He will keep it 'within the circle of mine arms' – and set it up on his tent for a war-goddess when he goes into the field. Erasmus once mocked at Christians who put saints' images on their tent flaps.[52]

The death of Zenocrate not only introduces for the first time a large element of pathos in the treatment of Tamburlaine; it sharpens the contradictions in his attitude towards Zenocrate herself. It is Tam-

burlaine, not Marlowe, who concentrates on the appearance of Zenocrate and treats it as a symbol.[53] She is, to begin with, the daughter
of a monarch 'rich and brave', who signifies future good fortune when
she falls into his hands. Hers is the 'fair face and heavenly hue / Must
grace his bed that conquers Asia' (1:1.ii.36–7). Marlowe may hint
at Tamburlaine's presumption when Tamburlaine (echoing Wisdom
7:29) terms her 'lovelier than the love of Jove / Brighter than is the
silver Rhodope' (1.ii.87–8), for in the *Metamorphoses* (Bk. VI; 11.
105–7) Rhodope, a barren mountain in Thrace, had once been a
proud mortal who took the name of Juno, just as Zenocrate will do
(III.ii.54). As Tamburlaine enlarges Zenocrate's symbolic role, his
stage-poetry deteriorates into brutality. So far as the imaginative
Tamburlaine is concerned, his divinely beautiful wisdom-figure lives
on as the portrait on his tent or as the sheet of gold which shrouds her
corpse. But the audience has observed that his resplendent symbol
can cry, curse, suffer, and finally die. After her death Tamburlaine
becomes even more violent; without the mediating forces of wisdom
and love, tension between his conceits and the intransigent matter of
experience grows stronger. The tragic folly of literally acting out a
poetic vision becomes increasingly evident.

As he continues with the education of his sons, Tamburlaine again
fails to find ways of translating his improbable deeds into precepts for
his heirs. The father who bears no scars must cut his arm so that
his sons will no longer fear death. Tamburlaine insists on an emblematic interpretation of his gesture. 'Blood is the god of war's rich
livery' (2:III.ii.116). His son, Calyphas, who is anything but a war
god, misses the allegorical significance and sees only the 'pitiful
sight' which the other characters ignore. It was suggested earlier
that Calyphas becomes a wise coward because he has been dismayed
by his father's figures. In that sense he is a victim of his father's
imagination or conceiving power even before Tamburlaine drags him
from his tent, exclaiming –

> Image of sloth, and picture of a slave,
> The obloquy and scorn of my renown!
> IV.ii.16–17

Calyphas yields without further protest to the requirements of the
spectacle and dies a ceremonial death. Not so the famous 'pampered

jades of Asia'. By harnessing conquered kings to his chariot, Tamburlaine fulfills the warning he uttered when he defeated them:

> And now, ye cankered curs of Asia
> That will not see the strength of Tamburlaine,
> Although it shine as brightly as the sun,
> Now, you shall feel the strength of Tamburlaine,
> And, by the state of his supremacy,
> Approve the difference 'twixt himself and you.
>
> IV.ii.57–62

Presumably the two kings in harness cannot speak. For Tamburlaine had promised:

> Well, bark, ye dogs. I'll bridle all your tongues
> And bind them close with bits of burnished steel,
> Down to the channels of your hateful throats:
>
> IV.ii.107–9

But King Orcanes who follows them has not yet been silenced. When he calls on the underworld god to abduct Tamburlaine, Theridamas suggests:

> Your majesty must get some bits for these,
> To bridle their contemptuous cursing tongues,
> That, like unruly never-broken jades,
> Break through the hedges of their hateful mouths
> And pass their fixed bounds exceedingly.
>
> IV.iv.43–7

Conflict among characters remains an important part of this scene, as it might not do if Marlowe were simply attempting to create a barbaric sensation. Tamburlaine insists upon actualizing his bridle metaphor because, like Faustus, he knows that demi-deities require the faith of witnesses and converts. If his victims refuse to see his power as divine, he will make them feel it. Tamburlaine's comparison of his team with the horses of Apollo's sun-chariot or the 'pampered Jades of Thrace' tamed by Hercules could prompt the audience to note how weak and exhausted the kings in harness actually are. Perhaps an Elizabethan audience might also have noted that Tamburlaine speaks of himself in terms which recall the homilies against rebellion:

> Thus am I right the scourge of highest Jove,
> And see the figure of my dignity,
> By which I hold my name and majesty!
>
> IV.iv.24–6

These lines parallel a justification of kings as gods on earth bearing God's figure, sword, and name, found in the section of *Sir Thomas More* often attributed to Shakespeare, and based upon the Homilies.[54] The chariot device is for Tamburlaine a reliable mirror for his belief in himself as 'scourge of God and terror of the world' (IV.ii.79).

Just how many other figures can be seen in Tamburlaine's mirror? A triumphal chariot would have been an icon particularly rich in its associations. The main factors in determining which ones might be most relevant to a comprehension of this show are its specific context and other references to chariots in the *Tamburlaine* plays. Within the dramatic situation as just described, bridling seems to be emphasized. This emphasis might have recalled to some spectators the application of the bridle metaphor in the Epistle of St James:

For in manie things we sinne all. If anie man sinne not in worde, he is a perfect man, and able to bridel all the bodie.

Beholde, we put bits into the horses mouthes that they shoulde obey vs, and we turne about all their bodie.

......

Euen so the tongue is a litle member, and boasteth of great things: beholde, how great a thing a litle fyre kindleth.

And the tongue is fyre, *yea*, a worlde of wickednes: so is the tongue set among our members, that it defileth the whole bodie, and setteth on fyre the course of nature, and it is set on fyre of hel.

3:2–3; 5–6

Marlowe appears to allude to the third and fourth chapters of this Epistle in both *The Jew of Malta* and *Doctor Faustus*. The observation that 'Out of one mouth proceedeth blessing and cursing' (3:10) could describe many of the speeches in the *Tamburlaine* plays. In the scene at hand, Tamburlaine most emphatically does not bridle his *own* tongue; he restrains only the 'contemptuous cursing tongues' of mirror-image kings who refuse to 'see' as he does, and would gladly bridle him.

In the course of the two plays other rulers have mentioned chariots pulled by men as symbols of power. The audience would probably not recall that in Part One Tamburlaine compared himself with Phaeton, and they would not yet have heard his references to both Phaeton and Hippolytus at the conclusion of Part Two. In any event, Tamburlaine's team of kings shows no signs of running away with

him as the teams of Hippolytus and Phaeton had done. If the charioteer were to signify only reason, and the horses, will or passion, as
they did for Plato or Erasmus, Tamburlaine would seem to be in full
control.[55] In fact, because he is driving and tormenting human
beings, his control may appear too full. What, after all, is he controlling? In the triumph of Sesostris, long before presented as a
dumbshow in Gascoigne's *Jocasta*, a chariot drawn by kings had been
used to signify 'unbridled ambitious desire' on the part of the
charioteer himself.[56] Marlowe's show may have a similar reflexive
meaning. When he bridles tyrants who resemble him, Tamburlaine
dramatizes his own lack of restraint. The charioteer is as wilful as the
team.

It would be misleading to suggest that an audience need feel great
sympathy for Tamburlaine's team of kings. Unlike Barabas, these
victims do not force us to recognize that the extreme right their
persecutor justifies is equalled by their own extreme wrong. Tamburlaine might convince a number of spectators that the chariot means
what he says it does. After all, victims like the kings, or their concubines punished later in this scene, do seem to deserve a scourging
for their pride and lust. We cannot regard Tamburlaine as a simple
example of 'unbrideled wickedness' (Sidney) in a 'foolish world'.
Marlowe's emblem provides the vehicle for a more complex and
tragic kind of irony. We see the suffering created by Tamburlaine's
unbridled poetic madness. But if we admire the speech which concludes the scene – Tamburlaine imagining his triumph in Samarkand
and his final apotheosis – then this poet's assault on the temple of the
muses will have succeeded. If we could judge the *Tamburlaine* plays
by the norms implicit in *The Jew of Malta*, Tamburlaine would lose
much of his power to perplex us. We might turn over his proud mind
and promptly discover that it conceals a denial of God. What prevents us from doing just that is the scrupulously pagan, agnostic
context which always surrounds Tamburlaine. Even when he be-
haves with outrageous cruelty to the proud Babylonians in Act v,
scene i, and burns Mahomet's 'superstitious books', Heaven and
Hell are silent. Neither by vision nor speech does Jove ever say 'Cease,
my Tamburlaine', as Tamburlaine trusts that he will (iv:ii.125).
Tamburlaine's conduct could more easily be regarded as a baffling
imitation of divinity, than as an inversion of it; echoes of the books

of Nahum and Revelation confirm his identity as a scourge on an
apocalyptic scale.

Tamburlaine so constantly acts out the established images of
conquest and triumph because he wishes to follow the highest gods
in at least three respects – as an heroic candidate for apotheosis, as an
avenging scourge, and as a miracle-worker or changer of shapes. As I
suggested earlier, it is only his success in this third respect which the
plays make accessible to the critical judgment of the audience. What
we finally see in Tamburlaine's shows may tell us almost as much
about ourselves as it does about Tamburlaine. John Russell Brown
has observed that the conclusion of *Tamburlaine* Part Two leaves us
with 'more ideas, questions, and undefined responses...than the
*character* has "thoughts to put them in, imagination to give them
shape, or time to act them in"'.[57] Will poetry and history always be
at odds? Are vengeful gods bad examples for men? Does proud
idealism generate religion? Is God a poem, the Bible a collection of
conceits? Would Marlowe have agreed with Montaigne that men
who attempt to imitate angels will only behave like devils?

Such challenges to the authority of our understanding can coexist
with a tragic attitude towards Marlowe's hero. Without Tamburlaine's shows, his world might be more foolish than ever – and it
would certainly be more barren. For a man of Tamburlaine's extraordinary imagination, history proves to be a tragic experience. The
greater his efforts to make it fit his own 'best wisedome', the more
destructive and foolish he appears. Allusions to wisdom add further
weight to the possibility that Marlowe could have viewed his conqueror's career as a tragedy of mind. Tamburlaine himself is allowed
to distort the accepted version of the soul's ascent towards God when
he replaces God with another goal – the 'sweet fruition of an earthly
crown' (1:II.vii.29). His shows make prominent motifs, situations,
and people which could refer us ironically to true wisdom – a variety
of crowns, the sun-chariot mishandled by Phaeton, the wise virgins,
the 'education' of princes, the idealization of Zenocrate as muse.

Tamburlaine's final speech to Amyras closely parallels the admonition with which Arthur Golding concluded the Epistle of his
*Metamorphoses*:

> The use of this same booke therefore is this; that every man
> (Endevoring for to know himself as neerly as he can,)

(As though he in a chariot sate well ordered,) should direct
His mynd by reason in the way of vertue, and correct
His feerce affections with the bit of temprance, lest perchaunce
They taking bridle in the teeth lyke wilfull jades doo praunce
Away, and headlong carie him to every filthy pit
Of vyce, and drinking of the same defyle his soule with it:
Or else too headlong harrie him uppon the rockes of sin,
And overthrowing forcibly the chariot he sits in,
Doo teare him woorse than ever was Hippolytus the sonne
Of Theseus when he went about his fathers wrath to shun.

p. 421

For Tamburlaine the same images and allusions become a way of
describing an all-powerful imagination. He tells Amyras that the
'steeled stomachs' of the jades are to be bridled by 'silken reins'
(2:v.iii.292–3). This would be a curious image for him to choose if he
were still regarding the chariot as a mirror for his dignity as scourge
of God. In order to drive this chariot, 'More than heaven's coach the
pride of Phaeton', and control the 'proud rebelling jades', Amyras
must, like his father, be 'full of thoughts / As pure and fiery and
Phyteus' beams'. Phyteus – or Apollo – the author of 'dreaming
prophecies', seems to have been this poet's true patron all along.

Tamburlaine does not share Golding's concern with self-knowledge
and self-control. The 'latest benefit' he desires for his 'eyes' is that
his soul will have the virtue of their sight:

Pierce through the coffin and the sheet of gold,
And glut your longings with a heaven of joy.

v.iii.226–7

In death, as in life, Tamburlaine desires to identify physical eyesight with the eye of his mind. We know that there is really a corpse
within the sheet of gold. Tamburlaine cannot overcome time, change,
and death with his remarkable imagination. But while we use imagination ourselves, can we entirely blame him for trying? His pride is
indeed like the pride of Phaeton. We must always be dazzled by it
until it dips closer to us and scorches a ground more familiar than
Marlowe's land of fortune.

# 7

# The difference of things in *Edward II*

*Edward II* presents a hero whose destruction can evoke our strong sympathy. It thereby reverses the pattern of response which occurs in the two *Tamburlaine* plays. We may observe with some detachment the stylized sequence of anarchies and outrages in Acts I and II. Edward, Gaveston, and the barons fall far short of Tamburlaine's heroic grandeur. They behave with as much conceit as Faustus does, and with far less plausibility. Yet from their noisy brawls will grow Marlowe's most powerful and tragic play. It engages characters and audience in a process which finally drives the hero into the grip of the dilemma Tamburlaine could evade by 'conceiving and subduing both' – by imposing his imagination upon his experience.

Deaf to the 'sun-bright' Virgins of Damascus with their pleas for mercy, Tamburlaine defined this dilemma as a conflict between the warrior's honour and his instinctive desire for beauty. *Edward II* suggests that such conflicts may arise whenever a powerful man extends and reduces his own strong identity through pity or friendship or love. Unlike Tamburlaine, Edward cannot avoid the problem. After the whirlwind confusion of the play's first four Acts, Act V slows to accommodate the patient deliberation of the King's torturers. Through his protracted agony, Edward acquires more awareness of his own identity than do Marlowe's other heroes. The audience which attends to his suffering may see beyond Edward towards an order which makes his suffering significant. We glimpse the fact that Marlowe has framed this tragic history to 'the example of that which is most reasonable'.

I do not wish to imply that Marlowe's frame resolves all ambiguities, or that it mitigates the effect of Edward's terrible death. Quite the contrary. His frame intensifies conflicts and speeds the mechanisms of destruction. These function as ruthlessly as in *The Jew of Malta*. But, unlike Malta, Edward's England is peopled by characters capable of change. They challenge us to join with them in making the most difficult judgments and discriminations. No longer can we enjoy the freedom to speculate which protects us from the full shock of Tamburlaine's barbarity. There are few allusions or emphatic analogies to guide us through the shadows of Edward's reign. A strong witness to its intellectual and moral chaos is the Earl of Kent, who swings helplessly back and forth between King Edward and his rebel barons. Marlowe stresses Kent's effort to be rational – as he does *not* stress Abigail's when she attempts to escape the follies of her world:

> Now experience, purchasèd with grief
> Has made me see the difference of things.
> III.iii.61–2

*The Jew of Malta* sweeps violently on, destroying both Abigail and our confidence that worldly wisdom is possible. *Edward II* destroys Kent but finally permits the audience to notice essential differences which Kent has missed.

That Kent serves to deepen the obscurity of the action becomes more obvious if we compare his function with that of similar characters in *King Lear*. *Edward II* anticipates *King Lear* because it often forces us to infer, after the dramatic fact, the motives and transformations of the King and of the evil characters. But *King Lear* also contains a whole series of Abigails, outsiders whose capacity for reliable discrimination illuminates the play from beginning to end:

> *Cordelia:*    Sure I shall never marry like my sisters,
> To love my father all.
> *Kent:* (to Oswald) I'll teach you differences.
> *Fool:* (to Lear)    Dost thou know the difference, my boy,
> between a bitter fool and a sweet one?
> *Edgar:* (to Albany and Kent) The weight of this sad time we must
> obey,
> Speak what we feel, not what we ought to say.
> The oldest hath borne most; we that are young
> Shall never see so much, nor live so long.

Marlowe's Kent sees far more darkly than any of the virtuous characters in *King Lear*. After fighting with Mortimer and the barons

in the battle which defeats Edward, his brother, Kent reveals his
desperate confusion:

> This way he fled, but I am come too late.
> Edward, alas, my heart relents for thee.
> Proud traitor, Mortimer, why dost thou chase
> Thy lawful king, thy sovereign, with thy sword?
> Vile wretch, and why hast thou, of all unkind,
> Borne arms against thy brother and thy king?
> Rain showers of vengeance on my cursed head,
> Thou God, to whom in justice it belongs
> To punish this unnatural revolt.
> Edward, this Mortimer aims at thy life.
> O fly him, then! But, Edmund, calm this rage;
> Dissemble, or thou diest, for Mortimer
> And Isabel do kiss while they conspire;
> And yet she bears a face of love forsooth.
> Fie on that love that hatcheth death and hate.
>
> IV.V.10–24

This soliloquy expresses the agony of a man trapped in an impossible
situation. It is hardly a reliable, objective assessment of that situation. Kent's revolt has not been as thoroughly unnatural as he says.
In this tragedy, revolt grows out of order by a process which seems
almost organic, so comprehensive is Marlowe's vision of the social
relationships involved. Love *does* hatch death and hate. Caught up in
such a process, Kent, neither a saint nor a fool, rarely knows what he
is doing.[1] He insists upon choosing one side or the other in the civil
conflict between Edward and his barons. We can't expect him to
recognize that his dilemma makes a meaningful choice impossible.

Kent, a rational man, epitomizes the situation of many other less
thoughtful, less scrupulous characters in *Edward II*. Throughout the
anarchy which follows upon Edward's love for Gaveston and hatred
for established order, confusions and 'unseen hypocrisies' abound.
In Act I, scene iv, Lancaster points out that it cannot be right to
banish Gaveston, then bring him back immediately, which is what
Mortimer and Queen Isabella advocate. 'In no respect can contraries
be true', insists the logical Lancaster (249). But repeatedly the characters in *Edward II* must live as if they *were* true. '*Quam male con-
veniunt*', quips the senior Mortimer when King Edward places the
commoner Gaveston upon Queen Isabella's throne (I.iv.13). 'How
ill-suited!' According to W. Moelwyn Merchant, he alludes to Ovid's
comment upon Jove's transformation into a bull for Europa's sake:

> Betweene the state of Majestie and love is set such oddes,
> As that they cannot dwell in one.[2]

Faced with this fundamental contradiction between Edward's royalty and his dangerous passion for Gaveston, the English peers defend England by attacking its King. Later, the barons and Edward go off to battle with one another, crying 'Saint George for England, / And the barons' right', 'Saint George for England, and King Edward's right' (III.iii.33–5). Isabella loves her husband and helps his enemies. Prince Edward takes leave of his father with the following speech:

> Commit not to my youth things of more weight
> Than fits a prince so young as I to bear,
> And fear not, lord and father, heaven's great beams
> On Atlas' shoulder shall not lie more safe
> Than shall your charge committed to my trust.
>                                        III.ii.74–8

Even after he is crowned, the young King's mind seems to waver:

> *Queen Isabella :*    Fear not, sweet boy, I'll guard thee from thy foes.
>                   Had Edmund lived, he would have sought thy death.
>                   Come son, we'll ride a-hunting in the park.
> *King Edward III :*  And shall my uncle Edmund ride with us?
>                                        v.iv.110–13

It is no wonder that characters repeatedly attempt to end their baffling conflicts by shouting, 'Off with his head!'

What is wonderful is that Marlowe can successfully end the play by having Edward III decapitate Mortimer. This ending boldly risks parody. It succeeds, instead, as a tragic affirmation because Edward III and the audience have at least begun to escape from the darkness of contrarieties and see 'the difference of things'. The fact that Marlowe ends his play by suggesting a worldly alternative to a blind or conceited vision distinguishes *Edward II* from his other plays. Abigail's alternative – withdrawal to a nunnery – is a negative, unworldly one. *Doctor Faustus* hints that real wisdom is attainable, but emphasizes the shows which are caused by folly. The *Tamburlaine* plays, as we have just seen, encourage the audience to perceive contradictions, not to resolve them.

In *Edward II*, discrimination and greater clarity are, to quote Abigail once more, 'purchased with grief', with the suffering and passion of the hero, King Edward. Only at the last moment does

Faustus become consciously tangled in the riddle of his own responsibility ('Curse thyself, curse Lucifer'). Tamburlaine creates a riddle in himself, as he dies magnificently unaware of the gaps between his poetry and his history. Edward more fully experiences contradictions. Edward can say:

> Commend me to my son, and bid him rule
> Better than I. Yet how have I transgressed,
> Unless it be with too much clemency?
>
> v.i.121–3

This question is tragic in spirit. It characterizes a hero who is belatedly starting to know the world he is bound to by examining himself. Like King Lear, Edward finally undergoes a contradiction of the most absolute and ironic kind. A demonic riddler, Lightborn, punishes him by methods exactly appropriate to the man he was, but is no longer.

Marlowe has thoroughly prepared us for this wrenching disparity between character and destiny. One can regard the entire action of *Edward II* as a tight-knit system of rackings and wrenchings. Trapped by contrarieties, characters alter more quickly than the terms of the oppositions they inflict on one another. Consequently, the action of *Edward II* resembles that of *King Lear* in being generally either behind or ahead of itself. At first the attitudes of the characters appear simply extreme, unwarranted by events. Later, after murderous motives ripen beneath a surface of anarchic relationships, events overwhelm their inventors. No one character can comprehend what has happened until the whole terrible process has exhausted itself. By then not only the reasonable Kent but many other characters as well have lost their heads. Marlowe provides no reassuring signs that Edward III is right when he uses Mortimer's 'accursed head' as a sacrificial offering:

> Sweet father, here unto thy murdered ghost
> I offer up this wicked traitor's head,
> And let these tears, distilling from mine eyes,
> Be witness of my grief and innocency.
>
> v.vi.99–102

Instead, he relies upon the very action of his play to distill a sense of justice from irony. He permits us to observe how a process that has engendered contradictions, finally drives them out.

This objective, tragic action may presuppose a set of ideas which make its dynamic structure intelligible. The 'tendency' which struck Bradley as novel in *King Lear* is more normal in Marlowe's plays. This is:

The tendency of imagination to analyse and abstract, to decompose human nature into its constituent factors, and then to construct beings in whom one or more of these factors is absent or atrophied or only incipient. This, of course, is a tendency which produces symbols, allegories, personifications of qualities and abstract ideas; and we are accustomed to think it quite foreign to Shakespeare's genius, which was in the highest degree concrete. No doubt in the main we are right here; but it is hazardous to set limits to that genius. The Sonnets, if nothing else, may show us how easy it was to Shakespeare's mind to move in a world of 'Platonic' ideas.[3]

Surely Marlowe's mind, when he wrote *Edward II*, was moving in a world similar to that of Sonnet 147:

> My reason, the physician to my love,
> Angry that his prescriptions are not kept,
> Hath left me, and I desperate now approve
> Desire is death, which physic did except.

Such worlds provide an intensely concentrated space within which characters behave like lines of great force. We find them not only in Shakespeare's sonnets, but also in 'Venus and Adonis', *Titus Andronicus*, and the first tetralogy. The abundance of puns, animal images, and double or even multiple identities in these works suggests that, so conceived, characters become capable of extraordinary transformations. These transformations actually disguise the 'tendency of imagination to analyse and abstract' which has produced them. Therefore it may seem dogmatic to suggest that a set of 'Platonic ideas' can explain the structure of Marlowe's plot. But without paying some attention to these ideas, however briefly, we may not understand the relationships which make the action of the play so inevitable.

In Act I, scene iv, Edward enters, mourning for Gaveston, just after the barons have agreed to call the exiled favourite home again:

> My heart is as an anvil unto sorrow,
> Which beats upon it like the Cyclops' hammers
> And with the noise turns up my giddy brain
> And makes me frantic for my Gaveston.
> Ah, had some bloodless Fury rose from hell

> And with my kingly scepter struck me dead,
> When I was forced to leave my Gaveston.
>
> I.iv.311–17

'*Diablo!* What passions call you these?' says a hostile observer, Lancaster. If we could pause to answer this rhetorical question, we might well call them 'brainsick' – young Mortimer's favourite term for Edward's attitudes throughout the play. Edward's speech suggests that his passions overwhelm his reason. This spiritual disorder within the ruler himself is mirrored by the disorders in his realm. An observation from the *Enchiridion* of Erasmus can help us to see how pervasively the schemes of microcosm and macrocosm define Edward's psychological and political dilemmas. Describing the soul and body, Erasmus writes: 'Now they can neither be separated without the utmost torment nor live together without continuous warfare. Obviously, as the saying has it, each in the other is holding a wolf by the ears; and a very clever bit of verse applies equally well to both: "I can live neither with you nor without you."'[4]

When Mortimer eventually justifies to Isabella their vengeful treatment of Edward, he appeals to the same proverb:

> In any case take heed of childish fear,
> For now we hold an old wolf by the ears,
> That, if he slip, will seize upon us both,
> And gripe the sorer, being griped himself.[5]
>
> v.ii.6–9

Gloriously oblivious to the traditional wisdom condensed in his proverb, Mortimer thinks he can kill Edward without being finally 'griped' in return. He is mistaken, because relations between the barons and Edward are as interdependent as relations between body and soul in the Platonic microcosm. Body and soul will always differ, according to Erasmus; the mortal, downward-tending body prefers the visible and temporal, while the aspiring soul seeks the true and eternal. Following Plato's *Timaeus*, Erasmus says that these jarring faculties will turn the breast of man into a 'factious commonwealth', 'Unless one man has the supremacy of power, and unless that man has such character that he imposes only what is conducive to the well-being of the state' (pp. 64–5).

The righteousness of Marlowe's political antagonists may be wilful and cruel. But, as usual, such righteousness represents the defect of an inverted virtue; it acquires much of its energy from the internal dynamics of the order which Edward himself has over-turned. In the 'commonwealth' of the microcosm, described by Erasmus, the 'one man' who has both power and concern for the well-being of the state is reason, or the 'immortal soul', whose seat is fixed 'in the brain, like the residence of a king in the citadel of our state' (p. 66). Immediately below him are those passions of the body which may be considered 'nobles'. These include 'manly courage and wrathfulness, emotions certainly factious and to be kept in check' (p. 66). At the bottom of the psychological hierarchy belong 'those passions which jar strongly against the principles of reason and grovel abjectly at brute level' (p. 65). With Plato, Erasmus agrees that 'sensual appetite' was deliberately placed

> Below the midriff and far from reason's stronghold – like some kind of untamed and intractable beast; there it should be penned, since it was in the habit of causing the most violent upheavals and was not at all amenable to rational control. Just how beastly and intractable this lowest part of our nature is, the pudenda of the body can demonstrate, in which area it exercises the most absolute tyranny. With its foul incitements it, alone of all the members, continually promotes rebellion in spite of the king's fruitless protests.
>
> pp. 66–7

Marlowe's characters are partially aware of what their psychological relationships ought to have been in a healthy social order. Why, Lancaster asks the King, does he 'incense' the peers who would 'naturally love and honor' him 'but for that base and obscure Gaveston?' (I.i.99–101). Their resentment of Gaveston carries from the beginning the energies of thwarted natural affection. 'If you love us, my lord, hate Gaveston' (I.i.80). Even as the barons' party urges Edward to sign the decree banishing Gaveston, Mortimer Junior pauses to wonder, 'why should you love him whom the world hates so?' (I.iv.76). In dramatizing Edward's reconciliation with the peers in Act I, scene iv, Marlowe emphasizes the proper balance of love and martial duty. When Edward goes in to feast and await the return of Gaveston from Ireland, leaving Mortimer Senior in charge of a war which agrees with his 'nature', King and barons may appear to be playing their appointed roles.

As a group, the barons are probably necessarily factious, even provoking. Between their natures and the King's some degree of antagonism might be present under the best of circumstances. The needs of the realm would always draw them together again. Significantly, this is in fact what happens when the rebellious Mortimer Junior later requires crown money for the ransom of his uncle from the Scots. King and barons cannot live without each other.

Why, then, does this new obligation quickly serve to drive Edward and his dependents still further apart? Edward's attachment to the truly Protean Gaveston has all but destroyed his responsiveness to his peers, his wife, and his brother. He infuriates the already angry barons, first by suggesting that they ransom Mortimer Senior themselves, then by mocking them with the offer of a royal licence to beg alms throughout his kingdom. Thereupon Mortimer and Lancaster insult Edward with a long litany of social and political abuses. They, too, speak in the scornful tone which accompanies the derangement of natural relationships throughout the play. After they leave, promising war, Kent takes up the basic theme of their tirade:

> My lord, I see your love to Gaveston
> Will be the ruin of the realm and you,
> For now the wrathful nobles threaten wars,
> And therefore, brother, banish him for ever.
> II.ii.206–9

This had been the chronicler Holinshead's judgment concerning the trouble between King Edward and his peers. Like all simple attitudes and judgments, it seems to have been displaced through Marlowe's dynamic, psychological treatment of politics.[6] Edward's enemies use the condition of England as the pretext for a revolt on which they have already determined.

If the barons were motivated only by disinterested concern for the realm, what would we make of the following exchange when they invade the fortress of Tynemouth two scenes later?

> *Mortimer Junior :*  Cease to lament, and tell us where's the king?
> *Queen Isabella :*   What would you with the king? Is't him you seek?
> *Lancaster :*    No madam, but that cursèd Gaveston.
> Far be it from the thought of Lancaster
> To offer violence to his sovereign.
> II.iv.30–4

Lancaster cannot be assumed to speak for Mortimer, whose real antagonist, almost from the beginning, appears to have been Edward – 'another Gaveston', as the King has ecstatically called himself

(1.i.143). Not that Mortimer is at first deliberate in his political opportunism or even conscious that his aversion to Gaveston is almost phobic. Rather, it seems that by passionately identifying with Gaveston, Edward touches off a depth charge which will bring about his own destruction through the transformation of his dependents. At the end, Mortimer will see no difference between Edward and the 'base commoner' Gaveston. The audience, however, may see that both Mortimer and Edward have changed, and that Gaveston has never fully absorbed Edward's identity.

These transformations are what make the action of the play tragic. We can only appreciate how momentous they are if we understand that pressures which can reshape nature have been generated through the inversion of a comprehensive and satisfying order of life.[7] Like the fall of the tragic hero described by Northrop Frye, Edward's 'is involved both with a sense of his relation to society and with a sense of the supremacy of natural law, both of which are ironic in reference'.[8] Eugene Waith has observed: 'The most powerful feelings in *Edward II* are aroused by the desire to break out of some constriction – a desire which increasingly seems doomed to disappointment.'[9] Constrictions, contradictions, a few allusive references, and a brutally 'appropriate' ending – these are Marlowe's negative, ironic images of the natural law:

> Ah, had some bloodless Fury rose from hell
> And with my kingly scepter struck me dead,
> When I was forced to leave my Gaveston.
>
> 1.iv.315–17

Lightborn's literal fulfillment of Edward's brainsick desire is quasi-logical. It parodies the rule of reason itself. Here again the *Enchiridion* can give us a 'Platonic' context for the metaphors which Marlowe uses in ironic ways:

That divine counselor, presiding in the lofty citadel, mindful of his origin, purposes nothing sordid or base. His mark of distinction is an ivory sceptre, because he never misgoverns; and Homer writes that on his head an eagle sits; soaring up toward the heavens, reason looks down with piercing eyes upon things of earth. Finally, he wears a golden crown. In mystical literature gold commonly signifies wisdom. The circular shape of the crown, moreover, symbolizes perfection and completeness in every respect.

p. 67

Let us observe one by one the major transformations which so thoroughly disfigure this Platonic ground. Mortimer is a difficult character to understand because for much of the play his motives remain uncertain. His wilful acts seem to have momentum or potential, but no definite intention. Although he will eventually resemble his theatrical prototype, Richard of Gloucester, he has not, like Richard, been born with inhuman traits and a claim to the English throne.[10] He may not realize that in opposing Gaveston he is threatening Edward's crown and life.[11] The episode in which Isabella persuades Mortimer to advocate repealing Gaveston's banishment suggests that Marlowe was trying to characterize an unconscious opportunist. It resembles a scene in *2 Henry VI*, Act III, scene i; there Henry's councillors, clearly bent on removing Duke Humphrey, had attempted to find 'color' for murdering him. We do not know what Isabella tells Mortimer in Marlowe's council scene, because we hear only her promise to give him 'reasons of such weight / As thou wilt soon subscribe to his repeal' (I.iv.226–7). The argument which Mortimer then urges on the doubting barons is that if Gaveston's banishment be repealed, they will find it easier to murder him. Isabella stands by while Mortimer produces another, very different reason – namely, that if Gaveston continues to be proud, the nobles will have 'color' for rising against Edward himself. 'For howsoever we have borne it out, / 'Tis treason to be up against the king' (I.iv. 280–1). Marlowe does jog our attention to these twists of reason by having the barons suspect 'contrarieties' and sophistry, and by making Mortimer speak of 'color'. But he leaves us to infer for ourselves the full significance of Mortimer's argument. Mortimer will probably use Gaveston to catch Edward. Instead of killing Gaveston because he threatens king and country, Mortimer will keep him alive as a means of provoking war.

Not until he escapes from the Tower – to which he exits proclaiming his 'virtue that aspires to heaven' and his hope that 'surmounts his fortune far' – does Mortimer fit the outline of the ambitious dissembler. In retrospect, we may question his argument that by using Gaveston's pride as a colour for rebellion, the barons will win the support of the commons who 'cannot brook a night-grown mushrump' (I.iv.284). It is proud Mortimer himself who cannot 'brook' Gaveston, the base commoner; he finds the minion's birth and costume as aggravating as his wastefulness. Had Mortimer been conceived by Marlowe as a more thorough hypocrite like Ferneze or Sigismund, he would probably have produced his social critique of Edward and Gaveston before, not after, his rebellion. Surely he would not have complained to his uncle that Edward and Gaveston

> From out a window laugh at such as we,
> And flout our train, and jest at our attire.
> 1.iv.416–17

We are meant to see, I think, that Edward's perversely exclusive attachment to Gaveston injures Mortimer personally. Because Edward consistently incenses him, exacerbating his natural and noble pride, we find his reactions sympathetic, even when his motives grow dubious.

After Gaveston's banishment is repealed, Mortimer joins in the general reconciliation, graciously accepting from Edward the role of Lord Marshall. He replies to his uncle's remark that 'the king is changed', with 'Then so am I, and live to do him service' (1.iv.420). Yet the senior Mortimer's suggestion that even wise men have had their foolish Gavestons seems to fall on his nephew's deaf ears. 'I will not yield to any such upstart', exclaims Mortimer Junior. 'You know my mind.' Does he? Who does? In the ensuing scene Spencer takes it for granted that the King and Mortimer are 'enemies'. 'A factious lord / Shall hardly do himself good, much less us' (II.i.5–6). And of course, when Gaveston does return to court, Mortimer in quick succession stabs him, exclaims against the King ('moved may he be, and perish in his wrath!'), waves a sword at Edward, and finally exits on a promise of civil war.

The Mortimer who eventually triumphs over Edward II is a far simpler character. That love which 'hatcheth death and hate' has produced another of Marlowe's wicked fools. Mortimer congratulates himself (and Isabella) on his skill at dissembling, but manages to deceive himself as well. For the first time he explicitly commends himself through soliloquy. He celebrates his own cunning in sending to Gurney and Matrevis an unpointed letter which both 'contains Edward's death' and 'bids them save his life' (v.iv.7). Mortimer might convince other characters that he has mastered fortune, but his boast, 'Feared am I more than loved; let me be feared, / And when I frown, make all the court look pale' (v.iv.52–3), could warn an audience that they are now watching a typical tyrant villain or

Machiavel. He betrays the folly appropriate to this type when he announces:

> I view the prince with Aristarchus' eyes,
> Whose looks were as a breeching to a boy.
> They thust upon me the protectorship
> And sue to me for that that I desire,
> While at the council-table, grave enough,
> And not unlike a bashful Puritan,
> First I complain of imbecility,
> Saying it is *onus quam gravissimum*;
> Till, being interrupted by my friends,
> *Suscepi* that *provinciam* as they term it;
> And to conclude, I am Protector now.
>
> v.iv.54–64

Superficial Latin learning and excessive trust in 'shows' are two 'imbecilities' which Mortimer probably does not intend to reveal, when he plays the fool to his councillors. By concluding his soliloquy with, '*Major sum quam cui possit fortuna nocere*', he echoes the over-weening words of Niobe in the *Metamorphoses* immediately before Diana and Apollo kill her fourteen children.[12]

Young Edward III, the child who restores justice, is not fooled by Mortimer's riddling, unpointed letter to Gurney and Matrevis. From Mortimer's hand-writing he immediately infers his responsibility for the death of Edward II; he does not concern himself with the absence of the literal murderer, Lightborn, cleverly disposed of by Mortimer. His behaviour reveals how monstrously 'brainsick' Mortimer and Isabella have been, when they assume that murder, indirect and unseen, ceases to be murder. Lightborn represents no more than the shadow of a demonic will that can ultimately be exorcized. Edward III orders his attendants to execute and dismember Mortimer. Then he turns to his mother, whose case scarcely warrants such a solution. Justly, Edward perceives the difference between Mortimer and his mother; he commits her to the Tower until 'further trial may be made' of her role in her husband's murder.

What is this difference? In Act I the situations of Isabella and Mortimer seem similar. Both are thrown into a welter of emotional contradictions by Edward's attachment to Gaveston – a truly Protean figure who usurps their rightful place in the King's affections. This attachment actually pushes Isabella towards the barons, who are the only people with enough power to injure her enemy. Isabella herself

fails to recognize that her course is dangerously antagonistic to
Edward, whom she loudly professes to love. Like the frustrated
lovers in *Dido Queen of Carthage*, she often surfeits on self-conceit.
If Marlowe felt sympathy for such characters, we can infer it only
from his careful design of predicaments which make them foolish.
Mortimer, to begin with, avoids suspicion of folly. He even gains
identity through his fierce reactions to Gaveston. But Isabella, re-
acting to Gaveston as a rival, as well as an enemy, loses it. When
Edward places her in a dilemma by enjoining her to beg the barons
for Gaveston's repeal, she laments to herself:

> O miserable and distressed queen!
> Would, when I left sweet France and was embarked,
> That charming Circes, walking on the waves,
> Had changed my shape, or at the marriage-day
> The cup of Hymen had been full of poison,
> Or with those arms that twined about my neck
> I had been stifled, and not lived to see
> The king my lord thus to abandon me.
>
> I.iv.170-7

Gaveston has just come from France. He has been seated upon her
throne. As Gaveston embraces Edward, Edward has said to Isabella,
'Fawn not on me, French strumpet.' But who is really the French
strumpet, Gaveston or Isabella? The bleak irony here lies in the fact
that the muddled contents of her marriage cup have poisoned Isabella already. She corruptly longs for her share of Edward's dotage,
and she does indeed begin to change her shape. With savage economy,
Marlowe uses her as the first 'shadow' Gaveston – those avatars of
his passion which ultimately destroy Edward.

Mortimer appears to catch a glimpse of her terrible situation when
she pleads for Gaveston's recall, but insists, ''Tis for myself I speak,
and not for him.' 'Fair queen', he warns her,

> Forbear to angle for the fish
> Which, being caught, strikes him that takes it dead.
> I mean that vile torpedo, Gaveston,
> That now, I hope, floats on the Irish seas.
>
> I.iv.221-4

Promptly forgetting his own wisdom, Mortimer allows her to persuade him with her 'reasons of such weight'. We hear of these
'reasons' only through Mortimer's sophistical speeches to the barons.

After the barons have actually exploited Gaveston as tinder to spark
their revolt, Edward again thrusts Isabella into Mortimer's way. This
time the change in her 'shape' is more obvious. Within some fifty
lines, Isabella weeps for Edward, who has abandoned her, advises
Mortimer on how to trap Gaveston, and begins to think about leaving the King. She conducts her weeping in a fantastically conceited
classical style, showing that as a 'frantic Juno' she can match her
'Jovial' husband's outbursts:

> O that mine arms could close this isle about,
> That I might pull him to me where I would,
> Or that these tears that drizzle from mine eyes
> Had power to mollify his stony heart,
> That when I had him we might never part.[13]
>
> II.iv.17–21

By the end of the scene she is calmly describing the facts of her situation, and calculating her future course:

> In vain I look for love at Edward's hand,
> Whose eyes are fixed on none but Gaveston.
>
> II.iv.61–2

If Edward continues to hate her, she decides, she will complain to her
brother, the King of France.

Through action, Mortimer eventually escapes from his own limbo
of contradictory motives, achieving the radical – and sub-human –
freedom of the Machiavel. Isabella never reaches such simplicity,
but she is also spared the evil and folly which accompany it.[14] Her
soliloquy at the end of Act II, scene iv, decisively sets out three clear
options for action – alliance with Mortimer, reconciliation with
Edward, or, should Gaveston continue to dominate Edward, an
expression of grievance to her brother. Thereafter Isabella seems to
act without definitive, responsible choice. She concludes her speech
by hoping that Gaveston will be slain. We never see her 'importune'
Edward, as she promises. Instead, he sends her to France to parley
about his own affairs, and she exits willingly – just one line before she
would have learned that her wish for Gaveston's death has come true.
Perhaps only her ambiguous role as a 'shadow Gaveston' – an agent
of destructive passion – can explain why her political loyalty to
Edward should seem to die when Gaveston does. The next we hear of
her (III.iii.85), an incalculable, but significant, period of time has

passed. The Spencers have replaced Gaveston with Edward, and Isabella is said to be building a force with which to enthrone her son. Edward now bribes the French King so that he will deny aid to Isabella. The only explanations Isabella gives for her altered attitude towards Edward are her words to her son, 'No, no, we jar too far' (IV.ii.10).

It is never clear whether Isabella's deceptions in Act V are primarily motivated by vindictiveness against Edward, lust for Mortimer, or concern for her son's and England's security. Using the balance of faculties in the psychic microcosm as a metaphor of social life, one might suggest that by the time of their triumph over Edward, Isabella and Mortimer actually parody the correct relationship of passion and reason. Isabella remains a passionate lover to the end; her grief in the concluding scene for her son's suspicion and her husband's death rings thin but true.[15] Mortimer, who calls himself an 'Aristarchus' or school-master to the Prince, schools the irrational Isabella as well. 'Be ruled by me, and we will rule the realm.' He interrupts her 'passionate' speech to her victorious soldiers, and coaches her in her dissembling. A hypocrite she may be, but she cannot be judged guilty of Mortimer's far greater sin – that intellectual pride which he shares with Marlowe's other over-reachers. And so, she goes finally off to the Tower as the prisoner of her own child. There would be little poetic justice in hanging or decapitating a character who, figuratively speaking, lacks a head of her own.

Only in the character of Edward do we see reason gather strength through its contest with passion. The other characters in the play lack this kind of psychic integrity; they appear to function as parts of Edward which split off when he overturns the orders of mind and society. They change by hardening into extreme positions, but he alone grows. In his scene with Lightborn, Edward sees more accurately than ever before:

> Small comfort finds poor Edward in thy looks.
> Villain, I know thou com'st to murder me.
>
> V.v.43–4

> These looks of thine can harbor nought but death.
> I see my tragedy written in thy brows.
> Yet stay awhile; forbear thy bloody hand,
> And let me see the stroke before it comes,

> That even then when I shall lose my life,
> My mind may be more steadfast on my God.
>
> v.v.72–7

His tormentors Gurney and Matrevis have wondered at the strength of this king, 'brought up so tenderly':

> He hath a body able to endure
> More than we can inflict, and therefore now
> Let us assail his mind another while.
>
> v.v.10–12

Pathetically exhausted and 'over-watched' he may be, but Edward's mind easily matches his body in strength:

> Know that I am a king. O, at that name
> I feel a hell of grief! Where is my crown?
> Gone, gone, and do I remain alive?
>
> v.v.88–90

For ten days this grief – a protracted recognition of his own royal nature – has kept his eyes wide open.

Edward manages to strike off a mordantly sardonic bit of irony at his own expense, as he concludes his account of ten days in the castle cess-pool:

> Tell Isabel, the queen, I looked not thus,
> When for her sake I ran at tilt in France
> And there unhorsed the Duke of Cleremont.
>
> v.v.67–9

In all probability, Edward used to look a great deal like Gaveston, described by Mortimer with satiric over-precision:

> He wears a lord's revenue on his back,
> And, Midas-like, he jets it in the court
> With base outlandish cullions at his heels,
> Whose proud fantastic liveries make such show,
> As if that Proteus, god of shapes, appeared.
> I have not seen a dapper Jack so brisk.
> He wears a short Italian hooded cloak,
> Larded with pearl, and in his Tuscan cap
> A jewel of more value than the crown.
>
> i.iv.406–14

Later Mortimer criticizes Edward because his soldiers marched to battle dressed as players –

> With garish robes, not armor, and thyself,
> Bedaubed with gold, rode laughing at the rest,

Nodding and shaking of thy spangled crest,
Where women's favors hung like labels down.
II.ii.182–5

We can trace Edward's growth, his approach to reason and royalty, by observing the shift in his attitudes towards ceremony and dress. Edward is the only one of Marlowe's heroes capable of criticizing, however tentatively, his own fascination with shows.

If the significance of the shows in *Edward II* were always more evident to the audience than to the characters, we might congratulate ourselves on our superior wit and decide that Edward's world is decidedly foolish. Or, if the sense of its shows lay regularly in the eyes of different beholding characters, *Edward II* might cause us to doubt the validity of our *own* wit. In either case – a case like that of *The Jew of Malta* on one hand, or of the *Tamburlaine* plays on the other – wit itself would tend to become an issue rivalling in interest the hero himself. Its very existence would be precarious, its uses doubtful. The shows in *Edward II*, however, reveal a more positive attitude towards wit. I have already suggested that in making Edward's tragic situation invert an ideal microcosm, Marlowe framed his history play to 'the example of that which is most reasonable'. We glimpse something of this reasonable frame and its decided firmness in his treatment of spectacle. Minor characters appear who reliably guide the audience in understanding particular shows.[16] Simultaneously, major characters experience confusions of eyesight without seeming altogether foolish. And, most important, the hero proves capable of learning to see more accurately. Disparate as these instances are, all express an implicit confidence in worldly wit. Without such confidence, Marlowe could never have discovered tragic qualities in Edward's fall.

Early in the play Edward's own mind (to quote from Folly herself) is 'taken far more with disguises than with realities' (p. 63). Like Faustus, he reacts to these eye-pleasing 'disguises' with Epicurean gusto. Gaveston returns from France planning to entertain Edward with shows by day and by night. We never see how Edward actually responds to such courtly revels; Gaveston's private project for a glittering show about the death of Actaeon immediately gives way to the noisy jars between Edward and his peers – all of whom are probably clad in drab mourning. The extended spectacles which we soon

behold on stage – the fouling of a bishop and Gaveston's enthrone-
ment – conspicuously violate order, rather than celebrating it. But
Gaveston's soliloquy does prepare us for Edward's more or less
'theatrical' attachment to Gaveston himself. Pleasure in show seems
to account for much of Edward's feeling towards Gaveston. He greets
his returning minion as if he were a mirror image:

> What, Gaveston! Welcome! Kiss not my hand;
> Embrace me, Gaveston, as I do thee.
> Why shouldst thou kneel? Knowest thou not who I am?
> Thy friend, thyself, another Gaveston!
>
> I.i.140–3

'I have my wish in that I joy thy sight', he exclaims. When Edward is
forced to part from Gaveston in scene iv, he laments, 'Thou from this
land, I from myself am banished', and Gaveston grieves 'to forsake
you, in whose gracious looks / The blessedness of Gaveston remains'.
They exchange portraits, and Edward beseeches Gaveston, 'give me
leave to look my fill' (I.iv.139). When Gaveston returns again (Act II,
scene ii), Edward says –

> And now thy sight
> Is sweeter far than was thy parting hence
> Bitter and irksome to my sobbing heart.
>
> 56–8

After the barons have captured Gaveston, both the King and his
minion vent their passionate longings for each other in images of
vision.

Edward and Gaveston treat their union as Paradise, their separa-
tion as Hell; Gaveston even describes these states in language which
closely parallels the language of *Doctor Faustus*:

> The sight of London to my exiled eyes
> Is as Elysium to a new-come soul
>
> I.i.10–11
>
> Is all my hope turned to this hell of grief?
>
> I.iv.116

Does this mean that Edward must be punished, like Faustus, for a
surfeit of conceit? Does his delight in appearances suggest that he is a
voyeur – one who mistakes the letter for the spirit, because self-love
corrupts his reason? Efforts have been made to apply the Actaeon

myth and its Renaissance rationalizations to the action of *Edward II*.[17] Perhaps the one thing we can say confidently about the meaning of this myth is that because Actaeon sees Diana in her forest bath, she punishes him. If the play follows the myth, then Edward's love of show should cause *his* punishment. Looking at Gaveston, profanely baptizing the Bishop of Coventry, and, of course, wearing Italian clothes in the Puritanical English court should all be regarded as symptoms of a fatal flaw.

We can indeed emphasize the parallel between Edward's punishment and Actaeon's, but only if we are also willing to applaud the remorselessly clever logic of the Fury who destroys Edward. Marlowe's tragedy upsets all exact identifications between his characters and the characters of the myth, just as surely as it displaces all choral statements and explanations. It thoroughly transvalues the narrow, barbaric legalism which informs the old Actaeon story.[18] Even in the first two Acts there are factors which should discourage us from seizing upon Edward's conceit as the single 'cause' of his doom. The King must always be the one who is most to blame. But Marlowe shows us that the other characters speak, and therefore reason, in much the same manner Edward does. Isabella's laments contain many references to seeing, looks, appearances, and heads. Perhaps the general reliance upon signs, oaths, sureties, proverbs, prognostications, and traditional experience (such as the senior Mortimer's reassuring lore about the minions of great men, I.iv.390) might be interpreted as an expressive device suggesting disorders of mind and spirit. Figures of testimony, said the rhetorician Sherry, 'are not fet by the wytte of hym that disputeth but are ministred otherwyse'.[19] Faustus at Rome has already shown us that fools become difficult to criticize when the worlds they inhabit complement their folly. In *Edward II*, the other characters seem to complement the hero's personal, tragic responsibility for his fate.

Moreover, Edward can already see and reason well enough whenever his own royal authority is seriously questioned. He immediately recognizes the meaning of the devices which Mortimer and Lancaster have painted on their shields as insults to Gaveston:

> They love me not that hate my Gaveston.
> I am that cedar, shake me not too much;
> And you the eagles; soar ye ne'er so high,

I have the jesses that will pull you down;
And *Aeque tandem* shall that canker cry
Unto the proudest peer of Britainy.
                                   II.ii.37–42

Edward swiftly turns the conceits of the barons against them, reminding these would-be eagles that they are hunting falcons whom he can
control. He speaks a language of wilful assertion – one of the simpler
languages which provide a regular counterpoint to the more artificial
languages of courtliness, amorous love, and satiric scorn. Because
Marlowe foreshortens Edward's history, there will never be time to
test Mortimer Senior's belief in the King's future promise. But at
such moments his optimism about Edward seems to be partly
justified.

In discussing Isabella, I mentioned the disparity between Marlowe's extraordinary grasp of tragic situations, and his belittling of
the characters who endure them. In order to comprehend the full
scope of Edward's offence against reason, we must patiently observe
what time will 'hatch' from it. As the play begins, Edward is very
young; under Gaveston's 'light-brained' influence he quickly becomes giddy and politically careless. The two men wish to die to the
world through their passion for one another, to become erotic monks.
They resemble another 'votary' of love, the Hero of 'Hero and
Leander'. Retrospectively, we come to understand that Edward's
tragedy originates in his failure to control his dependents. Loving
Gaveston is what he does *instead* of ruling vigilantly and wisely.

Given Elizabethan attitudes towards sexual perversion, Marlowe
could have presented Edward's addiction to Gaveston as bestial and
'demonic'. But because he actually presents it as something far more
trivial (a 'toy', in Mortimer Senior's words), it cannot be regarded as
the only cause of the high tragedy of civil rebellion and regicide
which follows. By replacing his complex social obligations with a
simple, absolute emotional commitment, Edward gives his wrathful
nobles an irresistibly simple weapon. Gaveston provides them with
an excuse for their rebellion. Just how adept they have become at
their game is suggested when Edward learns of Gaveston's death,
vows vengeance upon the barons, and adopts Spencer in Gaveston's
place. Immediately the Herald of the barons arrives to demand that
Edward renounce Spencer. The barons protest that they –

> Lovingly advise your grace
> To cherish virtue and nobility,
> And have old servitors in high esteem,
> And shake off smooth dissembling flatterers.
>
> III.ii.166–9

At this point in the play we may surmise that the watchdogs of the realm are deliberately failing to recognize their old master. Another opportunist he may be, but Spencer is not merely another foolish Gaveston; he urges Edward to rule his barons with greater severity, and his father leads a 'band of bowmen and of pikes', much in the manner of a trusty George a Greene. If Edward is Actaeon, then his noble hounds have glimpsed the man beneath the deerskin, and have chased him all the faster for it. They will only kill him when the skin drops away altogether. The hunting of Edward by Mortimer would be quite obvious during a performance; in rapid succession, Mortimer wounds Gaveston with his sword, and threatens the King about his uncle's ransom. 'Shall I still be haunted thus?' rages the provoked King (II.ii.152). 'Defend me, heaven, shall I be haunted still?' exclaimed Benvolio in *Doctor Faustus*, his head crowned with horns.[20] After his defeat by Mortimer, Edward must 'fly' about the stage, demanding, 'What, was I born to fly and run away, / And leave the Mortimers conquerors behind?' (IV.v.4).

Unlike so many of Marlowe's rhetorical questions, this one may be unanswerable. By asking such questions, Edward involves the audience in the riddles of his character and fate. These riddles include, as we have seen, his mutually dependent relationship with his barons. They also include the strong possibility that between his defeat and his death Edward too begins to change. The last we see of the former Edward is when he disguises himself as a monk and tries to escape from the world around him, by laying down his head in the Abbot's lap:

> O might I never open these eyes again,
> Never again lift up this drooping head,
> O never more lift up this dying heart!
>
> IV.vi.41–3

His posture may be regarded as emblematic of his fall; Leicester interprets it that way when he enters with the King's pursuers:

> Alas, see where he sits, and hopes unseen
> T' escape their hands that seek to reave his life.

Too true it is, *Quem dies vidit veniens superbum,*
*Hunc dies vidit fugiens jacentem.*[21]
IV.vi.51–4

It may also be regarded as the end of one movement in the play, and
the beginning of another. When he parts with the friends in whom
he has sought to mirror, even to lose, his own identity, Edward
exclaims, 'Hence feigned weeds! Unfeigned are my woes.' He then
throws off his monk's disguise. For Tamburlaine a similar gesture
had initiated two processes – his growing power over others and his
increasing ignorance about himself. But for Edward it marks the
onset of his confrontation with his own royal qualities.

During the deposition scene which follows, Edward acts out an
exhausting struggle between his reason and his passions. He compares himself with a lion, whose nature it is to aggravate its own
wounds rather than to nurse them. By this conceit he seems to
mean that when Mortimer 'curbs' his 'dauntless spirit', it falls back
upon the awareness of its own royalty:

> For such outrageous passions cloy my soul,
> As with the wings of rancor and disdain
> Full often am I soaring up to heaven,
> To plain me to the gods against them both.
> But when I call to mind I am a king,
> Methinks I should revenge me of the wrongs
> That Mortimer and Isabel have done.
v.i.19–25

Here we have still another version of that false or Icarian transcend-
ence which preoccupied Marlowe; the passions soar, while the
reason stays below. Rational enough to remember who he is, Edward
at least anticipates the just revenge which King Edward III will have
on Mortimer and Isabella. Again he poses one of his unanswerable,
tragic questions:

> But what are kings when regiment is gone,
> But perfect shadows in a sunshine day?
v.i.26–7

Growing less like a 'perfect shadow', Edward seems to realize that
his royalty has been no mere costume. Always stubborn, never
strong, he now clings to his crown as he had earlier clung to 'my
Gaveston':

> But stay awhile; let me be king till night,
> That I may gaze upon this glittering crown;
> So shall my eyes receive their last content,
> My head, the latest honor due to it,
> And jointly both yield up their wished right.
>
> v.i.59–63

Edward's desire to stop the sun while he looks at his crown sounds idolatrous, Faustian. According to a stage direction, he 'rageth' in response to the question, 'will you resign or no?' Later he actually gives up his crown, not, it seems, to save his son's 'right', but to avoid looking at the faces of Isabella and Mortimer. He sends Isabella a tear-drenched handkerchief, and tears up a letter bearing Mortimer's name, saying, 'This poor revenge hath something eased my mind.' Marlowe emphasizes the continuity in Edward's emotional character. But at the same time he allows us to observe differences between Edward's earlier passion for Gaveston and his passion for his crown. The first passion is at odds with Edward's royal disposition. The second is inseparable from it. As Edward handles his crown, as the words 'king' and 'kingdom' echo through his speeches, he restores the full meanings to what had been mere shows and conceits. He is furious and desperate, not because he has lost his royal identity, but because he cannot lose it. He knows himself better than he has before.

Harry Levin writes that: 'Rhetoric and pageantry existed on the surface in *Tamburlaine*, objective and unreal; but in *Edward II* they are of the essence, subjective and real. Here the theatricality is not conventional but psychological, conceived as a trait of Edward's character.'[22] This useful, thought-provoking distinction needs to be qualified. Tamburlaine cannot bring his stage images and metaphors to life. 'Objective' his pageantry may be, but with an inflexible, literal quality which measures the growing ironic tension between his history and his poetic vision, his bare fortune and his ideas. The English crown, on the other hand, means what Edward wants it to – 'last content', 'latest honor', 'comfort' – because his history objectively supports his 'conceits'. His crown *does* preserve his sanity and life:

> And in this torment comfort find I none,
> But that I feel the crown upon my head,
> And therefore let me wear it yet awhile.
>
> v.i.81–3

So deep is his attachment to his crown, that he cannot at first choose to give it away, but prefers that it be taken from him:

> Here receive my crown.
> Receive it? No, these innocent hands of mine
> Shall not be guilty of so foul a crime.
> He of you all that most desires my blood
> And will be called the murderer of a king,
> Take it. What, are you moved? Pity you me?
>
> v.i.97–102

Edward yields his crown just as he seems to have convinced even his stage audience that it is a valid symbol of his physical and spiritual strength:

> Then send for unrelenting Mortimer
> And Isabel, whose eyes, being turned to steel,
> Will sooner sparkle fire than shed a tear,
> Yet stay, for rather than I will look on them,
> Here, here!
>
> v.i.103–7

What has happened? Isn't Edward once again making far too much of appearances and shows? I think not. With brilliant economy, Marlowe has used the weakness of human folly to create a tragic experience. Edward fears their looks because these looks are accurate signs of a 'strange exchange' in love and power too great for his mind to bear. 'Ah, Leicester', he has exclaimed,

> Weigh how hardly I can brook
> To lose my crown and kingdom without cause,
> To give ambitious Mortimer my right,
> That like a mountain overwhelms my bliss,
> In which extreme my mind here murdered is.
>
> v.i.51–5

Edward fails to understand his initial responsibility for the baffling transformations in Isabella and Mortimer. But then, so does his more reasonable brother Kent, when he terms the revolt against Edward 'unnatural'. Edward's protecting crown finally exposes him to contradictions which injure him more than anyone else, and he collapses beneath the burden. It is not Mortimer who really wears the crown of fire or 'snaky wreath of Tisiphon' which Edward wishes upon him. Only Edward can wear it. Bert O. States has argued in his *Irony and Drama: A Poetics:*

The idea that the victory inherent in tragedy arrives primarily in the earned nobility of the defeated-victorious hero is actually much overrated as the key to catharsis; the victory is rather in the poet's having framed the definitive fate for his hero-victim. In turning the tables on his hero so *exactly*, getting the all into his one, he shows wherein the imagination is a match for nature in getting her to participate so thoroughly in the fault.[23]

Lion-like in his royal mind, Edward passionately hastens his own destruction.

By the end of this extraordinary scene Edward has moved by a path which anticipates Hamlet's, from mind-murdering awareness, to madness, to acceptance of his fate:

> Of this am I assured,
> That death ends all, and I can die but once.
> v.i.152–3

Mortimer continues to hunt him because now Mortimer is the fool whose mind is 'taken far more with disguises than with realities'. He writes an unpointed letter, '*Edwardum occidere nolite timere bonum est*', on the assumption that truth lies only in the eyes of the beholder. He pursues the phantom Gaveston through the agency of Lightborn – another phantom Gaveston, and an incarnation of the bloodless fury whom Edward has conjured to rise from Hell. Lightborn's pleasure in puns, riddles and secret tricks represents the logical culmination of a growing evil. 'None shall know my tricks', he tells Mortimer, and Mortimer replies, 'I care not how it is, so it be not spied.' He pushes the deceptions of more warm-blooded hypocrites to an abstract extreme when he tells the terrified Edward:

> These hands were never stained with innocent blood,
> Nor shall they now be tainted with a king's.
> v.v.80–1

At the end of *The Jew of Malta* no character within the play itself can judge that the final confounding of identities and dispensations is evil. Only an audience, reminded for five Acts of 'another foundation' than the 'superficial part' promises, has the awareness to recognize that such mere anarchy foretells apocalypse. No solution can possibly come from within such a fallen world. At the end of *Edward II*, however, Edward stands before the audience, sinned against as well as sinning. History has destroyed his youth but partly redeemed his promise. He has enacted in that inner theatre, his own spirit, the defeat and rebirth of reason. His transformation joins the play's foundation to its 'superficial' part. Edward's unjust suffering, which we see so well, overwhelms us with the presence of evil; we are not dependent upon what we already know or remember. Marlowe's tragedy deprives the audience of a privileged, speculative position. It even grants us the option of regarding Edward's catastrophe from Lightborn's position or from Edward's. The clever Lightborn inside of us tempts us to relish an ironic comparison between the young Edward and the old one who offers Lightborn his last jewel. The ragged, dripping Edward who moves and speaks before us permits us to realize that he has outlived the selfish, brainsick actor he once was:

> O, if thou harbor'st murder in thy heart,
> Let this gift change thy mind and save thy soul.
> Know that I am a king. O, at that name
> I feel a hell of grief! Where is my crown?
> Gone, gone, and do I remain alive?
>
> v.v.86–90

The manner of his death is just as appropriate to his character as was the manner of his tragic deposition. But this time only a demon could have contrived it.

Edward III, once so confused and helpless, seems to inherit both the crown and the moral vision 'purchased' by his father through grief. He finally plays the just Diana to Mortimer's proud, conceited Actaeon, hoisting this last shadow of Gaveston with his own petard. The final tableau in which young Edward offers up Mortimer's head to Edward's ghost is the last round in a familiar vengeful game of extreme right and exceeding wrong. Edward III obeys the rules of the game, bidding Mortimer to his last 'base', the block, with characteristic speed. But no one pities Mortimer's wrong any longer. *Edward II* has revealed great differences within its powerfully framed consistencies. Its blind furies die at last into the convincing ceremonies of funeral and sacrifice.

# 8

## The prophetic spirit

In her study, *Paradoxia Epidemica*, Rosalie Colie refers to the important 'question in logic' raised by the use of a paradoxical encomium:
'Can a thing unpraisable in fact be praised? If it can, then it is not
unpraisable; if it cannot, then a vast number of pieces of paradoxical
prose do not exist.'[1] By applying these alternatives to the poetic
praises of folly in Marlowe's plays, we find that they may not be
essentially paradoxical. Folly, understood as an inversion or parody of
wisdom, cannot be completely 'unpraisable'. We have seen that the
more wicked follies reduce existence to illusion. Only within this
illusory state, itself the consequence of moral attitudes and acts, does
Colie's 'question in logic' appear to arise. Although Marlowe involves us in shows, he suggests that his showmen misdirect the
divine power in all men. They unnecessarily darken their minds
through self-righteousness, making them subservient to will. Even
when Marlowe punishes 'conceit' with artfully conceited precision,
something of this power seems to survive the character. After the
tricks of Merlin we are left with a sense of his prophecy. Although
the individual hero may fall, the values of mind and language do
not.

With this general view of Marlowe's achievement as a background,
I wish to re-examine two closely related topics: the obscurity of his
ironic methods, and the prophetic vision they create. We have seen
that his methods are almost always oblique. The allusions, analogies,
and emblematic shows in more satiric plays based on a Christian
foundation never fully prepare us for the disasters which match so
precisely the errors of the characters. Like all of Marlowe's plays,
*The Jew of Malta* and *Doctor Faustus* move with whirlwind rapidity,
depriving us of leisure with which to ponder references and relation-

ships. For Marlowe, the mythical figures Icarus and Phaeton seem to have symbolized a tragic conflict between self-centred idealism and the objective, heliocentric triumphs of time. Speed and obliquity in the art of his plays force the audience to experience this conflict as a profound disturbance in the seasons of its own understanding. Marlowe does not resolve his ironic Winter's Tales gradually; his endings scorch through the plausible darkness with relentless light. History apocalyptically overwhelms those who have tried to ignore or suspend its necessities. Surely the twenty-four-year bond in *Doctor Faustus* is no mere hypothetical device. It defines the term of an anti-life, cleverly enacted by a hero who lacks faith in fulfilment through time. Barabas destroys his own 'child of the promise', Abigail. Faustus parodies Christian redemption by signing a contract which promises that his life will be shallow and short.

I have employed a generic distinction between satiric and tragic irony in order to emphasize the importance of Marlowe's relationship with his audience. In *The Jew of Malta* and *Doctor Faustus* Marlowe 'raises the mind and carries it aloft'; he finally urges his audience up into a watch-tower, whence it may glimpse the Christian 'foundation' revealed through speech and spectacle. In the *Tamburlaine* plays and *Edward II* he places a greater burden on his audience because he immerses it in the subjective element along with his characters. I hope that my discussions of these three plays have made the point that such a strategy actually implies greater confidence in the wit of the audience. Marlowe trusts us to keep the eyes of our own minds on the sun, so to speak, to develop a consciousness of historical necessity by observing the changes in the lives of his characters. By comparison with the development and transformation of characters in Shakespeare's two tetralogies, these changes are slight. But within a rigorously designed history like *Edward II* they appear momentous indeed.

Because Marlowe's ironic relationship with his audience varies from play to play, we probably cannot expect to infer his personal attitudes from any one work. For example, G. K. Hunter concludes his study of theology in *The Jew of Malta* by suggesting, 'The world of Marlowe is a completely fallen world; but so is the world of Calvin.'[2] Marlowe's art certainly encourages us to take a lofty and pessimistic view of Malta. His irony in *The Jew of Malta* resembles the modern variant, described by Søren Kierkegaard as 'a determination of subjectivity'. Unrestrained by any actuality in the content of his work, Kierkegaard's ironist 'hovers' over it, 'negatively free'.[3] What the modern and the Calvinistic ironist seem to share is the will to humiliate a world which frustrates their enormous idealism. They secure their 'negative freedom' by erecting labyrinths of poetry or theology. A writer who risks misunderstanding of his art, as Marlowe does, can easily be suspected of wishing to be a Magus alone on his watch-tower.

But when we turn from Barabas to Faustus or Tamburlaine, we must revise our estimation of Marlowe's 'negativity'. Although these heroes may wrench true wisdom from her heavenly throne, they do not prove that she is completely beyond human comprehension. They err by giving her a literal form, not by seeking her on earth. Faustus is a 'branch that might have grown full straight', had he not exchanged wisdom's 'fruitful plot' for his narrow conjuring circle. Wisdom remains a strong presence in the world of Faustus; it is the grace he repeatedly rejects, the intuitive love of God which, but for his folly, might have informed his learning and saved his soul. Tamburlaine's word-magic has a more puzzling relationship to true wisdom than does the demonic magic of Faustus. We have seen that while Zenocrate, Tamburlaine's wisdom-figure, lives, she seems to check the evil violence of his spectacular conceits. In any case, the very abuse of wit by both Faustus and Tamburlaine insinuates the potential greatness of the wit abused. The specious freedom of these characters affirms through energetic parody that spiritual man is indeed free.

Marlowe extends the sense of freedom from characters to audience. That is why we can conclude that he is not always one of the negative ironists – ironists who hold the world and their audiences in contempt. By appealing to our memories of literature and tradition, by inviting us to ponder analogies and scrutinize shows, Marlowe stimulates our imaginations. By praising folly he exercises our wisdom. He invites us to use those faculties of choice and recognition which his heroes neglect. Marlowe creates in his audience the prophetic spirit lacking in his heroes. He may expect too much of his audience, rather than too little. His 'hard' or 'proverbial' irony is never dark because it conceals insights beyond our powers of understanding. The darkness is instead a constant testimony to the ease with which our minds may be distracted and beguiled. Like his hero Tamburlaine, Marlowe really serves the god of light and poetry, Apollo. But he doesn't forget that votaries of Apollo resemble physicians. They must depend on the patient for much of the cure.

Marlowe's willingness to dose foolishness with folly may tempt us to confuse him with Sidney's 'Poet-haters' – or at least with that splenetic, scoffing voice which still harangues us so directly from the notorious Baines note. Then again, we may observe that the poetry of his plays seems to grow more glorious, even as the folly of his characters increases. Here, we might decide, is evidence of far more serious 'poet-hating'. Marlowe has caught the true Platonic contagion and learned to view the letter of poetic language as a lie, or, at best, as a veil for higher truths. Scoffing trickster or Platonizing saint? Marlowe's irony constantly threatens to pitch us upon these limiting interpretations of his genius. In order to steer a course between them I have regularly compared Marlowe with Erasmus – an ironist all too commonly regarded as superficially clever or profoundly mystical. Of course Erasmus often dropped his ironic mask. Letters, adages, tracts, and colloquies criticize the spiritual outrages celebrated by Marlowe's heroes. Erasmus can exhort us to the very attitudes conspicuously omitted by Marlowe. But when he writes ironically Erasmus resembles Marlowe in several essential ways. Indeed he is one of the few major Renaissance writers whom it is profitable to associate with Marlowe. The ironic moralist can help us recognize the true distinction of the more sardonic and passionate dramatist.

Both Marlowe and Erasmus are keenly interested in charlatans who can persuasively substitute conceits for realities. Both allow their charlatans to fool us when they 'rejoice after the flesh'. *The Praise of Folly* and Marlowe's plays put fools – figures who are generally static outsiders – at the centre of a dramatic process. The process moves from ironic obscurity toward clarity, sometimes transforming the fool himself. To reckon with either Erasmus or Marlowe we must admit their capacity for commitment, detachment, and, perhaps their most puzzling quality of all, indifference. When T. S. Eliot wrote in 'Little Gidding' that these three distinct conditions 'flourish in the same hedgerow', he identified 'indifference' with the 'use of memory' –

> For liberation – not less of love but expanding
> Of love beyond desire, and so liberation
> From the future as well as the past.

Defined in this manner, indifference can be separated from cynicism or mysticism, and approached as a kind of tragic awareness. Without such indifference, how could Marlowe have characterized his warrior poet Tamburlaine – the master of an art which expands desire beyond love?

Through his ironic art Marlowe shows how letter and spirit inter-animate one another. Faustus does not founder on the letter of St Paul for want of spirit. But the spirit with which he throws open his copy of Jerome is his own self-righteous one. Although Faustus may not know what he desires to discover, his Bible does. It greets him with a text appropriate to his disposition and prospects – just as it had greeted the convert Augustine when he threw open Paul's Epistles to the final verses of Romans 13. The games played by Faustus or by Barabas deny the prophetic spirit. They are sterile pastimes or 'sports', expressive of wit without wisdom. Although these pastimes may seem more trivial than the characters who pursue them, the disproportion has been caused by rhetorical sleight of hand. Barabas would fit his cauldron and Faustus his Hell-Mouth had Marlowe not allowed them to commend themselves so plausibly. When we turn from the more satiric plays to the more tragic ones, tensions between the vitality of the characters and the deadliness of their game-like destinies become more painful. Because Edward has grown and changed, Mortimer's hunt-game can strike us as a cruel injustice. Mortimer's praise of his wicked folly cannot prevent us from regarding the vicious circle of the plot as a sign of his own sick spirit. In *The Jew of Malta*, Barabas passes on his wicked folly to his heir, Ferneze. In *Edward II*, wicked folly dies with Mortimer, and wisdom lives through the righteousness of Edward III. Tragic law has finally been extricated from game.

When Friar John denied that Gargantua's engraved plate contained a Christian allegory, he suggested that the riddle merely concealed a description of a tennis game. If his absurdly sceptical remark comes close to describing one effect of the *Tamburlaine* plays, it may be because within these plays tragic law and game are still entangled. Although the contexts of Tamburlaine's shows increasingly suggest that he, too, is a literalist, seeing by the light of his own proud spirit, Marlowe never offers us unquestionable evidence that Tamburlaine is thoroughly wicked or foolish. Apocalyptic allusions do not definitely indicate whether Tamburlaine is a god of anger and power, or whether he merely worships one. Allusions to the wisdom he lacks imply criticism of Tamburlaine if we regard him as a conqueror. Marlowe's method here resembles the method of Rabelais, whose bloody tyrant, Picrochole, is made to swear by Solomon and St James. But if we regard Tamburlaine as primarily a poet, his madness may become a source of strength. Can we really expect Tamburlaine to control himself, when other monarchs echo his ambitions and pretensions? The *Tamburlaine* plays are tragic riddles. They presuppose the value of history and continuity; Tamburlaine's political conquests and family relationships equip us to regard him as a tragic figure. But at the same time the plays make Tamburlaine insensitive to the tragic elements in his own life; his imagination always gets the last triumphant word.

Experience, said the humanists Ascham and Erasmus, is 'the common school-house of fools and ill-men'.[4] Marlowe often betrays the humanist's exasperation with worldly follies, but he values experience because it tests the will of his heroes. Generations of readers and spectators have been moved by the passionate energy of these characters. Their vitality dominates our first impressions and memories; it 'proves', more effectively than any allusion, that the folly the characters praise is not unpraisable. I have reserved the significance of this vitality for the end, because it returns me to an important point with which I began – the strength of more traditional, even Romantic responses to Marlowe's air and fire.

Fredson Bowers has said that Marlowe's 'protagonists are interesting personalities in themselves, regardless of what they specifically do'.[5] But doing, negligible as it might seem, amplifies personality. Marlowe collaborates with his proud and eloquent fools when they attempt to suspend necessity and control fate. Here we encounter the most prophetic of Merlin's tricks. Dame Helen Gardner treats *Doctor Faustus* as a 'tragedy of damnation' and its hero as a man incapable of change. But she observes, at the same time, that Marlowe is 'more merciful, as he is always more metaphysical, than Shakespeare'.[6] Marlowe's general treatment of dramatic action supports her perception about his mercy. Characters conceived as statically paradoxical – wicked and wise fools, passionate princes, a mad poet – are nevertheless made to run. For all their blind will, they participate in a dynamic process which has only one truly inevitable phase – the last. In Marlowe's plays a single disastrous choice or fatal turning point is difficult to discover. Even in *Doctor Faustus* he can make us feel that the tragic sequence might have gone another way. Faustus, after all, passes up one occasion to repent after another, yet retains an 'amiable soul' for most of the five Acts and twenty-four years. Like Faustus, Marlowe's other heroes are given opportunities to alter their purposes. Aeneas, his first hero, receives not one (as in Virgil) but two divine behests to leave Dido. Tamburlaine is constantly placed in situations demanding personal decision. Barabas regains his wealth before he begins his vengeance. Edward proceeds through a series of quarrels and reconciliations with his barons, his wife, and his brother.

Marlowe's merciful treatment of his characters suggests that they are obsessively self-bound. But it also implies that all are, like Faustus, potentially amiable, open, responsible, and capable of using their extraordinary freedom to change themselves. Through his mercy his characters gain much of their power to fascinate us. He brings to life, as no scholastic argument ever has, the metaphysical dilemmas of free-will. That is why the spirits of his heroes seem to survive the traps which punish and destroy their bodies. After so much mercy, which of us can fully accept harsh justice? The chorus of *Doctor Faustus* tries to teach us detachment:

> Cut is the branch that might have grown full straight,
> And burnèd is Apollo's laurel bough
> That sometime grew within this learnèd man.
> Faustus is gone. Regard his hellish fall,
> Whose fiendful fortune may exhort the wise
> Only to wonder at unlawful things,
> Whose deepness doth entice such forward wits
> To practise more than heavenly power permits.

But the warning comes too late. Marlowe has already enticed us far beyond mere wonder. He has killed his hero, then passed Apollo's green laurel on to his audience.

# Notes

## 1 INTRODUCTION

1 W. F. Smith, trans., *Rabelais*, 2nd edn (2 vols., Cambrioge, 1934), I, 273–4. Smith observes, concerning this 'Prophecy in Riddles' (p. 269, n. 1), 'This poem, with the exception of the first two and the last ten lines, is borrowed from Mellin de Saint-Gelais. It is intended as a protest against the persecution of the Protestants proceeding at that time, under pretence of describing a game of tennis, the more so because of the great pains taken both by Saint-Gelais and Rabelais to shew that the allusion throughout is to tennis.' For additional commentary on the riddle and its genre, see Mikhail Bakhtin, *Rabelais and His World*, trans. Helene Iswolsky (Cambridge, Mass., 1968), pp. 232–9, Thomas M. Greene, *Rabelais: A Study in Comic Courage* (Englewood Cliffs, New Jersey, 1970), pp. 55–8, and M. A. Screech, 'L'Évangélisme de Rabelais: Aspects de la Satire Religieuse au XVIe Siècle', *Travaux d'Humanisme et Renaissance*, 32 (1959), 64–6.

2 Biographical interpretation originates with Robert Greene's admonition to 'thou famous gracer of Tragedians' in his *Groatsworth of Wit*, Richard Baines's 'Note' about the 'Atheist Lecture', and Thomas Kyd's letter to the Lord Keeper, Sir John Puckering. The most influential of modern biographical interpreters has been Una Ellis-Fermor, whose edition *Tamburlaine the Great in Two Parts* (London, 1930), helped persuade future scholars that Marlowe was an uncommonly learned young man. Although she admired his poetry and his antinomian radicalism, Ellis-Fermor discounted his dramatic art. In *Christopher Marlowe* (London, 1927), she wrote, in reference to *Tamburlaine* and *Doctor Faustus*, 'the form tends to betray the idea rather than to elucidate it' (p. 79). Her spirit lingers on in those who stress either the power of Marlowe's lyricism or, negatively, the obsessive personal concerns which distort his craftsmanship.

3 *Marlowe: A Critical Study* (Cambridge, 1964), p. 17. The best accounts of the historical evidence are still those by C. F. Tucker Brooke, in *The Life of Marlowe and The Tragedy of Dido Queen of Carthage* (London, 1930), and by Frederick S. Boas in *Christopher Marlowe: A Biographical and Critical Study* (Oxford, 1940).

4 See, for example, Nicholas Brooke, 'Marlowe as Provocative Agent in Shakespeare's Early Plays', *Shakespeare Survey*, 14 (1961), 34–44.

5 From the epistle 'To My Most Dearely-Loved Friend Henery Reynolds Esquire, of Poets and Poesie', J. William Hebel, ed., *The Works of Michael Drayton* (5 vols., Oxford, 1931), III, 228–9.

6 Alexander B. Grosart, ed., *The Life and Complete Works in Prose and Verse of Robert Greene, M. A.* (15 vols., London, 1881–6; reprinted, New York, 1964), VII, 7–8. For an extended discussion of 'Galfridian' prophecies, including the folklore visions of Merlin which were troublesome to Elizabethan authorities because of their concern with foretelling the royal succession, see chapter 13, 'Ancient Prophecies', in Keith Thomas's *Religion and the Decline of Magic* (Penguin Books, 1973), pp. 461–514.

7 *Lives of Eminent Philosophers*, trans. R. D. Hicks, Loeb Classical Library (2 vols., London, 1958), II, 61.

8 I shall use the terms 'audience' or 'reader' when speculating about the rhetorical effects of ironic techniques; the term 'spectator' will generally be reserved for conjectures about how Marlowe's irony might affect a respondent who could actually test his senses on the performance he watches.

9 Until the revision of the Church of England calendar for 1561, this passage from Second Corinthians would have been paired as a lesson with Job 1. (The Old Testament was read through once a year, the New, three times.) The characters of *The Jew of Malta* do of course allude emphatically to Job 1, encouraging the audience to compare the Jew's partial losses with Job's total ruin. Would Marlowe's play also have reminded some listeners of St Paul's paradoxical fooling? After 1561 Job 23 replaces Job 1.

10 All Biblical references in this study are to the Geneva edition of 1560. (*The Geneva Bible: A Facsimile of the 1560 Edition*, introd. by Lloyd E. Berry [Madison, 1969]). Scholars agree that Marlowe seems to have based his Biblical allusions on this version. See G. K. Hunter, 'The Theology of Marlowe's *The Jew of Malta*', *Journal of the Warburg and Courtauld Institutes*, 27 (1964), 212, n. 5, and James H. Sims, *Dramatic Uses of Biblical Allusion in Marlowe and Shakespeare*, University of Florida Monographs, Humanities, no. 24 (Gainesville, 1966), Preface.

11 See the analysis of prophetic rhetoric in chapter 2, 'Allegory and Prophecy in the Ancient World', of Michael Murrin's *The Veil of Allegory* (Chicago, 1969), p. 21.

12 In his excellent study, *The Rhetoric of Irony* (Chicago, 1974), Wayne Booth notes, 'There is no point in quarrelling about definitions, so long as we remember that in almost all discussions of "irony" and "the ironist" we must figure out what silent modifiers, like stable or satiric or ambiguous or metaphysical, are implied' (p. 179). Booth helped me to define difficulties I had already encountered in selecting 'satiric' and 'tragic' as explicit modifiers, when he pointed out that we grow less confident of our bearings as we move from local ironies and ironies created by the speeches of characters, towards consideration of authorial tone, and of effect and world vision (pp. 148–50).

13 Perhaps the distortion of Marlowe's dramatic temper has been a consequence of the much needed emphasis on his skill as a dramatist of ideas. The work of such scholars as Douglas Cole in *Suffering and Evil in the Plays of Christopher Marlowe* (Princeton, 1962) and G. K. Hunter (see note 10) ought to have banished from Marlowe studies that restless ghost, the angry, artless young playwright. It may be unfair to expect that Cole or Hunter would have paused to explain why this ghost has lived so long in our imaginations. Here the school of Ellis-Fermor can provide invaluable assistance. Those who find Marlowe in his heroes have been attentive to what Harry Levin, following

David Masson, terms 'fervors' and 'recurrences' ('Marlowe Today', *Tulane Drama Review*, 8 [1964], 26). (This issue, devoted to Marlowe, will hereafter be cited as 'Marlowe *TDR*'.) This ear for intensities genuinely distinguished the work of Levin in *The Overreacher: A Study of Christopher Marlowe*, British ed. (London, 1954), of Paul Kocher in *Christopher Marlowe: A Study of His Thought, Learning and Character* (Chapel Hill, 1946), and of J. B. Steane. And it also marks the criticism of L. C. Knights and Wilbur Sanders, even while they insist upon Marlowe's uncontrollable obsessions ('The Strange Case of Christopher Marlowe', in *Further Explorations* [London, 1965], pp. 75–98; *The Dramatist and the Received Idea: Studies in the Plays of Marlowe and Shakespeare* [Cambridge, 1968]).

## 2 MARLOWE'S PROPHETIC STYLE

1 'Marlowe and the Actors', Marlowe *TDR*, 168.

2 Cole, p. 254.

3 *Ibid.* p. 257, p. 259. The general tendency in studies of Marlowe's irony has been to stress the boldness of his effects and the detachment they produce. To this date, the best studies have been brief: Clifford Leech's 'Marlowe's Humor', in Richard Hosley, ed., *Essays on Shakespeare and Elizabethan Drama: In Honor of Hardin Craig* (Columbia, 1962), pp. 69–81; Eugene M. Waith's 'Marlowe and the Jades of Asia', *Studies in English Literature*, 5 (1965), 229–45; Katherine Lever's 'The Image of Man in *Tamburlaine* Part I', *Philological Quarterly*, 35 (1956), 421–7; and Michael Hattaway's 'Marlowe and Brecht', in Brian Morris, ed., *Christopher Marlowe* (London, 1968), pp. 95–112. (This useful collection will hereafter be cited as *Morris*.)

4 All references to Marlowe's plays are to the one volume edition by Irving Ribner, *The Complete Plays of Christopher Marlowe* (New York, 1963). Rhetorically such questions illustrate either the figure of 'interrogatio' by which 'the Orator doth affirme or deny something strongly', or the figure of 'percontatio', by which we 'chide, and set forth our griefe with more vehem-encie'. The definition of 'interrogatio' comes from Peacham's *The Garden of Eloquence*, and the definition of 'percontatio' from Wilson's *The Arte of Rhetorique*. Both are reprinted and discussed in Sister Miriam Joseph's *Shakespeare's Use of the Arts of Language* (New York, 1947), p. 390 and p. 392.

5 I have found the most helpful discussions of relationships between conven-tions and audiences in Bernard Beckerman, *Shakespeare at the Globe 1599–1609* (New York, 1962), in S. L. Bethell, *Shakespeare and the Popular Dramatic Tradition* (London, 1945), and in Anne Righter, *Shakespeare and the Idea of the Play* (London, 1962).

6 G. Gregory Smith, ed., *Elizabethan Critical Essays* (2 vols., Oxford, 1904), I, 181.

7 *Ibid.* pp. 181–2. Wayne Booth seems to use a similar (and ancient) conception of irony when he draws upon metaphors from the 'building trades' – re-construction, location, and platform – to characterize the ideal meeting ground where readers of 'stable' irony share common assumptions revived in their minds by the ironic writer (p. 33).

8 *Elizabethan Critical Essays*, I, 182.

9 In the adage 'Ollas ostentare' ('to make a show of kitchen pots'), Erasmus says of his critics who confused him with Folly herself, 'They are not giving full weight to something which is very important in a dialogue, the fitness of the speech to the speakers...It is just as if one were to write a dialogue between a pagan and a Christian, and be told it was sacriligious to make the pagan say anything against Christian doctrine' (Margaret Mann Phillips, *The 'Adages' of Erasmus: A Study with Translations* [Cambridge, 1964], p. 356.)

10 An extended discussion of the Renaissance wisdom tradition may be found in Eugene F. Rice Jr's, *The Renaissance Idea of Wisdom* (Cambridge, Mass., 1958). Frank Manley has recognized the importance of this tradition for an understanding of Donne's *Anniversaries*. His Introduction to *John Donne: The Anniversaries* (Baltimore, 1963) provides an excellent account of the wisdom types on which the celebration of Elizabeth Drury relies (pp. 20–40).

11 Hooker justifies the inclusion of readings from books like Wisdom and Ecclesiasticus in the Church calendar, pointing out that the Church Fathers termed a number of such Old Testament books 'ecclesiastical' rather than 'canonical', reserving the term 'apocrypha' for matter *not* to be read in church. Hooker's defence of these 'ecclesiastical' books against their Puritan critics is an eloquent one: 'So little doth such their supposed faultiness in moderate men's judgment enforce the removal of them out of the house of God, that still they are judged to retain worthily those very titles of commendation, than which there cannot greater be given to writings the authors whereof are men.' Citing the Preface to Ecclesiasticus, and the book's purpose to help men live by the Law, he states: 'Their end in writing and ours in reading them is the same. The books of Judith, Toby, Baruch, Wisdom, and Ecclesiasticus, we read, as serving most unto that end. The rest we leave unto men in private' (Rev. John Keble, ed., *The Works of that Learned and Judicious Divine, Mr. Richard Hooker*, 7th edn [3 vols., Oxford, 1888], II, 82–3; hereafter cited as *Works*).

Learned fooling is a field in which the Renaissance genius for classical–Christian syncretism is practically a forced growth. To account for exact sources will, where many allusions are concerned, be as profitable as identifying Feste's Quinapalus. On the antecedents of folly, see Kenneth Walter Cameron, *The Background of John Heywood's 'Witty and Witless'* (Raleigh, 1941), Robert Hillis Goldsmith, *Wise Fools in Shakespeare* (Liverpool, 1958; reprinted, 1974), and the introductions by Hoyt Hopewell Hudson and Leonard F. Dean to their translations of *The Praise of Folly* (New York, 1941, and New York, 1946).

12 The definition cited here corresponds to the ancient Stoic definition, rediscovered and repeated by Renaissance humanists (see Rice, p. 2). Especially pertinent to Marlowe's dynamic plays is Rice's sixth chapter, which describes the 'transformation of wisdom from contemplation to action, from a body of knowledge to a collection of ethical precepts, from a virtue of the intellect to a perfection of the will' (p. 149).

13 Chapter 6 of the *Enchiridion Militis Christi* has as its heading: 'The First Point of Wisdom is to Know Yourself: Concerning Two Kinds of Wisdom: Seeming and Real' (Raymond Himelick, trans. and ed., *The Enchiridion of Erasmus* [Bloomington, 1963], p. 59). On the Christian wisdom with which *The Praise of Folly* concludes, Eugene Rice comments, 'This wisdom is no

rustic piety. It is a *sancta eruditio* rather than a *sancta rusticitas*, a *scientia* whose source is not only Scripture but the classics also. Erasmus warns his readers against those who oppose learning on the authority of Paul's *scientia inflat*, or say that immortality was promised to the innocent not to the learned, and that if you know Christ well you need know nothing else. It is ignorance, not learning which causes pride; for, like Socrates, the more a man knows the more he knows that he does not know' (p. 159).

At no point will I argue that the writings of Erasmus provided actual sources for Marlowe, but it is likely that he knew them. In a list of earlier sixteenth-century 'best-sellers' referred to by T. W. Baldwin, we find the *Colloquies*, *Enchiridion*, and *Adages*. According to Baldwin, all the volumes mentioned were grammar school texts (*William Shakspere's Small Latine & Lesse Greeke* [2 vols., Urbana, 1944], I, 103). What Baldwin describes as a 'very full list of grammar school texts, published in London in 1581' includes the *Moriae Encomium* (I, 436). The *Institutio Principis Christiani* had a place in more aristocratic education, and Baldwin mentions it in this connection. The *Adages*, *Colloquies*, *Enchiridion* and *Praise of Folly* were all translated and reprinted in England throughout the sixteenth century. Boas points out that Erasmus's New Testament in Greek and his Paraphrases were included in Archbishop Parker's divinity collection for the use of his scholars at Corpus Christi College (*Christopher Marlowe*, p. 20).

14 This allusiveness has long been recognized, but there have been few studies of its implications as a dramatic technique. I have referred, particularly in chapters 3 and 4, to a number of allusions first pointed out by Sims. Sims suggests that Marlowe used Biblical allusions to imply reversals of role, value, and meaning (p. 16). He finds no 'consistent pattern' in the allusions of *Tamburlaine* or of *Edward II*, and concentrates, therefore, on *Doctor Faustus* and *The Jew of Malta*. Most of the allusions Sims mentions are to the New Testament, and he does not attempt to relate allusiveness to other aspects of Marlowe's dramatic style.

15 Cf. Eric Rothstein, who postulates an 'unwritten but always heard counterpoint that Elizabethan culture ideally provided' ('Structure as Meaning in *The Jew of Malta*', *Journal of English and Germanic Philology*, 65 [1966], 261). Somewhat idealized assumptions about the audience may also have influenced G. K. Hunter's discussion of its role in 'Theology', pp. 211–13. According to Sims, 'The dramatists in the late sixteenth and early seventeenth centuries could be *sure* [italics mine] that their audiences would recognize and respond to Biblical allusions' (p. 8).

16 William Gillis, trans. (London, 1971), p. 3.

17 James Sanford, trans. (London, 1575), sig. Aiv v.

18 Brant, p. 4.

19 Cole has pointed out (p. 199): 'The second of the official Elizabethan sermons and homilies opened with a series of scriptural references to the sinful condition of man, among them the very one Faustus uses: "So doth blessed Saint Iohn the Euangelist, in the name of himselfe, and of al other holy men (be they neuer so iust) make this open confession: if we say we haue no sinne, we deceyue ourselues, and the truth is not in vs: If we knowledge our sinnes, God is faythfull and iust to forgiue our sinnes, and to cleanse vs from all vnrighteousness."'

20 *The Praise of Folly*, trans. Hudson, p. 96. Unless otherwise indicated, all references will be to this translation. Folly does not always warn the reader that she is quoting selectively. For example, to prove the superiority of the fool to the wise man (pp. 107–8), she quotes from Ecclesiasticus 20:30: 'Better is he that kepeth his ignorance secret, then a man that hideth his wisdome.' Given her assumption that what we hide must be more valuable than what we do not, the quotation appears to support her case. But she leaves out the context provided by verse 29 immediately preceding 'Better': 'Wisdome that is hid, and treasure that is horded vp, what profite is in the(m) bothe?' Cf. her similar treatment of Ecclesiastes 1:17, discussed by Goldsmith, p. 13.

21 See Eleanor O'Kane, 'The Proverb: Rabelais and Cervantes', *Comparative Literature*, 2 (1950), 365. DeWitt T. Starnes includes a helpful survey of how proverbs were used, as well as a bibliography, in his Introduction to the facsimile *Proverbs or Adages. By Desiderius Erasmus. Gathered Out of the Chiliades and Englished (1569) by Richard Taverner* (Gainesville, 1956).

22 All references to Shakespeare's plays are to the revised Pelican text, Alfred Harbage, ed., *William Shakespeare: The Complete Works* (Baltimore, 1969).

23 F. P. Wilson cites this passage as 'The most famous reference to a proverb in the whole of Shakespeare', and suggests that 'in his day the saying that "the cat would eat fish yet dare not wet its feet" was in such common use that he could refer to it thus obliquely' (*The Proverbial Wisdom of Shakespeare*, Presidential Address of the Modern Humanities Research Association [Cambridge, 1961], p. 3).

24 Cole, p. 92.

25 As expository devices, Marlowe's soliloquies therefore lack the quality which Dieter Mehl, considering choral figures, finds typical of the popular Elizabethan drama – the 'tendency...to make everything as clear and impressive as possible' (*The Elizabethan Dumb Show* [London, 1965], p. 12). They are impressive at the expense of being clear.

26 *The Arte of English Poesie*, in *Elizabethan Critical Essays*, II, 159–60.

27 That Marlowe's use of these praising soliloquies links him to Erasmus has not been observed. Walter Kaiser writes, 'Erasmus' book is a mock encomium – but at the same time the mocking is mocked. I know of no other mock encomium before the *Moriae encomium* that employs this subtle device, and after Erasmus only Swift successfully approximates it' (*Praisers of Folly: Erasmus, Rabelais, Shakespeare* [Cambridge, Mass., 1963], p. 37). Sister Geraldine Thompson has asked what happened to English irony after Erasmus, and has concluded that 'his imitators only partially recognized the ironic techniques he was using' (*Under Pretext of Praise: Satiric Mode in Erasmus' Fiction* [Toronto, 1973], p. 14; cf. p. 54). She comes tantalizingly close to Marlowe when she calls Nashe (Marlowe's sometime collaborator?) a 'kindred spirit' with Erasmus (p. 12) and when she states, 'late in the century there is a resurgence of dramatic irony – which indeed Erasmus' near-dramas may have helped to promote' (p. 14). Emphasis on the secular spirit of the later English Renaissance has perhaps discouraged the search for its connections with the earlier one. Cf. Enid Welsford's conclusion in *The Fool* (London, 1935), p. 242: 'Nothing could be more sharply contrasted than the fool of the sottie, and the aspiring tragic hero of Marlowe, or the self-satisfied

courtier of Spenser. Nothing could be more incompatible than the respective tempers of Erasmus in his *Praise of Folly*, and Bacon in his *Advancement of Learning.*'

28 'It is the method of Lyly's art to accumulate parallels', writes G. K. Hunter, in *John Lyly: The Humanist as Courtier* (London, 1962), p. 172. Cf. Cole's remark on the construction of *Tamburlaine* Part Two: 'Marlowe, in putting together his play from diverse sources, has again fallen back on the principle of analogy as a unifying structural force, a tendency also evident in *Dido* and *Doctor Faustus*, and firmly implanted in the English dramatic tradition of his time' (p. 116).

29 *Of the Dignity and Advancement of Learning*, in James Spedding, Robert Leslie Ellis, and Douglas Denon Heath, eds., *The Works of Sir Francis Bacon* (7 vols., London, 1858-74; reprinted, 14 vols., Stuttgart, 1963), IV, 316.

30 The modern editors of *Dido* have agreed that the play is early (1585-6). Cole has surveyed the date question and argued for an early one (n. 1, pp. 75-6). Leonora Leet Brodwin places the play among Marlowe's last works ('*Edward II*: Marlowe's Culminating Treatment of Love', *Journal of English Literary History*, 31 [1964], 139-55). Another argument for a later date, based on discovery of sophisticated staging techniques, and on close parallels with *The Spanish Tragedy* and *Soliman and Perseda*, may be found in T. M. Pearce's 'Evidence for Dating Marlowe's *Tragedy of Dido*', in Josephine W. Bennett et al., eds., *Studies in the English Renaissance Drama* (London, 1961), pp. 231-47. Obviously the argument gains in force if one accepts, with Philip Edwards, a date of around 1590 for *The Spanish Tragedy*. See Edwards's edition of this play for the Revels series (London, 1959), p. xxvii.

31 Most commentators recognize that *Dido* emphasizes psychology, not history. Boas offers a brief but excellent discussion of this emphasis (pp. 65-6). Brooks Otis has shown how Virgil used *his* gods as genuinely fatal-historical daimons, in *Virgil: A Study in Civilized Poetry* (Oxford, 1964), p. 68, pp. 79-80, p. 92.

32 Una Ellis-Fermor believes the 'supernatural apparatus' is actually played down (*Christopher Marlowe*, p. 19). For Levin, however, the induction is an 'unambiguous comment upon the sexual climate of the play' (*The Overreacher*, p. 32). Steane thinks Jupiter's perversion merely foreshadows Dido's in courting Aeneas (p. 34). Might it not as easily foreshadow Aeneas's short-term dalliance with Dido? The Revels editor, H. J. Oliver, argues that Marlowe manages to depreciate the gods without depreciating his heroes at the same time (*Dido Queen of Carthage, The Massacre at Paris* [London, 1968], p. xli). Don Cameron Allen feels that divine interference, which he takes to be genuine and powerful, reduces the characters. 'They lend their ears and then their hearts to the advice and direction of the silly hulks they have themselves created' ('Marlowe's *Dido* and the Tradition', in *Essays on Shakespeare and Elizabethan Drama*, p. 68). In their thoughtful essays, both Brian Gibbons and Brian Morris have indicated that the Induction has powerful, even ecstatic, as well as absurd qualities. See Gibbons's 'Unstable Proteus: Marlowe's *The Tragedy of Dido Queen of Carthage*', in *Morris*, pp. 45-6, and Morris's 'Comic Method in Marlowe's Hero and Leander', in *Morris*, pp. 127-8. The play's sub-plot and its conclusion have produced similar diversity in interpretation.

33 It is curious to note that after his departing mother, Venus, this unhappy hero sends a despairing cry reminiscent of that which his prototype addresses to Dido's shade in Elysium. See H. Rushton Fairclough, ed., *Aeneid*, Loeb Classical Library (2 vols., New York, 1916), I, Bk. VI, ll. 465–6.

34 *An Apology for Poetry, Elizabethan Critical Essays*, I, 180. Here Virgil's epic spirit may have been tempered by medieval tradition. Oliver correctly argues, I think, that Marlowe does not particularly emphasize the 'medieval' cowardice and weakness of his hero in the account of the fall of Troy (pp. xxxviii–xxxix). A more genuinely medieval aspect of Marlowe's play would seem to lie in the fact that Aeneas is subordinated to Dido. According to Douglas Bush, Chaucer and the writers of romance rationalized divine agency and depicted Dido as a 'faithful saint of Cupid deceived and abandoned by a treacherous man' (*Mythology and the Renaissance Tradition in English Poetry* [Minneapolis, 1932; reprinted, New York, 1957], p. 20). This conception, he adds, resembles Ovid's. The most helpful summary of the traditional growth of the story is that by Allen (pp. 55–64).

35 Where Cole maintains that 'dramaturgy insists on the ironic implications of destruction or sorrow, hidden to the characters but revealed to the audience' (p. 75), I am suggesting that, until the ending of the play, the secondary lovers may function to suspend our awareness of potential fatality by complicating the emotional predicament. They make more probable Dido's swift infatuation. Cf. W. J. Harvey on the function of the 'ficelle' character in Henry James's fiction: 'The more exceptional the experience embodied in the protagonist the greater become the problems of mimetic adequacy and hence the more important are the mediating and choric functions of the ficelle' (*Character and the Novel* [London, 1965], p. 63).

36 Ovid's Dido had also emphasized her beguilement by Venus and the thousand suitors from whom she might have chosen a husband. Otis, discussing Virgil's 'subjective style', observes that Virgil's Dido seems attracted to Aeneas before the gods intervene (p. 67) – a fact which might make us aware how far the epic had already tended to rationalize the role of the gods. Marlowe, however, *irrationalizes* his gods; he creates tragic suffering within a framework which seems almost gnostic in its cosmic triviality. For example, by moving Juno's speech of vengeful purpose from *Aeneid*, Bk. I, ll. 37–8, to Act III.ii.14–15, and making her threaten the sleeping child Ascanius, he turns her into a petty nemesis, obsessed with her personal wrongs, not with Jupiter's historical scheme for Roman grandeur.

37 *Death and Elizabethan Tragedy* (Cambridge, Mass., 1936), p. 219.

38 This is Levin's attitude in *The Overreacher*, p. 66. His biographical approach to spectacle has in effect been controverted by studies like Jocelyn Powell's which rely on iconography and pageantry to argue that Marlowe's spectacle is consistently allegorical, like that in the morality plays ('Marlowe's Spectacle', Marlowe *TDR*, 195–210).

39 Cf. Lyly's use of symbolic deities to externalize and abbreviate emotional experience. Cupid in *Sappho and Phao* anticipates Cupid–Ascanius in wanting to call Sappho his mother. But when he sits in Queen Sappho's lap, when she holds him and kisses him, it is because reason has triumphed over passion and Sappho has got Cupid away from Venus (v.ii.15, 45). (R. Warwick Bond, ed., *The Complete Works of John Lyly* [3 vols, Oxford, 1902], II, 412.) In

*Gallathea* (v.iii.42) Diana actually refuses to 'dandle' the tricky god in her lap (*Works*, 11, 467).

40 Gibbons describes the 'metamorphosis' of harsh reality into court art as primarily 'a passionate expression of Dido's wholly erotic being' (pp. 36–7). Powell treats the sequence in which Dido knots her lover's ropes and shears his sails (iv.iv) as an emblem which externalizes Dido's predicament (pp. 199–200). Like most discussions of Marlowe's spectacle, these two apparently fall just short of recognizing how his irony combines both internal and external kinds of significance.

41 *The Praise of Folly*, p. 63.

42 Bacon's definition of 'emblem' is cited from *The Advancement of Learning* (1605) by the *OED*.

43 For all the popularity of emblems in decorative art and the prevalence of the emblematic spirit in literature, England produced few emblem books and little theoretical discussion about emblems. See G. Pellegrini, 'Symbols and Significances', *Shakespeare Survey*, 17 (1964), 181.

44 Whitney's volume was published in Leyden. See his address 'To the Reader'.

45 We have to infer Marlowe's flexible, often sceptical attitude towards the sense of sight from his plays. E. H. Gombrich has shown how the passion for emblems among the Florentine neo-Platonists derived from their confidence that symbolic images, rather than words, permitted an intellectual intuition of essence; through visual symbols, they believed, one might nondiscursively 'contemplate the whole of a proposition in a flash' ('*Icones Symbolicae*: The Visual Image in Neo-Platonic Thought', *Journal of the Warburg and Courtauld Institutes*, 11 [1948], 163–92). But other emblem-makers may have relied on the eye for illustration rather than for inspiration, believing with Richard Hooker that 'That which we drink in at our ears doth not so piercingly enter, as that which the mind doth conceive by sight' (*Works*, iii, 605). Rosemary Freeman refers to this somewhat pedagogical attitude towards sight in her *English Emblem Books* (London, 1948), p. 89.

46 Cf. Angus Fletcher, who points out a connection between Merlin's glass in *The Faerie Queene*, Bk. iii and an emblem from Carolus Bovillus's *Liber de sapiente* (1511), reproduced by Rice, which shows Fortune, crowned and blindfolded, holding a wheel, and Sapientia, surrounded by sun, moon and stars, holding a mirror in which she regards herself (*The Prophetic Moment: An Essay on Spenser* [Chicago, 1971], p. 110).

## 3 WICKED FOOLS OF FORTUNE

1 The translation of Job is that of the Douai Old Testament. See note 49 for a discussion of the military metaphor in Job's phrase, and its preservation in Elizabethan Bibles.

2 *Illuminations* (London, 1970), p. 108.

3 My method of analysis has little bearing on the question of the play's chronological place in the Marlowe canon. I approach differences between this play and others in terms of genre, not the playwright's artistic growth. Therefore, while I believe the arguments of Leo Kirschbaum, supplemented by those of J. C. Maxwell on the dating of *Titus Andronicus*, imply that the play was

almost certainly written by 1589-90 (when it was imitated by *Titus Androni-cus*, according to Kirschbaum), my interpretation of the play as a dark, satiric proverb does not depend on or challenge any arguments about its exact date. (See Kirschbaum's 'Some Light on *The Jew of Malta*', *Modern Language Quarterly*, 7 [1946], 53-6, and J. C. Maxwell's introduction to the New Arden *Titus Andronicus* [London, 1953] p. xx). Because my interpretation suggests that the instability of the Jew's character and the sudden shift of the play into farce must have been deliberate, it has more relevance to another problem, the soundness of the text. For a survey of arguments against and for the reliability of this text, see David M. Bevington, *From Mankind to Marlowe: Growth of Structure in the Popular Drama of Tudor England* (Cambridge, Mass., 1962), pp. 218-19.

4 Levin recognizes that profession is a 'key-word', suggests that it expresses ambiguity either as to 'religious conviction' or 'practical employment', and applies this ambiguity to the usury question (*The Overreacher*, p. 82). See also Howard B. Babb, 'Policy in Marlowe's *Jew of Malta*', *Journal of English Literary History*, 24 (1957), 88.

5 Ellis-Fermor praises Barabas for his 'clear-sightedness'. 'At the crisis of his fortunes he is revealed as a man whose habit of thought is honest' (*Christopher Marlowe*, p. 98). Babb argues that for a time Barabas has 'stature' because, unlike the Christians, he lacks 'moral ambiguity' and has 'self-awareness' (p. 89). M. M. Mahood writes: 'As in Jonsonian comedy, the rogue who deceives everybody except himself is far more acceptable than the self-deceiving hypocrite who flatters himself that his own shady deeds are directed by the highest motives' (*Poetry and Humanism* [London, 1950], p. 78). Even G. K. Hunter implies that the Jew is superior to his enemies in his freedom from 'the cant of idealism' ('Theology', p. 231).

6 Those who have observed the corruption generally attribute it to the Jew's humour and vitality, but do not suggest that he takes in himself as well as the audience. Cf. Steane's brilliant account: 'What one quick-witted part of the head conspires with the heart to support is exactly what another morally-directed part tells the feelings to condemn. Laughter will by-pass that countering reason and carry our inner allegiances into places where we have no sober intention of their going' (p. 172).

7 Sims was the first to notice that Barabas has here planned 'to carry out his fiendish schemes in accord with his version of an injunction of Christ' (p. 22).

8 'As an over-all ironic formula here, and one that has the quality of "in-evitability", we could lay it down that "what goes forth as A returns as non-A." This is the basic pattern that places the essence of drama and dialectic in the irony of the "peripety", the strategic moment of reversal' ('Four Master Tropes', *A Grammar of Motives* [Berkeley, 1945; reprinted, 1969], p. 517).

9 R. Mark Benbow, ed., *The Longer Thou Livest and Enough Is as Good as a Feast*, Regents Renaissance Drama Series (London, 1968), ll. 1875-80. Bevington has pointed out structural similarities between these plays and *The Jew of Malta* (p. 219).

10 Coming from a morality vice or a Martin Marprelate, such ebullient chop-logic would provoke little criticism of its user. Cf. Martin's argument in 'An Epistle to the Terrible Priests' that 1) 'petty popes and petty antichrists

ought not to be maintained in any Christian commonwealth', 2) all the bishops are 'petty popes and petty antichrists', 3) bishops are therefore not to be 'tolerated in any Christian commonwealth'. See William Pierce, ed., *The Marprelate Tracts 1588, 1589* (London, 1911), p. 23. But Barabas always boasts of his wisdom. Therefore his syllogism is a self-reflexive satire, as well as a mordant thrust at the 'notorious Catholic doctrine that promises made to heretics need not be kept' (Kocher, *Christopher Marlowe*, p. 123).

11  From the John Wilson translation of 1668 (Ann Arbor, 1965), p. 124. Thomas Chaloner 'englished' this 'olde sawe' as, 'how wheras the thyng selfe wanteth, there it is best at lest to countrefaict the same' (London, 1549, sig. Qi v).

12  *Elizabethan Dramatists* (London, 1963), pp. 63–4.

13  See especially chapter 6, 'Religious Laughter' (London, 1966). Using a similar approach, Paula Neuss has shown how the audience is implicated in the sins of 'Mankind', another hero who parodies Job ('Active and Idle Language: Dramatic Images in *Mankind*', in Neville Denny, ed., *Medieval Drama* [London, 1973], pp. 41–67).

14  Steane notices that Barabas can profit from the 'simple self- (and others-) deception' of his enemy's statements (p. 180), and Kocher observes that Ferneze, although arguing seriously, 'darts in some derisive thrusts' (p. 282).

15  Cited in Joseph, p. 374.

16  Steane, p. 179.

17  'Theology', pp. 237–8.

18  Kocher suggests Proverbs 10:2 and 12:28 (*Christopher Marlowe*, p. 128); Sims refers to Isaiah 33:15–16a – 'often regarded as a Messianic prophecy' (p. 17); Hunter interprets the Jew's religious legality in light of the Geneva gloss on Romans 11 and 10:3–4, and the texts of Tobit 4:6 and Ezekiel 18:5–9 ('Theology', p. 237).

19  The Revised Standard Version is verbally closer to the Jew's profession: 'He who through faith is righteous shall live' (Galatians 3:11).

20  Sims, p. 20.

21  In particular, see the work of Hunter, Cole, Rothstein and Sims.

22  Phillips, p. 347.

23  See Hunter's discussion of the purpose of the 'Christian appropriation of Job', in 'Theology', pp. 219–20.

24  Thomas Harding, ed., *The Decades of Henry Bullinger*, the Fourth Decade, Sermon no. 1, Parker Society Publications (Cambridge, 1851), p. 53.

25  *Works*, I, 194.

26  After 1561 the Church calendar pairs Second Corinthians 11 with Job 23 rather than with Job 1, when Job is given its yearly reading. Chapter 23 powerfully expresses Job's need to find God in order to present his case, and his faith both in God and in himself. I do not suggest that Marlowe or his auditors *had* to be aware of this connection, only that they might have been. Hooker refers to the cause of the ancient practice in reading both Old and New Testament lessons as that given by both Justin Martyr and St Augustine. According to Augustine, 'What the Old Testament hath, the very same the New containeth; but that which lieth there as under a shadow, is here brought forth into the open sun. Things there prefigured, are here performed' (*Works*, II, 75).

27 Those who have regarded the early Barabas as a great and potentially tragic figure include Boas (p. 142) and Fredson Bowers, in *Elizabethan Revenge Tragedy 1587–1642* (Princeton, 1940), p. 108. Bernard Spivack writes that the Jew's stratagems 'do not belong to the tragic plot, they invade it, and move by a momentum outside the premises set up in the first part of the play' (*Shakespeare and the Allegory of Evil* [New York, 1958], p. 351). Similar antitheses appear in Muriel Bradbrook's *Themes and Conventions in Elizabethan Tragedy* (Cambridge, 1935), p. 156 and in Bevington's study ('the conflict between the intricacy of character portrayal and inherited moral structure', p. 222).

28 Alfred Harbage's comment on this opening is a strong testimony to its plausible character: 'Wealth, as the idea of it is here invoked, remains one of the Aristotelian *good things*, like health, unsicklied o'er with the pale cast of moralistic brooding' ('Innocent Barabas', Marlowe *TDR*, p. 57).

29 The translation of the epigram used here is that printed in Michel Poirier's *Christopher Marlowe* (London, 1951), pp. 48–9.

30 Irving Ribner points out that the political ideas in the Prologue are contradicted by Machiavelli himself; see 'Marlowe and Machiavelli', *Comparative Literature*, 6 (1954), p. 352. Kocher earlier argued with much more detail that these ideas owe little to Machiavelli or Gentillet: 'Marlowe's Prologue seems to be composed partly of subjective elements, partly of commonplace ideas which might possibly have been suggested by Gentillet and quite as possibly by a hundred other originals' (*Christopher Marlowe*, p. 200). A great number of such originals (in many tongues) have been drawn together by Nigel Bawcutt in order to recreate the contexts in which Machiavelli was read and Machiavel heard, in 'Machiavelli and Marlowe's *The Jew of Malta*, *Renaissance Drama*, n.s. 3 (1970), 3–49. Especially pertinent to the Prologue is Bawcutt's demonstration (p. 16 and p. 42) that a classical context was often involved. Perhaps because he continues to regard Marlowe as an *enfant terrible*, Bawcutt fails to see that the way in which Machiavel exactly inverts the views of Erasmus on the tyrant Phalaris (p. 45) could be as deliberately ironic on Marlowe's part as are inversions of Biblical passages. In *The Education of a Christian Prince* Erasmus gives as a favourite expression of tyrants, 'Let them hate, if only they fear' (p. 190). L. K. Born's long Introduction to his translation of this work (New York, 1936) refers several times to the tyrannical attitude; Caligula was said to have quoted much the same line Erasmus cites (p. 70). Born also includes references to tyranny and fear by Seneca in *De Ira* (p. 69) and Cicero in *De Officiis* (p. 65).

31 George Bull, trans. (Penguin Books, 1961), pp. 96–7.

32 'Theology', pp. 216–17.

33 *The Praise of Folly*, p. 43. References following will be included in the text.

34 It is important to remember, as Kocher points out (*Christopher Marlowe*, n. 7, p. 124) that the fruits image was very common and might come from any number of texts.

35 The texts from which later formulations of pride seem to derive are Ecclesiasticus 10:7–8 and 14–15. See Cole's summary of Augustine's views on pride, and n. 11, p. 195.

36 Rothstein, p. 267.

37 Hunter believes that the image in line 37 draws upon paradoxes used to

describe Christ within the Virgin's womb ('Theology', p. 221). If we are dealing here with a proverbial style of writing (or in Hunter's 'Empsonian terms' with 'an extended pun on the word "treasure"' (p. 220), we may expect to find many layers of meaning – all suggested by an image quite possibly too simple and familiar to create a strong ironic shock. To Hunter's examples from theological tradition one might add the observations on more secular uses of the image in John Bakeless, *The Tragicall History of Christopher Marlowe* (2 vols., Cambridge, 1942), I, 373–4.

38 *The Overreacher*, p. 88.

39 Cf. the 'Aristophanic' plot described in *Bartholomew Fair* by Ray L. Hefner: 'In each of his major plays he explores an idea or a cluster of related ideas through a variety of characters and actions. And the central expression of the unifying idea is usually not in a fully developed plot but in a fantastic comic conceit, an extravagant exaggeration of human folly, to which all of the more realistically conceived characters and incidents have reference' ('Unifying Symbols in the Comedy of Ben Jonson', in W. K. Wimsatt, ed., *English Stage Comedy* [New York, 1955], p. 75).

40 Here, perhaps for the first time in the play, the distortion becomes quite obvious. An excellent discussion of avarice as a symptom of 'Spiritual Jewishness' may be found in Cole, p. 132.

41 Cited by Born, p. 19. The principle that *summum jus* may be equivalent to *summa injuria* is applied to the question of capital punishment in Sir Thomas More's *Utopia* (H. V. S. Ogden, trans., [New York, 1949], p. 12). Taverner translates the adage 'Summum ius, summa inuria'.

42 *The Prince*, pp. 65–6.

43 *Ibid.* p. 61. Ribner cites passages from *The Discourses* which make the same point ('Marlowe and Machiavelli', p. 353).

44 Machiavelli warns against these two policies in chapter 3 of *The Prince*.

45 Pp. 50–1. Glynne Wickham emphasizes the simplicity of Marlowe's stage and the speed of his style: 'Speed of delivery and action coupled with a firm grasp of rhythm are essential prerequisites for any realization of the effects aimed at. These go hand in hand with an emblematic stage that is simple enough to allow swift-moving action while still being supplied with scenic devices sufficient to identify each shift of locality for the spectator' ('*Exeunt to the Cave*: Notes on the Staging of Marlowe's Plays', Marlowe *TDR*, p. 194).

46 Productions may create this detachment by turning the play into a steel glass. See James L. Smith's account of how the Royal Shakespeare Company (1964) extended the mechanism of the sick joke to all the elements of the play, so that the 'audience accepted the play as a "black comedy" and untroubled by embarrassing uncertainties of *genre* were free to concentrate wholly on Marlowe's dramatic purpose' – which, according to the drama critics, was 'a vicious attack on the entire Establishment, satirising "the materialistic attitude of Christians and Turks, as well as Jews"' ('*The Jew of Malta* in the Theatre', *Morris*, p. 18).

47 Rothstein suggests that the play was anti-Catholic in its topicality and mentions the Babington plotters in connection with religious duplicity and self-inflicted punishment (p. 267).

48 Cole, p. 143.

49 A reader trained up on the King James Bible could scarcely be expected to recognize this image as an allusion. The King James version is: 'Is there not an appointed time to man upon earth? are not his days also like the days of an hireling?' It follows closely the Geneva version: 'Is there not an appointed time to man vpon earth? and *are not* his dayes as the dayes of an hyreling?' The Bishops Bible has 'hired servant'. The Vulgate is: 'Militia est vita hominis super terram: et sicut dies mercenarii, dies eius.'

50 P. 38.

51 H. D. Purcell suggests that in writing the *Jew*, Marlowe may have used Whetstone's *English Myrror*, which links the Magus and Machiavelli as 'the archetypes of self-destructive atheism' ('Whetstone's "English Myrror" and Marlowe's "Jew of Malta"', *Notes and Queries*, 211 [1966], 290). The *Myrror* was probably a source for *Tamburlaine*. In 'Marlowe, Faustus, and Simon Magus', *Publications of the Modern Language Association*, 54 (1939), 104, Beatrice D. Brown points out that Marlowe could have found an account of Simon modelled on the Acts of Peter in Caxton's *Golden Legend*, and that he could have read the account in the Latin Clementine *Recognitions* as well.

52 *Works*, III, 602.

53 Craig R. Thompson, trans., *The Colloquies of Erasmus* (Chicago, 1961), pp. 60–1.

54 In this rapid survey of densities, I am again indebted to Hunter's discussion of the Biblical contexts (Romans 4 and 9, and Galatians 3) in which Marlowe's 'promise' theme might be understood. He refers to Luther's ('patristic') idea that 'Jews were represented in the Abraham story by the figure of Ishmael, and the Christians by Isaac' ('Theology', n. 22, p. 217), but does not apply the idea to the actual 'children' of Barabas. Rothstein links Abigail to Isaac and sees Ithamore as her 'viler counterpart', but does not show how carefully Marlowe has structured their dramatic destinies as an ironic fulfilment of the 'promise'.

55 See Levin's *The Overreacher*, p. 98, Hunter's 'Theology', p. 233, Cole, p. 129. Kocher has pointed to an instance of poisoning a household with porridge as the basis of the 1530 treason law prescribing death by boiling for poisoners ('English Legal History in Marlowe's *Jew of Malta*', *Huntingdon Library Quarterly*, 26[1962–3], 155–63).

56 *Enchiridion*, p. 109.

57 'For as golde & siluer are tryed in the fyre, euen so are men acceptable in the fornace of aduersitie' (Ecclesiasticus 2:5). The just man proves to be gold (Wisdom 3:6, Job 23:10). In Ecclesiasticus, folly, the opposite of justice or piety, is signified by lead; 'What is heauier then lead? and what other name shulde a foole haue?' (22:14). That Marlowe is making an ironic use of this symbolism is suggested when Barabas calls his Jewish brethren earth-mettled, for submitting so 'basely' to Ferneze, or simple for thinking him a 'senseless lump of clay' (I.ii.217). In *Edward II* Gaveston will term his beef-eating enemies 'base leaden earls'. Cf. the Jew's boasting about his wealth at IV.i.65–9 and the metaphors of a treasure house or storage space used to describe wisdom in Proverbs 24:3–4 and Ecclesiasticus 1:21 and 31.

58 See Mary Mellen Wehling, 'Marlowe's Mnemonic Nominology with Especial Reference to *Tamburlaine*', *Modern Language Notes*, 73 (1958), 244.

59 P. 108.

## 4 THE TRAGIC FOLLY OF DR FAUSTUS

1 Mahood, p. 74.

2 Cf. Levin: 'The playwright not only takes part in the scholar's blasphemy, but also seems to enjoy his anathema' ('Marlowe Today', p. 28). In his earlier *Overreacher* he also finds Marlowe to be a poetic diabolist (p. 158). The most determined advocate for a diabolic interpretation of the play, on the grounds that Hell's voice, not Heaven's, carries conviction, is Nicholas Brooke, 'The Moral Tragedy of Doctor Faustus', *Cambridge Journal*, 5 (1952), 662–87. J. P. Brockbank's well-balanced exposition of the play's heroic and moralistic qualities concludes by suggesting that the heroism provides a criticism of the Augustinian morality (*Marlowe: Dr. Faustus*, Studies in English Literature, 6 [London, 1962], pp. 59–60).

3 Douglas Cole bases his study of the play on Augustine's theology, and his chapter contains much helpful information on the psychology of sin, temptation, and despair, which he buttresses with references to theologians of Marlowe's time.

4 Two studies which attempt to relate *Doctor Faustus* to an anti-intellectual tradition deriving from Augustine are James Smith's 'Marlowe's "Doctor Faustus"', *Scrutiny*, 8 (1939), 36–55, and Arpad Steiner's 'The Faust Legend and the Christian Tradition', *Publications of the Modern Language Association*, 54 (1939), 391–404.

5 Lynette and Eveline Feasey have recognized the allusion in Tamburlaine's praise of Zenocrate at III.iii.117 of Part I, immediately before his battle with Bajazeth ('Marlowe and the Christian Humanists', *Notes and Queries*, 196 [1951], 266–8). For a discussion of its significance in *Doctor Faustus*, see pp. 73–4 and notes.

6 I have relied here on the distinctions made by Rice in chapters 5 and 6 of *The Renaissance Idea of Wisdom*. The only attempt to study this play in terms of wisdom has been Michael Hattaway's 'The Theology of Marlowe's *Doctor Faustus*', *Renaissance Drama* 3 (1970), 51–78. Hattaway stresses doctrine, not dramatic effect, and the unworldly, even 'self-destructive' quality of the learned tradition implied by the play.

7 Nashe's query appears appropriately in the well-known passage on superficially learned writers who 'busie themselues with the indeours of Art' (*Elizabethan Critical Essays*, I, 311–12).

8 *Works*, III, 541.

9 I have been influenced by Harry C. Porter's discussion of the predestination controversy in *Reformation and Reaction in Tudor Cambridge* (Cambridge, 1958). Porter's excellent study portrays the intellectual ferment of Marlowe's Cambridge. It contains much evidence suggesting that 'the story of the theology of the Elizabethan Church of England was that of a debate, and not of an unchallenged Calvinist oration' (p. 287). I cannot agree with Pauline Honderich's conclusion that, for all the tension between Calvinist and moderate Anglican positions, the play supports the hero's own Calvinist attitude ('John Calvin and Doctor Faustus', *Modern Language Review*, 68 [1973], 1–13). Even the latitudinarian Hooker cautioned against the 'lewd collections' made on Paul's teaching that the greater is our misery over sin, the greater is God's mercy (*Works*, III, 545). Some of Faustus's sins are those

which Hooker puts into his third and worst category – namely 'infidelity, extreme despair, hatred of God and all goodness, obduration in sin'. From these, he believes, 'God shall preserve the righteous, as the apple of his eye, forever', and he argues that the truly justified may never fall so far as to deny the foundation of the Christian faith – that Christ is the only saviour of the world (*Works*, III, 519, 516).

My reading should not invalidate the conclusions of many scholars who have found in Faustus himself a bound or perverted will. But I hope it will suggest Marlowe's distance from those Reformation theologians who, in Levin's words, 'had made contrition so difficult that at times it seemed virtually unattainable' (*The Overreacher*, p. 156).

10 Two studies which emphasize analogues for this decline in established moral or doctrinal patterns are G. K. Hunter's argument for a 'Five-Act Structure in *Doctor Faustus*', Marlowe *TDR*, pp. 77–91, based on the interdependence of types of learning and the hierarchy into which they fall, and Gerald H. Cox's 'Marlowe's *Doctor Faustus* and "Sin against the Holy Ghost"', *Huntingdon Library Quarterly*, 36 (1972–3), 119–37, which uses sequential temptations from catechisms and the six sins of Matthew 12:31–2. My approach is closer to that of Brockbank, pp. 29–30.

11 Cited by Manley in his edition of the *Anniversaries*, p. 123.

12 (Madison, 1963), p. 85.

13 See Cole's exposition of Augustinian theory, p. 195, and Helen Gardner, 'Milton's "Satan" and the Theme of Damnation in Elizabethan Tragedy', *Essays and Studies*, n.s.1 (1948), 48–9.

14 Aquinas, cited by Manley, p. 37. The preceding discussion of will is indebted to Manley's concise exposition of the three parts of the rational soul – mind, understanding, and will – as formulated by Augustine in *De Trinitate* (pp. 41–2).

15 John Frederick Nims, ed., *Ovid's Metamorphoses: The Arthur Golding Translation, 1567* (New York, 1965), Bk. VIII, 1. 291, 1. 299. References to this edition will be included in the text.

16 Robert Krueger, ed., *The Poems of Sir John Davies* (Oxford, 1975), p. 7.

17 This is perhaps one source of the tension which David Bevington finds between 'moral structure and secular content' (p. 261).

18 In 'Dr Faustus and Renaissance Learning', *Modern Language Review*, 51 (1956), 9–10, Joseph T. McCullen points out that like Ralegh and Bacon, Faustus questions the method of learning, but that he also discards its ends, which were to find truth – and then uses the rejected logic to dismiss divinity. Hattaway has neatly placed Faustus's Ramist definition of logic, 'Bene disserere est finis logices', in a context of opinion identifying Ramus with superficial scholarship. ('The Theology of Marlowe's *Doctor Faustus*', pp. 55–6.)

19 Cole, p. 199.

20 The second omission was earlier noted by Helen Gardner, in 'Milton's "Satan"', n. 2, p. 49; Virgil Whitaker briefly discusses both of them in *Shakespeare's Use of Learning: An Inquiry into the Growth of His Mind and Art* (San Marino, 1953), p. 242.

21 Hunter writes, 'The fallacy of the argument here needs no subtle doctor to expose it; I suspect that most Elizabethans would have recognized it'

('Theology', p. 212). The responses of interpreters who are sensitive to logical and theological distortions suggests, however, that at this point in the play the audience might have been disposed to take Faustus seriously – and sympathetically. Cf. Gardner: 'Divinity, which he comes to last, holds the greatest disappointment: it is grounded in the recognition of man's mortality and his fallibility' ('Milton's "Satan"', p. 49). Cole views Faustus as a desperate reprobate (p. 200). And Mahood, who regards the entire play as an intense and gloomy tragedy of Promethean humanism, believes that the syllogism was motivated by spiritual despondency (p. 67).

22 There is a parallel to (and perhaps a conscious imitation of) Faustus's attitude in that of Carew Ralegh, brother of Sir Walter, during the dinner party (summer, 1593) later scrutinized by the Cerne Abbas investigators. '"Some loose speeches of Mr. Carew Ralegh's being gently reproved by Sir Ralph Horsey", Carew inquired of the preacher Ironside what danger he might incur by such speeches. He scoffed at the reply, that "the wages of sin is death", since death is the common lot of sinner and saint; but Ironside answered further, "That death which is properly the wages of sin, is death eternal, both of the body and of the soul also." "Soul", asked Carew Ralegh, "What is that?" And Ironside remarked that knowledge of how the soul was to be saved was preferable to close inquiry into its essence.' Ernest Strathmann, who refers to this incident in *Sir Walter Ralegh: A Study in Elizabethan Skepticism* (New York, 1951), p. 47, observes that Carew 'may have been deliberately baiting his companion.' With Faustus, however, ignorance is no mere pretence.

23 The folly of Faustus has been recognized, but has not been used for an interpretation of the whole play. See Brockbank, p. 29; J. C. Maxwell, 'Two Notes on Marlowe's "Faustus"', *Notes and Queries*, 194 (1949), 334–5; John M. Steadman, 'Averroes and Dr. Faustus: Some Additional Parallels', *Notes and Queries*, 207 (1962), 327–9; James L. Smith, 'Marlowe's "Doctor Faustus"', pp. 54–5; Cyrus Hoy, '"Ignorance in Knowledge": Marlowe's Faustus and Ford's Giovanni', *Modern Philology*, 57 (1960), 145–54. A. L. French gives an extended, often keen account of Faustus's stupidity in 'The Philosophy of *Dr. Faustus*', *Essays in Criticism* 20 (1970), 123–42. Unfortunately he identifies Faustus with Marlowe and fails to observe the hero's change by Act v.

24 Sims, p. 24.

25 *The Praise of Folly*, p. 83. Further references will be included in the text. Agrippa, linked by Sidney with Erasmus, seems to have written his own maddening anatomy of abused learning in order to confound proud philosophers who held simple Scripture 'in greate contempte' (sig. Aiv r). Especially pertinent to *Doctor Faustus* are his arguments that all science is only as good as those who use it (chapter 1) and his criticism 'Of Sophistrie' (chapter 8).

26 *The Enchiridion of Erasmus*. Further references will be included in the text. The fact that the *Enchiridion* should also provide a number of analogues for Faustus's activities is less surprising when we recall that Erasmus, in his often-cited letter to Martin Dorp, treated *The Praise of Folly* as an ironic presentation of the same ideas he had discussed in his other works. 'Nec aliud agitur in Moria sub specie lusus quam actum est in Enchiridio'

(P. S. and H. M. Allen, eds., *Opus Epistolarum*, [12 vols. Oxford, 1910], II, 93).

27 See note 18 and Hunter's 'Five-Act Structure in Doctor Faustus', p. 82. In his edition for the Revels series John D. Jump has compared the survey of the professions in *Doctor Faustus* to that in *Euphues* (*Doctor Faustus* [London, 1962], notes, p. 6). The comparison is an apt one, for Euphues is also witty but unwise. Jump also notes that the two 'medical' quotations which follow 'Galen come' are still from Aristotle, while the Greek reference, in 'Bid *On cay mae on* farewell', is from Plato's *Gorgias* (p. 7). French sees a revealing confusion here; Faustus says 'farewell' to being and metaphysics, when he should have said farewell to logic and analytics (p. 128). The *Gorgias*, to be sure, is much concerned with the sophistical abuse of rhetoric.

28 For Rabelais, see Bk. III, chapter 29, 'How Pantagruel made a Convocation of a Theologian, a Physician, a Lawyer and a Philosopher, to give Opinion on the Perplexity of Panurge', and chapters following. By approaching witch-craft as one of those mechanizations of spirit traditionally attacked by anti-scholastic satirists, Marlowe anticipated H. R. Trevor-Roper's rationalistic explanation: 'The growth of belief in witchcraft is a by-product, in specific social circumstances, of that hardening and extension of Aristotelianism (or rather, of the pseudo-Aristotelianism of the Schoolmen) which had begun in the later Middle Ages and was intensified both by Catholics and Protestants after the Reformation' (*The European Witch-Craze of the 16th and 17th Centuries* [Penguin Books, 1969], p. 8).

29 Here my argument coincides with that of T. McAlindon in 'Classical Mythology and Christian Tradition in Marlowe's *Doctor Faustus*', *Publications of the Modern Language Association*, 81 (1966), 220.

30 Sims, p. 20. He also refers us to Philippians 3:19. The same allusion occurs in Beza's second sermon on the first chapter of the Song of Songs, when he is attempting to distinguish members of the true church (the Bride) who forget themselves in love of Christ (the Bridegroom) from self-interested world-lings: 'Nether are those they whose god is their belly, & who desire nothing els but to be kissing the cup: neither the covetous, which desire onely to be kissing of their gold, & their siluer' (John Harman, trans., *Master Bezaes Sermons Upon The Three First Chapters Of The Canticle of Canticles* [Oxford, 1587], p. 24).

31 The passage immediately precedes Panurge's famous praise of debtors and borrowers in Bk. III, chapter 3.

32 Sims, p. 25.

33 *Elizabethan Critical Essays*, I, 181.

34 These attitudes were judged characteristic of those who sin against the Holy Ghost. See Cole, p. 218, and Gardner, 'Milton's "Satan"', p. 50. As Mahood has put it so well, 'The cave of Despair lies at no great distance from the castle of Orgoglio' (p. 66).

35 Interpretations which stress the sinful desperation of Faustus at this point have failed to appreciate the small but still important extent to which he is capable of learning and change. See Lily B. Campbell, '*Doctor Faustus*: A Case of Conscience', *Publications of the Modern Language Association*, 67 (1952), 219–39, and Arieh Sachs, 'The Religious Despair of Doctor Faustus' *Journal of English and Germanic Philology*, 63 (1964), 625–47.

36 'Nashe's Authorship of the Prose Scenes in *Faustus*', *Modern Language Quarterly*, 3 (1942), 17–40.

37 Quoted from Anton C. Pegis, ed., *Basic Writings of St. Thomas Aquinas* (2 vols., New York, 1944), I, 1053.

38 Philip Mason Palmer and Robert Pattison More, *The Sources of the Faust Tradition from Simon Magus to Lessing* (New York, 1936), p. 195.

39 'The Damnation of Faustus', *Modern Language Review*, 41 (1946), 97–107. T. W. Craik finds Greg's 'demoniality' too literal and material a sin for a play dominated by the spiritual sins of pride and despair. See 'Faustus' Damnation Reconsidered', *Renaissance Drama*, n.s. 2 (1969), 189–96. But since it is in the hero's character to err by choosing the letter over the spirit, demoniality could be a particularly appropriate sin. Because of the fact that the play often suggests folly through an ironic use of 'oral' images, Greg's 'demonic' kiss may actually parody the kiss of genuine wisdom glossed by commentators on the Song of Songs.

40 See chapter 3, note 51, for Marlowe's familiarity with the Magus legend. Palmer and More reprint from the Clementine account of Magus the passage in which he places himself above the Creator and says that his mistress, Luna, is wisdom brought down from the heavens (p. 15). Hans Jonas speaks for the modern audience, but probably not for Marlowe's when he writes, 'Surely few admirers of Marlowe's and Goethe's plays have an inkling that their hero is the descendant of a gnostic sectary, and that the beautiful Helen called up by his art was once the fallen Thought of God through whose raising mankind was to be saved' (*The Gnostic Religion* [Boston, 1958], p. 111).

41 See the discussion in Manley's edition of the *Anniversaries*, p. 36. In a more recent article focused on the tragic ambiguity of Faustus as a man/spirit, Manley writes of the devil who appears in woman's dress: 'Like Helen of Troy, whom she prefigures, she is an inversion of the traditional image of wisdom, which has its modern counterpart in Jung's concept of the *anima*' ('The Nature of Faustus', *Modern Philology*, 66 [1968–9], 218–31). Manley, it seems to me, clarifies the *difference* between genuine wisdom-figures and Jung's *anima* when he writes, in his 'Introduction' to the *Anniversaries*, that such figures symbolize 'both the object and the wit: the realization as well as the means to realize it' (p. 19).

42 Manley, *Anniversaries*, p. 18, p. 36.

43 Palmer and More, p. 151.

44 *Basic Writings*, I, 596.

45 Rosalie Colie refers to the fate of this originally sophist paradox – the praise of a notoriously bad woman – in *Paradoxia Epidemica : The Renaissance Tradition of Paradox* (Princeton, 1966), on pp. 3, 8–9, and 278.

46 Luther charted the course of the man wise according to nature down into that ultimate spiritual blindness which was the destiny of knowledge without faith: 'Here empty of all truth, he wanders foolishly in darkness. The result is error toward God and his final perdition. Deep in sin and idolatry he worships no real God, but a foul creation of his own – Jupiter or some other. He has relinquished God and is now drawn into every devilish wickedness.' (Paraphrased by Rice, pp. 137–8.)

47 'The Rehabilitation of Faustus', from *Three Philosophical Poets: Lucretius, Dante, and Goethe* (Cambridge, Mass., 1910), reprinted in Willard Farnham,

ed., *Twentieth Century Interpretations of Doctor Faustus* (Englewood Cliffs, 1969), p. 13.

48 *Works*, III, 515. References following are included in the text.

49 *The Overreacher*, p. 157. As Helen Gardner points out, 'It is to Lucifer he prays' because 'it is the power of Lucifer and the bond with Lucifer which he really believes in' ('Milton's "Satan"', p. 50).

50 Brockbank, p. 57.

51 For another source of the hero's desire to die as a beast without a soul, see the *Faustbook*, Palmer and More, p. 224.

52 *The Vision of Tragedy* (New Haven, 1959), p. 66.


## 5 MIRRORS FOR FOOLISH PRINCES

1 'François Hotman and Marlowe's *The Massacre at Paris*', *Publications of the Modern Language Association*, 56 (1941), 349–68; 'Contemporary Pamphlet Backgrounds for Marlowe's *The Massacre at Paris*', *Modern Language Quarterly*, 8 (1947), 151–73; 309–18.

2 Steane, pp. 245–6.

3 When religious satirists contemporary with Marlowe 'spoke foolishly' to their audiences by adopting a pose, their deception seems to have been almost transparent. Cf. Richard Harvey's attack on the style of Martin Marprelate: 'Bot there remayneth yet a monstrous and a craftie anti-Christian practisser, not already touched to the quick, one and his mate compounded of many contraries, to breede the vulgar confusion in simple vulgar wits, who like *Pasauantius* is content to be ridiculous himself, so that his enuie in any sort make poore *Lysetus* contemptible.' (Cited by William Pierce in *An Historical Introduction to the Marprelate Tracts* [London, 1908], p. 240. Cf. p. 264.) In *The Beehive of the Romishe Church* by 'Aldegonde' (the seigneurial name of Filipe van Marnix), a long satire against Catholicism translated from the Dutch and dedicated to Sidney in 1579, the fictive author, a Flemish Franciscan, condemns himself and his cause through his attempt to confute Protestant beliefs by means of outrageous superstitions.

4 Kocher considers the blackening of the Guise and other characters in both of his studies. See also Cole, p. 150 and H. J. Oliver, ed., *Dido Queen of Carthage, The Massacre at Paris*, p. lxvii.

5 See especially *The Education of a Christian Prince*, p. 163, and the adages 'Sileni Alcibiadis' and 'Dulce bellum inexpertis' (Phillips, p. 280 and p. 321). The most relevant colloquies are 'The Shipwreck', 'A Fish Diet', 'Charon', and 'Cyclops, or The Gospel Bearer'.

6 For the background of this dialogue, see the Introduction by J. Kelley Sowards to *The Julius exclusus of Erasmus*, Paul Pascal, trans. (Bloomington, 1968).

7 Cole, p. 145. The indications that the play is a memorial reconstruction have been discussed at length by Oliver, p. lii. See also the Malone Society Reprint (Oxford, 1928), pp. ix–x, and the Introduction by H. S. Bennett to the Case edition of *The Jew of Malta and The Massacre at Paris* (London, 1931), pp. 173–4. The only critic who has argued with much enthusiasm for the play's stylistic integrity is Michael Hattaway in 'Marlowe and Brecht', pp. 103–4.

8 Sanders, p. 23, pp. 33–4.

9 Cole treats the Guise as a focus for 'furious indignation' and a symbol for a more personal evil than Barabas represents (p. 154). Kocher also suggests that Marlowe orders his material so as to group other characters around the Guise ('François Hotman', p. 368).

10 See Kocher, 'Contemporary Pamphlet Backgrounds', p. 155, and Oliver, p. lxxi.

11 *Rabelais*, I, 244.

12 *The Prince*, p. 90.

13 P. 203.

14 Phillips, pp. 229–63. Erasmus assimilates the classic proverb to his political philosophy; he ignores the eagle's common function in Christian iconography as a symbol of the resurrection, Christ, justice, or 'the virtues of courage, faith and contemplation'. He and Marlowe seem to choose instead the more unusual signification of the eagle as a 'demon who ravishes souls, or the sins of pride and worldly power'. See George Ferguson, *Signs and Symbols in Christian Art* (New York, 1954), p. 17.

15 Phillips, p. 243.

16 Oliver, who recognizes a resemblance between Navarre and Ferneze, suggests that the ironies in Ferneze's case might not strike an Elizabethan audience as they do us. He implies that Ferneze's righteousness is only a failing in modern eyes, and compares him with Cromwell, who 'was neither hypocritical nor irreligious when he gave his famous advice to trust in God and keep your powder dry' (p. lxv).

17 See Kocher, 'Contemporary Pamphlet Backgrounds', p. 167 and p. 170, where it is suggested that Marlowe retains Navarre's motive of self-preservation from Protestant accounts, and draws in others which anticipate the civil wars of 1585. Charles actually died in 1574, Navarre escaped from custody in Paris in 1576.

18 *Ibid.* 167–73.

19 *Christopher Marlowe*, p. 136.

20 Kocher shows that the Protestant pamphleteers believed the councillors to be in sympathy with the Guise's League ('Contemporary Pamphlet Backgrounds', p. 172).

21 P. 95.

22 Oliver notes the 'poetic justice' of the King's death, but implies that there might have been a 'repentence' in the 'full version' (p. lxxi).

23 F. S. Boas refers to Marlowe's 'snap-shot' method of handling the massacre, (p. 159). Oliver finds the technique of the massacre scenes 'sophisticated' (p. lxxiii).

24 Marlowe could have seen in Hotman the exact details of costume and procedure, along with the Guise's responsibility for them. See Kocher, 'François Hotman', pp. 356–7. The discrepancy at this point between attire and action seems to be Marlowe's independent emphasis.

25 The translation of Hotman's account recalls Marlowe's association of vision and conceit in *Doctor Faustus* and *Tamburlaine* when it describes Queen Catherine's desire to see the body hung on the common gallows outside Paris: 'The Queene mother', it says, 'to feede hir eyes with that spectacle, had a mind also to go thither' (Kocher, 'François Hotman', p. 361).

26 Phillips, pp. 339–40.

27 Kocher's quotation from Hotman indicates that the Admiral was shot when coming from a council meeting ('François Hotman', p. 353). Marlowe had historical warrant for the bride's separate mass, and for the theatrical murder of the Guise, but appears to have exaggerated conjunctions of ceremony and violence suggested by his sources.

28 Oliver treats the similar line, 'Yet Caesar shall go forth' (l. 67), as an example of corruption through memorial reconstruction (p. lvii).

29 'How Thrasonical the beast is acting', remarks the 'Genius' (p. 52) who has accompanied Pope Julius upon his vain expedition to the gates of Heaven. Sowards's Introduction to the satire cites a well-known epigram by Erasmus which compares Pope Julius to Caesar, harrier of the Gauls (pp. 18–19). There was apparently no sixteenth-century translation of this work into English, but its treatment of the proud pope suggests that the boasting Caesar alluded to in *As You Like It* (v.ii.34) may have been a familiar figure. He seems as likely a prototype for the Guise as does the opportunistic Caesar of Lucan's *Pharsalia* mentioned by Oliver (p. lxxi) and by D. J. Palmer ('Marlowe's Naturalism', *Morris*, p. 161).

30 P. 95.

31 Kocher, 'Contemporary Pamphlet Backgrounds', pp. 155–7.

32 Kocher notes that there were no 'exact' originals for the killing of the group of Huguenots or for the swimmers in the Seine who are shot at ('François Hotman', p. 363).

33 *Ibid.* p. 360, n. 26.

34 Pp. 54–5.

35 *The Colloquies of Erasmus*, pp. 388–94.

## 6 MERLIN'S PROPHECIES

1 P. 257.

2 See *Elizabethan Critical Essays*, I, 168 and 170. As a dramatic historian, Marlowe seems to have made much of his captivity, consulting, as Una Ellis-Fermor has shown, in *Tamburlaine the Great in Two Parts*, a number of sources. To the list of works provided by Ellis-Fermor and by Bakeless have been added Whetstone's *English Myrror* (which would eliminate whole chains of earlier source material) and Foxes's *Acts and Monuments*.

3 See Spencer, p. 223. A 'sensational' tragedy would be like that which Minturno defined: 'Whoever suffers a marvelous thing, if it is horrifying or causes compassion, will not be outside the scope of tragedy, whether he be good or whether he be evil.' (Quoted in Allan H. Gilbert, ed., *Literary Criticism, Plato to Dryden* [New York, 1940], p. 293.)

4 In *The Herculean Hero in Marlowe, Chapman, Shakespeare and Dryden* (London, 1962).

5 *Ibid.* p. 86.

6 *Ibid.* p. 63. For Waith, Marlowe's attitude is constant because it is defined by the tensions inherent in the paradox of the Herculean hero. Robert Kimbrough has reached a similar conclusion about the playwright by reasoning that although the picture of ambition in Part One is 'perfectly in keeping with sixteenth century moral thought', Marlowe leaves the audience free either to admire or hate Tamburlaine ('*1 Tamburlaine*: A Speaking Picture in a Tragic Glass', *Renaissance Drama*, 7 [1964], 31).

7 This anatomical tendency is especially marked in Part Two. As Clifford Leech has observed, 'For the most part we are not even sure where Tamburlaine is' ('The Structure of *Tamburlaine*', Marlowe *TDR*, p. 42). Ever since Dame Helen Gardner effectively challenged Ellis-Fermor's argument that Part Two is 'journeyman work', patched together after Marlowe had exhausted both sources and interest ('The Second Part of "Tamburlaine the Great"', *Modern Language Review*, 37 [1942], 18–24), it has been customary to regard Part Two as a deepening and complication of themes at least foreshadowed by Part One.

8 Cf. Gardner's argument concerning *Paradise Lost* that acts which bear their own significance impress us more strongly than do acts which stand for a significance. Satan's rebellion against God has a dramatic quality lacking in the disobedience of Adam and Eve, whose action is momentous *only* in symbolic terms ('Milton's "Satan"', pp. 60–1). Frances Yates has suggested the sense in which it is possible to separate the image and the idea of an emblem; the image in genuine allegory cannot be taken at its 'face value' – or at least, not for long – but the visual counterpart of an emblem can ('The Emblematic Conceit in Giordano Bruno's *De Gli Eroici Furori* and in the Elizabethan Sonnet Sequences', *Journal of the Warburg and Courtauld Institutes*, 6 [1943], 104). Writers like Bruno who employed emblems, as well as theorists who discussed them, seem to have been aware of this problem. See note 49.

9 From 'Dulce bellum inexpertis', Phillips, p. 330.

10 The writings of Euhemerus, as used by the Church Fathers, preserved the old gods and gave them dignity as benefactors and heroes. According to Jean Seznec, the career of Alexander and the deification of Seleucids and Ptolemies prepared many to believe that 'les dieux traditionnels étaient simplement des souverains que la gratitude – ou l'adulation – de leur sujets avaient élevés jusqu'aux cieux' (*La Survivance des Dieux Antiques* [London, 1940], p. 14). In the first chapter *Of the Trewnes of the Christian Religion*, Philip de Mornay mentions the view of the ancient 'atheist', 'Ewhemere of Tegea', as one which is acceptable to Christians (Albert Feuillerat, ed., *The Prose Works of Sir Philip Sidney* [4 vols., Cambridge, 1912; reprinted, 1962], III, 214–15.

11 While it is true that Marlowe's debates and sceptical models provide an 'intellectual challenge' (Hattaway, 'Marlowe and Brecht', p. 100), it is also true that his debates, like his 'praises of folly', inhibit detachment.

12 On the connection between Tamburlaine's control of fortune and the Machiavellian ideal, see Ribner's 'Marlowe and Machiavelli', p. 354, and Roy W. Battenhouse's *Marlowe's Tamburlaine: A Study in Renaissance Moral Philosophy* (Nashville, 1941), p. 209.

13 *Works*, III, 515.

14 W. K. Clay, ed., *Liturgies and Occasional Forms of Prayer Set Forth in the Reign of Queen Elizabeth*, Parker Society Publications (Cambridge, 1847), p. 523. The following exhortation to the English from John Aylmer's *Harborowe* (1559), a book widely advertised through its criticism by Martin Marprelate in the *Epitome* of October 1588, comes still closer in tone to Marlowe's prayers: 'Think not that God will suffer you to be foyled at their handes, for your fall is hys dishonour; if you lose the victory, he must lose the glory' (*The Marprelate Tracts, 1588, 1589*, pp. 133–4, n. 2).

15 As does Montaigne: 'This I have seen with my own eyes, that in public disorders men stunned by their fate will throw themselves back, as on any superstition, on seeking in the heavens the ancient causes and threats of their misfortune' ('Of Prognostications', in Donald M. Frame, trans., *The Complete Essays of Montaigne* [Stanford, 1958], p. 29).

16 'The Sceptic', *The Works of Sir Walter Ralegh, Kt.* (8 vols., Oxford, 1829), VIII, 554. Although Ellis-Fermor seems convinced of Marlowe's Satanism in *Doctor Faustus: The Frontiers of Drama* [London, 1945], pp. 141–3, she earlier stressed his intolerance of 'spiritual crimes' ('counterfeits, superstitions, traditional obscurities') his belief in a God of spirit, and his kinship with Ralegh (*Christopher Marlowe*, p. 156).

17 Cole points out in his speech 'a mingling of concepts connected with the Christian hell: chiefly, the privation of God and the eternity of a hopeless existence' (p. 96).

18 L. C. Knights, concerned with Marlowe's psychic urges rather than with his dramatic skill, nevertheless is close to the sense of this episode when he suggests that its climax presents an 'alternation of attitude rather than any real growth of understanding' ('The Strange Case of Christopher Marlowe', p. 89).

19 For a different interpretation, see Charles Masinton's *Christopher Marlowe's Tragic Vision* (Athens, Ohio, 1972), chs. 2 and 3, and D. J. Palmer's 'Marlowe's Naturalism', *Morris*, pp. 153–75.

20 Although David Daiches apparently identifies the poetic impulse with Marlowe, rather than with Tamburlaine, he recognizes the importance of language: 'It is made clear in innumerable ways that for Marlowe the proper kind of talk is both the precondition for and in a sense the equivalent of action. Soaring talk is the sign of the soaring mind, and only the soaring mind can achieve spectacularly successful action' (*More Literary Essays* [Edinburgh, 1968], p. 45).

21 This resemblance is pointed out by Lynette and Eveline Feasey in 'Marlowe and the Prophetic Dooms', *Notes and Queries*, 195 (1950), 419–21. Why, they wonder, should Mycetes be allowed to mock this theme so early if it is not to be criticized throughout?

22 *Rhetoric as Dramatic Language in Ben Jonson* (New York, 1948), p. 120.

23 'The Second Part of "Tamburlaine the Great"', p. 20.

24 Ellis-Fermor demonstrates how closely the arguments of Frederick and Baldwin follow the arguments for breaking faith with the Turk Amurath actually made by the Papal Legate Cardinal Julian to King Vladislaus, prior to the Battle of Varna (1444), as reported by Bonfinius, and reprinted by Lonicerus (*Tamburlaine the Great in Two Parts*, pp. 41–3). In 'Protestant Apologetics and the Sub-plot of 2 *Tamburlaine*', *English Literary Renaissance*, 3 (1973), 30–43, Battenhouse suggests that Marlowe may have been influenced by Foxe, who followed Luther in connecting Sigismund and Vladislaus as faith-breakers.

25 'Marlowe and the Commination Service', *Notes and Queries*, 195 (1950), 159. The same example is also used in the Sermon on 'falling from God', which emphasizes that God wants obedience, not offerings. See G. E. Corrie, ed., *Certain Sermons* (Cambridge, 1850), p. 80.

26 See the Biblical parallels suggested in L. and E. Feasey, 'Marlowe and the Prophetic Dooms', pp. 356–9; 404–7; 419–21.

27 Battenhouse, *Marlowe's Tamburlaine*, p. 106. This quotation from *Hercules Furens* is used to argue that 'psychological infelicity' is a 'form of retribution'.

28 Historically it had no relation at all. The various sources for the episode are discussed by Ellis-Fermor in her edition, pp. 44–5.

29 P. 170. Erasmus also returns again and again to the Platonic argument that because the king is the likeness of God on earth, he must imitate his wisdom and goodness as well as his power.

30 Seznec, p. 33. In this section I appeal regularly to evidence from Renaissance iconography, art, and pageantry, because I am trying to recreate probable Renaissance responses. In an interesting article, Nancy T. Leslie has tried to describe the responses of modern directors and theatre audiences to *Tamburlaine* ('*Tamburlaine* in the Theatre: Tartar, Grand Guignol, or Janus?', *Renaissance Drama*, n.s. 4 (1971), 105–20).

31 See Muriel Bradbrook, *Shakespeare and Elizabethan Poetry* (London, 1951), p. 18, and Frances Yates, *Astraea: The Imperial Theme in the Sixteenth Century* (London, 1975).

32 The poem is printed in John Nichols, ed., *The Progresses and Public Processions of Queen Elizabeth* (2 vols., London, 1788), II, 545.

33 For example, the painter Bronzino, designing tapestries in 1578, regrets that the life of Hercules is *too* well known, but finally decides that what is familiar will be more pleasing. See Seznec, p. 250, on the influence of manuals of iconography.

34 'Studies in Allegorical Portraiture', Part I, *Journal of the Warburg and Courtauld Institutes*, 1 (1937–8), 138–9.

35 The apocalyptic Christ is represented with flaming eyes in the Bishops Bible (1574) illustration for chapter 1 of Revelation. For a stimulating study of the influence of Biblical illustration on drama, see Helen Morris, 'Shakespeare and Dürer's Apocalypse', *Shakespeare Studies*, 4 (1968), 252–62. Marlowe seems to have used Revelation 19, where another flaming-eyed Christ is described, when in Part Two he reaches the mass drownings in Limnasphaltis lake and has Techelles refer to the 'amazed' fishes fed on carcasses (v.i.204–5). Ellis-Fermor points out that Perondinus refers to Tamburlaine's ferocious eyes, in the notes to 1:II.i.14–15 in her edition of *Tamburlaine*. Battenhouse suggests a similarity with the monstrous Machiavel of Harvey, who has furious eyes (*Marlowe's Tamburlaine*, p. 208).

36 Battenhouse stresses the Machiavellian purpose of the shows (*Marlowe's Tamburlaine*, p. 210). He considers only five spectacular sequences in Part One and treats them as detachable 'morality' additions to the historical sources (pp. 150–1).

37 On Biblical parallels, see L. and E. Feasey, 'Marlowe and the Prophetic Dooms', pp. 357–8. For Phaeton as a type of temerity and a warning to young princes, see *Emblèmes D'Alciat, En Latin Et François. Vers Pour Vers* (Paris, 1574), pp. 86–7. In *The Education of a Christian Prince*, the Phaeton story is suggested as an example of how 'a prince...with no supporting wisdom, seized the reins of government' (p. 147). Marlowe probably depends upon such associations, but the complex attitude implied by the scene may have been closer to Ovid's. In the *Metamorphoses*, Phaeton, for 'want of wit',

requests a charge 'greater...than any God could ever have as yet' (Bk. II, I. 77). Ovid concludes the incident, however, with an epitaph and the surmise, 'Yet that he gave a proud attempt it cannot be denide' (I. 415).

38 The ultimate source for Tamburlaine's device could be Psalm 110:1: 'The Lord said vnto my Lord, Sit thou at my right hand, vntil I make thine enemies thy footstole.' Histories of Tamburlaine mention the footstool, and critics have also discovered the motif in medieval romance and Reformation art. Ethel Seaton finds a footstool in *Godffrey of Boloyne* ('Marlowe's Light Reading', in Herbert Davis and Helen Gardner, eds., *Elizabethan and Jacobean Studies* [Oxford, 1959], p. 34). Muriel Bradbrook points out that a 1580 frontispiece of Foxe's martyrology has Henry VIII mounting on the back of the Pope to the throne ('Shakespeare's Primitive Art', *Proceedings of the British Academy*, 51 [1965], 216).

39 George Riley Kernodle, in *From Art to Theatre: Form and Convention in the Renaissance* (Chicago, 1944), pp. 139–40, observes how this scene combines the pageant motifs of the 'city-castle', throne, and banquet.

40 'What significance has the crown on his head, if not wisdom that is absolute?' asks Erasmus concerning his ideal ruler, in *The Education of a Christian Prince*, p. 187.

41 The presence of an allusion is suggested by L. and E. Feasey in 'Marlowe and the Commination Service', 156.

42 B. Jowett, trans., *Phaedrus*, *The Dialogues of Plato*, 4th edn (4 vols., Oxford, 1953), III, 151. Marlowe apparently alludes to the dialogue *Gorgias* when Faustus bids *On cay mae on* farewell. Robert Cockcroft includes the *Phaedrus* among the many sources and analogues for Tamburlaine's chariot in Part Two ('Emblematic Irony: Some Possible Significances of Tamburlaine's Chariot', *Renaissance and Modern Studies*, 12 [1968], 49.

43 The conflict of love and honour is discussed in most detail by G. I. Duthie, who treats it as a psychological crisis. Tamburlaine will not permit beauty to degrade him as it degraded Jove ('The Dramatic Structure of Marlowe's "Tamburlaine the Great", Parts I and II', *Essays and Studies*, n.s. I [1948], 101–26). Waith's approach in *The Herculean Hero* is similar (pp. 72–3).

44 In her editorial notes to these lines, Ellis-Fermor unfortunately concludes that they do not 'seriously affect the meaning of the whole passage'. Alternative readings to which she refers are Dyce's 'stoopt', for 'stopped', and Deighton's 'topmost' for 'tempest.' 'Lowly' has been frequently conjectured in place of 'lovely' (*Tamburlaine the Great in Two Parts*, p. 163). Duthie, who accepts the emendations 'stooped' and 'topmost', proposes that Marlowe is alluding to the wooing of Mnemosyne by Jove, disguised in a shepherd's dress (pp. 111–12).

45 A recent editor of the *Tamburlaine* plays, Tatiana A. Wolff, has also discovered the allusion here to Golding's Ovid, but she makes only one emendation (changing 'strowed weeds' to 'straw and reeds') and emphasizes the 'concluding moral' of the story, 'Let them whom God doth love be gods.' This, she states, was 'apt to Tamburlaine's present purpose – the extolling of humble virtue' (*Tamburlaine the Great, Parts I and II* [London, 1964], p. 246). Surely there is pathos, as well as irony, in Tamburlaine's allusion to a myth which concerns both apocalyptic violence and a direct, gentle relationship between gods and men.

46 Here my interpretation is in agreement with those of Battenhouse (*Marlowe's Tamburlaine*, p. 251) and Waith (*The Herculean Hero*, p. 74) rather than with that of Powell, who believes that the action of *Tamburlaine* can move from temporal fable to timeless symbol, without disturbing emotional consistency (p. 205).

47 Those who have observed either jarring discontinuities between narrative and symbolic sequences, or symbols which do not match their intended significance, include Clifford Leech, in his Introduction to *Marlowe: A Collection of Critical Essays* (Englewood Cliffs, 1964), p. 8; Lever p. 424, and Cole, pp. 102-3 and p. 108.

48 L. and E. Feasey find comparable images of carnage in Ezekiel 32:3-6 and Isaiah 34:2-7 ('Marlowe and the Prophetic Dooms', p. 405).

49 The use of this emblem is discussed by Battenhouse (*Marlowe's Tamburlaine*, p. 164) and by Powell (pp. 209-10). Tamburlaine, a literalist, is blind to a problem of which Renaissance artists (including Marlowe) were aware. Although learning and art might do their best to achieve an equation between visible attribute and idea, the reference of an emblem used for a pageant or show also had to be very obvious. Such emblems, according to Ben Jonson, were 'So to be presented, as upon a view they might, without cloud or obscurity, declare themselves to the sharp and learned; and for the multitude, no doubt but their grounded judgements did gaze, said it was fine, and were satisfied.' (Noted by Hal H. Smith, 'Some Principles of Elizabethan Stage Costume', *Journal of the Warburg and Courtauld Institutes*, 25 [1962], 246.) Because such emblems had to be clear, they were perhaps necessarily superficial. 'N. W.', in an epistle prefaced to Samuel Daniel's translation of a tract by Paolo Giovio, compares emblems with heraldic devices. Emblems, he suggests, 'giue credit to the wit', while devices 'reueale the secretes of the minde', and he seems to prefer this inward substance to the outward show of emblems. See Alexander B. Grosart, ed., *The Complete Works in Verse and Prose of Samuel Daniel* (5 vols., London, 1896; reprinted, New York, 1963), IV, 11. The English do not commonly make such a distinction. Puttenham, for example, gives as the purpose of both device and emblem 'to insinuat some secret, wittie, morall and brave purpose presented to the beholder' (Edward Arber, ed., *The Arte of English Poesie, 1589* [London, 1906], p. 121). I agree with those scholars who confirm N.W.'s observation on the witty properties of emblems by observing within the emblematic image an uneasy tension between esoteric and obvious elements, rather than with Dieter Mehl's emphasis on the organic interrelation of pictures and meanings, in 'Emblems in Elizabethan Drama', *Renaissance Drama*, n.s. 2 (1969), 41. See Freeman, p. 25 and p. 29, Seznec, p. 250, and Mario Praz, *Studies in Seventeenth Century Imagery*, *Sussidi Eruditi*, 16 (Rome, 1964), p. 23 and p. 169.

50 *Works*, III, 606.

51 Alciati, pp. 84-7.

52 See the colloquy 'Military Affairs', *The Colloquies of Erasmus*, p. 14.

53 C. L. Barber tentatively relates Tamburlaine's rebellious Oedipus complex to his attempt to create his own gods and to worship (rather frigidly) an idealized mother-figure ('The Death of Zenocrate: "Conceiving and Subduing Both" in Marlowe's *Tamburlaine*', *Literature and Psychology*, 16 [1966], 15-24). Surely Marlowe's vision was closer to Freud's own sense of

tragic irony than it was to Tamburlaine's 'conceited' heroism. One wonders whether modern psychology could have taught a Renaissance dramatist educated in Platonized Christianity much about desires and projections that he didn't already know. For his part, he might correct the psychologist's over-emphasis on determining origins through his own emphasis on choice, transformation, and destiny.

54 See the brief article by L. and E. Feasey, 'Marlowe and the Homilies', *Notes and Queries*, 195 (1950), 7–10.

55 Erasmus refers in the *Enchiridion* (p. 69) to 'Socrates' fable of the charioteers and their horses, good and bad' included in the *Phaedrus*. Cockcroft, well aware that not even the 'most exhaustive and sensitive analysis' (p. 34) can do justice to this complex and powerful symbol, includes the *Phaedrus* in his rich gathering of possible sources. Whitney had used a runaway wagon as an emblem (his sixth) of uncontrolled affections: 'Then bridle will, and reason make thy guide,/So maiste thou stande, when others doune doe slide.'

56 Cole (p. 109) and Cockcroft (p. 38) also regard *Jocasta* as a source for the scene.

57 P. 170.

## 7 THE DIFFERENCE OF THINGS IN *EDWARD II*

1 Cf. Toby Robertson's view of Kent: 'Unable to commit himself to either party for long, trusted by no one, his failure is that of the good man submerged by forces which he cannot control or understand' ('Directing *Edward II*', Marlowe *TDR*, p. 178). Some commentators treat Kent as a *raisonneur*, making him more reliable than the riddles of the play seem to warrant. For example, F. P. Wilson thinks he might be 'the only character in Marlowe's plays who may be regarded as a point of reference' (*Marlowe and the Early Shakespeare* [Oxford, 1954], p. 94). Kocher feels that his judgment 'represents a kind of ethical norm' (*Christopher Marlowe*, p. 205).

2 See Merchant's reference to the Golding translation, Bk. II, ll. 1057–8, in the New Mermaid edition of *Edward II* (London, 1967), p. 19.

3 *Shakespearean Tragedy*, 2nd edn (London, 1949), p. 264.

4 Pp. 63–4. Following references will be included in the text.

5 In his editorial notes to this line, William Dinsmore Briggs refers to the classical sources of the proverb and cites other uses in Renaissance drama (*Marlowe's Edward II* [London, 1914], p. 187).

6 Cole observes that Marlowe has 'significantly departed from his source in not making Edward realize his own responsibility' (p. 177). H. B. Charlton and R. D. Waller attribute Edward's failure to repent and apologize to Marlowe's own temperament. 'This stubborn self-assertion bears the mark of his creator' (R. H. Case edition of *Edward II* [London, 1933], pp. 37–8). A particularly detailed discussion of Marlowe's adaptation of chronicle matter, with extensive quotations from both Holinshed and Stowe, may be found in the Introduction to their edition.

7 Just how 'nature' is related to the general structure and vision of the play has been an important issue for many commentators. Charlton and Waller, who emphasize a 'naturalistic' quality, can find no 'moral pattern' (p. 55). They are followed by Steane and Sanders. Bevington believes that the moral

element is 'pronounced though vestigial' (p. 234) – a traditional theatrical convention inherited by Marlowe which is at odds with the plausibility of his characters. My own view is that by presenting political interactions as analogues of interactions within the microcosm, Marlowe subtly introduces moral order – similar to, yet far more rigorous than the order we might expect to find in a feudal society 'naturalistically' presented.

8 *The Anatomy of Criticism* (Princeton, 1957), p. 37. The best discussion of 'objective' tragic qualities in *Edward II* is that by Clifford Leech, in 'Marlowe's "Edward II": Power and Suffering', *Critical Quarterly*, 1 (1959), 181–96.

9 '*Edward II*: The Shadow of an Action', Marlowe *TDR*, p. 63.

10 Harold F. Brooks discusses the influence of *Richard III* on *Edward II* in 'Marlowe and Early Shakespeare', *Morris*, p. 72.

11 Levin writes that 'Originally, when the King is so unreasonable, Mortimer seems not merely reasonable but exceptionally downright and hearty' (*The Overreacher*, p. 121). Ribner feels that 'All of Edward's lack of public virtue is mirrored in Mortimer's supreme possession of it' ('Marlowe's *Edward II* and the Tudor History Play', *Journal of English Literary History*, 22 [1955], 248).

12 Brooks points out Marlowe's indebtedness to *Richard III* in this scene, (p. 74). Marlowe's independence is shown in the fact that whereas Richard's act fools everyone *but* Buckingham and Richard, Mortimer's fools Mortimer as well.

13 Wolfgang Clemen observes, regarding the soliloquies in this play, that 'the mythological imagery and classical parallels and the rhetorical exaggeration of the curses and protestations seem to be based on the stylistic pattern of the earlier classical tragedies, and they are curiously at variance with the very different language of their context' (*English Tragedy Before Shakespeare* [London, 1961], p. 157).

14 She does not change from 'forlorn wife' to 'scheming adulteress' within some forty lines of Act II, scene iv, as Levin argues in *The Overreacher*, p. 121. Both Leech and Waith stress the subtlety and psychological accuracy of Marlowe's art in characterizing her.

15 Cf. Waith, 'She is driven to pleading with her son for the life of her lover as once she pled with Mortimer for the return of her husband's lover' ('*Edward II*: The Shadow of an Action', p. 69).

16 The allegorical nature of the shows in *Edward II* is emphasized by John Russell Brown, p. 164, and by Powell, p. 204.

17 Levin notes that the masque imagined by Gaveston 'can be taken as a portent, since its hero, Actæon, was hunted down for having gazed on a sight forbidden to men' (*The Overreacher*, p. 114). Bent Sunesen, in 'Marlowe and the Dumb Show', *English Studies*, 35 (1954), 241–53, treats the fortunes of the myth in this play as an instance of the poetic integration of dumb show. The myth, he believes, suggests a needed, if hateful, corrective for sin. Martha Hester Golden thinks that as a type of Christ the hart forecasts a resurrection – the sudden emergence of Edward III ('The Iconography of the English History Play', Ph.D. thesis [Columbia, 1964], p. 215).

18 Ovid's account is a step in this direction. Golding himself moralizes Actaeon's death in the prefatory epistle to his translation of the *Metamorphoses*, treating it as the destruction of a riotous liver by his own vices (p. 408, l. 97). His

translation, on the other hand, preserves the indecisiveness of Ovid's approach to Actaeon's punishment:

> If you sift the matter well, ye shall not finde desart
> But cruell fortune to have bene the cause of this his smart.
>
> Bk. III, ll. 164–5

> Much muttring was upon this fact. Some thought there was extended
> A great deale more extremitie than neded. Some commended
> Dianas doing: saying, That it was but worthely
> For safe garde of hir womanhed.
>
> Bk. III, ll. 305–8

19 Quoted by Joseph, p. 309.
20 Although the verb 'haunt' was mainly used by Elizabethans to refer to habitual practices or associations with people and places, it could also suggest the ideas of pursuit and molestation, as by a disease or a ghost.
21 Waith finds the King's gestures and words, as he lays his head on the Abbot's lap, 'almost emblematic of the King's powerlessness and prophetic of his imminent death' (*'Edward II*: The Shadow of an Action', p. 73).
22 *The Overreacher*, p. 118.
23 (Ithaca, 1971), p. 50.

## 8 THE PROPHETIC SPIRIT

1 P. 5.
2 P. 240.
3 Lee M. Capel, trans., *The Concept of Irony with Constant Reference to Socrates* (London, 1966), p. 279.
4 The saying is attributed by Ascham to Erasmus in *The Schoolmaster* (Rev. Dr Giles, ed., *The Whole Works of Roger Ascham* [London, 1864], Part III, p. 137). (Cf. *De Pueris Instituendis*: 'They err, therefore, who affirm that wisdom is won by handling affairs and by contact with life, without aid from the teaching of philosophy' (William Harrison Woodward, ed., *Desiderius Erasmus Concerning the Aim and Method of Education* [New York, 1904; reprinted, 1971], p. 191).)
5 P. 105.
6 'Milton's "Satan"', p. 48.

# Select bibliography

## EDITIONS OF MARLOWE

*The Complete Plays of Christopher Marlowe*, ed. Irving Ribner. New York, 1963.
*Dido Queen of Carthage, The Massacre at Paris*, ed. H. J. Oliver, London, 1968.
*Doctor Faustus*, ed. John D. Jump. London, 1962.
*Marlowe's Edward II*, ed. William Dinsmore Briggs. London, 1914.
*Edward II*, ed. H. B. Charlton and R. D. Waller. London, 1933.
*Edward II*, ed. W. Moelwyn Merchant. London, 1967.
*The Jew of Malta and The Massacre at Paris*, ed. H. S. Bennett. London, 1931.
*Tamburlaine the Great in Two Parts*, ed. Una Ellis-Fermor. London, 1930.
*Tamburlaine the Great, Parts I and II*, ed. Tatiana A. Wolff. London, 1964.

## EDITIONS AND TRANSLATIONS OF OTHER WRITERS

Agrippa, Henrie Cornelius, *Of the Vanitie and Uncertaintie of Artes and Sciences*. Trans. James Sanford, London, 1575.
Beza, Theodore, *Master Bezaes Sermons Upon The Three First Chapters of The Canticle Of Canticles*. Trans. John Harman, Oxford, 1587.
Brant, Sebastian, *The Ship of Fools*. Trans. William Gillis, London, 1971.
Donne, John, *John Donne: The Anniversaries*. Ed. Frank Manley, Baltimore, 1963.
Erasmus, Desiderius, *The Colloquies of Erasmus*. Trans. Craig R. Thompson, Chicago, 1961.
—*Desiderius Erasmus Concerning the Aim and Method of Education*. Ed. William Harrison Woodward, New York, 1904 (reprinted, 1971).
—*The Education of a Christian Prince*. Trans. L. K. Born, New York, 1936.
—*The Enchiridion of Erasmus*. Trans. Raymond Himelick, Bloomington, 1963.
—*The Julius exclusus of Erasmus*. Trans. Paul Pascal, Bloomington, 1968.
—*Opus Epistolarum*. Ed. P. S. and H. M. Allen, 12 vols., Oxford, 1910.
—*The Praise of Folie. Moriae Encomium*. Trans. Sir Thomas Chaloner, London, 1549.
—*The Praise of Folly*. Trans. John Wilson, 1668, Ann Arber, 1965.
—*The Praise of Folly*. Trans. Hoyt Hopewell Hudson, New York, 1941.
—*The Praise of Folly*. Trans. Leonard F. Dean, New York, 1946.
—*Proverbs or Adages. By Desiderius Erasmus. Gathered Out of the Chiliades and Englished (1569) by Richard Taverner*. Facsimile. Introd. DeWitt T. Starnes, Gainesville, 1956.
*The Geneva Bible: A Facsimile of the 1560 Edition*. Introd. Lloyd E. Berry, Madison, 1969.

Greene, Robert, *The Life and Complete Works in Prose and Verse of Robert Greene*, *M. A.* Ed. Alexander B. Grosart, 15 vols., London, 1881–6 (reprinted, New York, 1964).

Hooker, Richard, *The Works of that Learned and Judicious Divine, Mr. Richard Hooker*. Ed. Rev. John Keble, 3 vols., Oxford, 1888 (7th edition).

Kyd, Thomas, *The Spanish Tragedy*. Ed. Philip Edwards, London, 1959.

Laertius, Diogenes, *Lives of Eminent Philosophers*. Trans. R. D. Hicks, 2 vols., Loeb Classical Library, London, 1958.

Lyly, John, *The Complete Works of John Lyly*. Ed. R. Warwick Bond, 3 vols., Oxford, 1902.

Machiavelli, Niccolò, *The Prince*. Trans. George Bull. Penguin Books, 1961.

Marnix, Filipe van, *The Beehive of the Romishe Church*. London, 1579.

Ovidius Naso, Publius, *Ovid's Metamorphoses: The Arthur Golding Translation, 1567*. Ed. John Frederick Nims, New York, 1965.

Plato, *The Dialogues of Plato*. Trans. B. Jowett, 4 vols, Oxford, 1953 (4th edition).

Rabelais, François, *Rabelais*. Trans. W. F. Smith, 2 vols., Cambridge, 1934 (2nd edition).

Shakespeare, William, *William Shakespeare: The Complete Works*. Ed. Alfred Harbage, Baltimore, 1969.

Wager, William, *The Longer Thou Livest and Enough Is as Good as a Feast*. Ed. R. Mark Benbow, London, 1968.

## STUDIES OF MARLOWE

Allen, Don Cameron, 'Marlowe's *Dido* and the Tradition'. *Essays on Shakespeare and Elizabethan Drama: In Honor of Hardin Craig*, ed. Richard Hosley, Columbia, 1962.

Babb, Howard B., 'Policy in Marlowe's *Jew of Malta*'. *Journal of English Literary History*, 24 (1957).

Bakeless, John, *The Tragicall History of Christopher Marlowe*, 2 vols., Cambridge, 1942.

Barber, C. L., 'The Death of Zenocrate: "Conceiving and Subduing Both" in Marlowe's *Tamburlaine*'. *Literature and Psychology*, 16 (1966).

Battenhouse, Roy W., *Marlowe's Tamburlaine: A Study in Renaissance Moral Philosophy*. Nashville, 1941.

—'Protestant Apologetics and the Sub-plot of *2 Tamburlaine*'. *English Literary Renaissance*, 3 (1973).

Bawcutt, Nigel, 'Machiavelli and Marlowe's *The Jew of Malta*'. *Renaissance Drama*, n.s. 3 (1970).

Bevington, David M., *From Mankind to Marlowe: Growth of Structure in the Popular Drama of Tudor England*. Cambridge, Mass., 1962.

Boas, Frederick S., *Christopher Marlowe: A Biographical and Critical Study*. Oxford, 1940.

Brockbank, J. P., *Marlowe: Dr. Faustus*. Studies in English Literature, 6, London, 1962.

Brodwin, Leonora Leet, '*Edward II*: Marlowe's Culminating Treatment of Love'. *Journal of English Literary History*, 31 (1964).

Brooke, C. F. Tucker, *The Life of Marlowe and The Tragedy of Dido Queen of Carthage*. London, 1930.

Brooke, Nicholas, 'Marlowe as Provocative Agent in Shakespeare's Early Plays'. *Shakespeare Survey*, 14 (1961).

—'The Moral Tragedy of Doctor Faustus'. *Cambridge Journal*, 5 (1952).

Brooks, Harold F., 'Marlowe and Early Shakespeare'. *Christopher Marlowe*, ed. Brian Morris, London, 1968.

Brown, Beatrice D., 'Marlowe, Faustus, and Simon Magus'. *Publications of the Modern Language Association*, 54 (1939).

Brown, John Russell, 'Marlowe and the Actors'. *Tulane Drama Review*, 8 (1964).

Campbell, Lily B., '*Doctor Faustus*: A Case of Conscience'. *Publications of the Modern Language Association*, 67 (1952).

Cockcroft, Robert, 'Emblematic Irony: Some Possible Significances of Tamburlaine's Chariot'. *Renaissance and Modern Studies*, 12 (1968).

Cole, Douglas, *Suffering and Evil in the Plays of Christopher Marlowe*. Princeton, 1962.

Cox, Gerald H., 'Marlowe's *Doctor Faustus* and "Sin against the Holy Ghost"'. *Huntingdon Library Quarterly*, 36 (1972–3).

Craik, T. W., 'Faustus' Damnation Reconsidered'. *Renaissance Drama*, n.s. 2 (1969).

Daiches, David, 'Language and Action in Marlowe's *Tamburlaine*'. *More Literary Essays*, Edinburgh, 1968.

Duthie, G. I., 'The Dramatic Structure of Marlowe's "Tamburlaine the Great", Parts I and II'. *Essays and Studies*, n.s. 1 (1948).

Ellis-Fermor, Una, *Christopher Marlowe*. London, 1927.

Farnham, Willard (ed.), *Twentieth Century Interpretations of Doctor Faustus*. Englewood Cliffs, 1969.

Feasey, Lynette and Eveline, 'Marlowe and the Christian Humanists'. *Notes and Queries*, 196 (1951).

—'Marlowe and the Commination Service'. *Notes and Queries*, 195 (1950).

—'Marlowe and the Homilies'. *Notes and Queries*, 195 (1950).

—'Marlowe and the Prophetic Dooms'. *Notes and Queries*, 195 (1950).

French, A. L., 'The Philosophy of *Dr. Faustus*'. *Essays in Criticism*, 20 (1970).

Gardner, Helen, 'The Second Part of "Tamburlaine the Great"'. *Modern Language Review*, 37 (1942).

Gibbons, Brian, 'Unstable Proteus: Marlowe's *The Tragedy of Dido Queen of Carthage*'. *Christopher Marlowe*, ed. Brian Morris, London, 1968.

Greg, W. W., 'The Damnation of Faustus'. *Modern Language Review*, 41 (1946).

Harbage, Alfred, 'Innocent Barabas'. *Tulane Drama Review*, 8 (1964).

Hattaway, Michael, 'Marlowe and Brecht'. *Christopher Marlowe*, ed. Brian Morris, London, 1968.

—'The Theology of Marlowe's *Doctor Faustus*'. *Renaissance Drama*, 3 (1970).

Honderich, Pauline, 'John Calvin and Doctor Faustus'. *Modern Language Review*, 68 (1973).

Hoy, Cyrus, '"Ignorance in Knowledge": Marlowe's Faustus and Ford's Giovanni'. *Modern Philology*, 57 (1960).

Hunter, G. K., 'Five-Act Structure in *Doctor Faustus*'. *Tulane Drama Review*, 8 (1964).

—'The Theology of Marlowe's *The Jew of Malta*', *Journal of the Warburg and Courtauld Institutes*, 27 (1964).

Kimbrough, Robert, '*I Tamburlaine*: A Speaking Picture in a Tragic Glass'. *Renaissance Drama*, 7 (1964).

Kirschbaum, Leo, 'Some Light on *The Jew of Malta*'. *Modern Language Quarterly*, 7 (1946).

Knights, L. C., 'The Strange Case of Christopher Marlowe'. *Further Explorations*, London, 1965.

Kocher, Paul H., *Christopher Marlowe: A Study of His Thought, Learning and Character*. Chapel Hill, 1946.

—'Contemporary Pamphlet Backgrounds for Marlowe's *The Massacre at Paris*'. *Modern Language Quarterly*, 8 (1947).

—'English Legal History in Marlowe's *Jew of Malta*'. *Huntingdon Library Quarterly*, 26 (1962–3).

—'François Hotman and Marlowe's *The Massacre at Paris*'. *Publications of the Modern Language Association*, 56 (1941).

—'Nashe's Authorship of the Prose Scenes in *Faustus*'. *Modern Language Quarterly*, 3 (1942).

Leech, Clifford, (ed.), *Marlowe: A Collection of Critical Essays*. Englewood Cliffs, 1964.

—'Marlowe's "Edward II": Power and Suffering'. *Critical Quarterly*, 1 (1959).

—'Marlowe's Humor'. *Essays on Shakespeare and Elizabethan Drama: In Honor of Hardin Craig*, ed. Richard Hosley, Columbia, 1962.

—'The Structure of *Tamburlaine*'. *Tulane Drama Review*, 8 (1964).

Leslie, Nancy T., '*Tamburlaine* in the Theatre: Tartar, Grand Guignol, or Janus?' *Renaissance Drama*, n.s. 4 (1971).

Lever, Katherine, 'The Image of Man in *Tamburlaine* Part I'. *Philological Quarterly*, 35 (1956).

Levin, Harry, 'Marlowe Today'. *Tulane Drama Review*, 8 (1964).

—*The Overreacher: A Study of Christopher Marlowe*. London, 1954 (British edition).

McAlindon, T., 'Classical Mythology and Christian Tradition in Marlowe's *Doctor Faustus*'. *Publications of the Modern Language Association*, 81 (1966).

McCullen, Joseph T., 'Dr. Faustus and Renaissance Learning'. *Modern Language Review*, 51 (1956).

Mahood, M. M., *Poetry and Humanism*. London, 1950.

Manley, Frank, 'The Nature of Faustus'. *Modern Philology*, 66 (1968–9).

Masinton, Charles, *Christopher Marlowe's Tragic Vision*. Athens, Ohio, 1972.

Maxwell, J. C., 'Two Notes on Marlowe's "Faustus"'. *Notes and Queries*, 194 (1949).

Morris, Brian (ed.), *Christopher Marlowe*. Mermaid Critical Commentaries, London, 1968.

—'Comic Method in Marlowe's Hero and Leander'. *Christopher Marlowe*, ed. Brian Morris, London, 1968.

Palmer, D. J., 'Marlowe's Naturalism'. *Christopher Marlowe*, ed. Brian Morris, London, 1968.

Pearce, T. M., 'Evidence for Dating Marlowe's *Tragedy of Dido*'. *Studies in the English Renaissance Drama*, ed. Josephine W. Bennett et al., London, 1961.

Poirier, Michel, *Christopher Marlowe*. London, 1951.

Powell, Jocelyn, 'Marlowe's Spectacle'. *Tulane Drama Review*, 8 (1964).

Purcell, H. D., 'Whetstone's "English Myrror" and Marlowe's "Jew of Malta"'. *Notes and Queries*, 211 (1966).

Ribner, Irving, 'Marlowe and Machiavelli'. *Comparative Literature*, 6 (1954).

—'Marlowe's *Edward II* and the Tudor History Play'. *Journal of English Literary History*, 22 (1955).

Robertson, Toby, 'Directing *Edward II*'. *Tulane Drama Review*, 8 (1964).

Rothstein, Eric, 'Structure as Meaning in *The Jew of Malta*'. *Journal of English and Germanic Philology*, 65 (1966).

Sachs, Arieh, 'The Religious Despair of Doctor Faustus'. *Journal of English and Germanic Philology*, 63 (1964).

Sanders, Wilbur, *The Dramatist and the Received Idea: Studies in the Plays of Marlowe and Shakespeare*. Cambridge, 1968.

Santayana, George, 'The Rehabilitation of Faustus'. *Three Philosophical Poets: Lucretius, Dante, and Goethe*. Cambridge, Mass., 1910. Reprinted in Willard Farnham, ed., *Twentieth Century Interpretations of Doctor Faustus*, Englewood Cliffs, 1969.

Seaton, Ethel, 'Marlowe's Light Reading'. *Elizabethan and Jacobean Studies*, ed. Herbert Davis and Helen Gardner, Oxford, 1959.

Sims, James H., *Dramatic Uses of Biblical Allusion in Marlowe and Shakespeare*. University of Florida Monographs, Humanities, no. 24, Gainesville, 1966.

Smith, James L., '*The Jew of Malta* in the Theatre'. *Christopher Marlowe*, ed. Brian Morris, London, 1968.

—'Marlowe's "Doctor Faustus"'. *Scrutiny*, 8 (1939).

Steadman, John M., 'Averroes and Dr. Faustus: Some Additional Parallels'. *Notes and Queries*, 207 (1962).

Steane, J. B., *Marlowe: A Critical Study*. Cambridge, 1964.

Steiner, Arpad, 'The Faust Legend and the Christian Tradition'. *Publications of the Modern Language Association*, 54 (1939).

Sunesen, Bent, 'Marlowe and the Dumb Show'. *English Studies*, 35 (1954).

Waith, Eugene M., '*Edward II*: The Shadow of an Action'. *Tulane Drama Review*, 8 (1964).

—*The Herculean Hero in Marlowe, Chapman, Shakespeare and Dryden*. London, 1962.

—'Marlowe and the Jades of Asia'. *Studies in English Literature*, 5 (1965).

Wickham, Glynn, '*Exeunt to the Cave*: Notes on the Staging of Marlowe's Plays'. *Tulane Drama Review*, 8 (1964).

Wilson, F. P., *Marlowe and the Early Shakespeare*. Oxford, 1954.

## GENERAL REFERENCE

Alciati, *Emblèmes d'Alciat, En Latin et François. Vers Pour Vers*, Paris, 1574.

Baldwin, T. W., *William Shakspere's Small Latine & Lesse Greeke*. 2 vols., Urbana, 1944.

Beckerman, Bernard, *Shakespeare at the Globe 1599–1609*. New York, 1962.

Benjamin, Walter, *Illuminations*. London, 1970.

Bethell, S. L., *Shakespeare and the Popular Dramatic Tradition*. London, 1945.

Booth, Wayne, *The Rhetoric of Irony*. Chicago, 1974.

Bowers, Fredson, *Elizabethan Revenge Tragedy 1587–1642*. Princeton, 1940.

Bradbrook, Muriel C., *Themes and Conventions in Elizabethan Tragedy*. Cambridge, 1935.

Burke, Kenneth, *A Grammar of Motives*. Berkeley, 1945 (reprinted, 1969).

Cameron, Kenneth Walter, *The Background of John Heywood's 'Witty and Witless'*. Raleigh, 1941.

Clemen, Wolfgang, *English Tragedy Before Shakespeare*. London, 1961.

Colie, Rosalie, *Paradoxia Epidemica: The Renaissance Tradition of Paradox*. Princeton, 1966.

Corrie, G. E. (ed.), *Certain Sermons*. Cambridge, 1850.

Eliot, T. S., *Elizabethan Dramatists*. London, 1963.

Frye, Northrop, *The Anatomy of Criticism*. Princeton, 1957.

Ferguson, George, *Signs and Symbols in Christian Art*. New York, 1954.

Fletcher, Angus, *The Prophetic Moment: An Essay on Spenser*. Chicago, 1971.

Freeman, Rosemary, *English Emblem Books*. London, 1948.

Gardner, Helen, 'Milton's "Satan" and the Theme of Damnation in Elizabethan Tragedy'. *Essays and Studies*, n.s. 1 (1948).

Golden, Martha Hester, 'The Iconography of the English History Play'. Ph. D. thesis, Columbia, 1964.

Goldsmith, Robert Hillis, *Wise Fools in Shakespeare*. Liverpool, 1958 (reprinted, 1974).

Gombrich, E. H., '*Icones Symbolicae*: The Visual Image in Neo-Platonic Thought'. *Journal of the Warburg and Courtauld Institutes*, 11 (1948).

Harvey, W. J. *Character and the Novel*. London, 1965.

Hunter, G. K., *John Lyly: The Humanist as Courtier*. London, 1962.

Jonas, Hans, *The Gnostic Religion*, Boston, 1958.

Joseph, Sister Miriam, *Shakespeare's Use of the Arts of Language*. New York, 1947.

Kaiser, Walter, *Praisers of Folly: Erasmus, Rabelais, Shakespeare*. Cambridge, Mass., 1963.

Kernodle, George Riley, *From Art to Theatre: Form and Convention in the Renaissance*. Chicago, 1944.

Kierkegaard, Søren, *The Concept of Irony with Constant Reference to Socrates*. Trans. Lee M. Capel, London, 1966.

Kolve, V. A., *The Play Called Corpus Christi*. London, 1966.

Mehl, Dieter, *The Elizabethan Dumb Show*. London, 1965.

Morris, Helen, 'Shakespeare and Dürer's Apocalypse'. *Shakespeare Studies*, 4 (1968).

Murrin, Michael, *The Veil of Allegory: Some Notes toward a Theory of Allegorical Rhetoric in the English Renaissance*. Chicago, 1969.

Neuss, Paula, 'Active and Idle Language: Dramatic Images in *Mankind*'. *Medieval Drama*, ed. Neville Denny, London, 1973.

O'Kane, Eleanor, 'The Proverb: Rabelais and Cervantes'. *Comparative Literature*, 2 (1950).

Otis, Brooks, *Virgil: A Study in Civilized Poetry*. Oxford, 1964.

Palmer, Philip Mason and More, Robert Pattison, *The Sources of the Faust Tradition from Simon Magus to Lessing*. New York, 1936.

Pellegrini, G., 'Symbols and Significances'. *Shakespeare Survey*, 17 (1964).

Phillips, Margaret Mann, *The 'Adages' of Erasmus. A Study with Translations*. Cambridge, 1964.

Pierce, William, *An Historical Introduction to the Marprelate Tracts*. London, 1908.

—(ed.), *The Marprelate Tracts 1588, 1589*. London, 1911.

Porter, Harry C., *Reformation and Reaction in Tudor Cambridge*. Cambridge, 1958.

Rice, Eugene F., Jr, *The Renaissance Idea of Wisdom*. Cambridge, Mass., 1958.

Righter, Anne, *Shakespeare and the Idea of the Play*. London, 1962.

Screech, M. A. 'L'Évangélisme de Rabelais: Aspects de la Satire Religieuse au XVIe Siècle'. *Travaux d'Humanisme et Renaissance*, 32 (1959).

Sewall, R. B., *The Vision of Tragedy*. New Haven, 1959.

Seznec, Jean, *La Survivance des Dieux Antiques*. London, 1940.

Smith, G. Gregory (ed.), *Elizabethan Critical Essays*. 2 vols., Oxford, 1904.

Smith, Hal H., 'Some Principles of Elizabethan Stage Costume'. *Journal of the Warburg and Courtauld Institutes*, 25 (1962).

Spencer, Theodore, *Death and Elizabethan Tragedy*. Cambridge, Mass., 1936.

Spivack, Bernard, *Shakespeare and the Allegory of Evil*. New York, 1958.

States, Bert O., *Irony and Drama : A Poetics*. Ithaca, 1971.

Strathmann, Ernest, *Sir Walter Ralegh : A Study in Elizabethan Skepticism*. New York, 1951.

Thomas, Keith, *Religion and the Decline of Magic : Studies in Popular Beliefs in Sixteenth- and Seventeenth-Century England*. Penguin Books, 1973.

Thompson, Sister Geraldine, *Under Pretext of Praise : Satiric Mode in Erasmus' Fiction*. Toronto, 1973.

Trevor-Roper, H. R., *The European Witch-Craze of the 16th and 17th Centuries*. Penguin Books, 1969.

Welsford, Enid, *The Fool*. London, 1935.

Whitaker, Virgil, *Shakespeare's Use of Learning : An Inquiry into the Growth of His Mind and Art*. San Marino, 1953.

Whitney, Geffrey, *A Choice of Emblemes and Other Devices*. Leyden, 1586.

Wilson, F. P., *The Proverbial Wisdom of Shakespeare*. Presidential Address of the Modern Humanities Research Association, Cambridge, 1961.

Wind, Edgar, 'Studies in Allegorical Portraiture', Part I. *Journal of the Warburg and Courtauld Institutes*, I (1937–8).

Yates, Frances, *Astraea : The Imperial Theme in the Sixteenth Century*. London, 1975.

—'The Emblematic Conceit in Giordano Bruno's *De Gli Eroici Furori* and in the Elizabethan Sonnet Sequences'. *Journal of the Warburg and Courtauld Institutes*, 6 (1943).

# Index